HIGH-YIELD Vegetable Gardening

Grow More of What You Want
in the Space You Have

Colin McCrate and Brad Halm

Storey Publishing

The mission of Storey Publishing is to serve our customers by publishing practical information that encourages personal independence in harmony with the environment.

Edited by Carleen Madigan
Art direction and book design by Alethea Morrison
Text production by Liseann Karandisecky
Indexed by Nancy D. Wood

Cover and interior illustrations by © Steve Sanford
Authors' photograph by © Hilary Dahl

Storey books are available for special premium and promotional uses and for customized editions. For further information, please call 1-800-793-9396.

Storey Publishing
210 MASS MoCA Way
North Adams, MA 01247
www.storey.com

Printed in China by Shenzhen Caimei Printing Co., Ltd.
10 9 8 7 6 5 4 3 2 1

Library of Congress Cataloging-in-Publication Data on file

Contents

INTRODUCTION
Becoming a High-Yield Vegetable Gardener

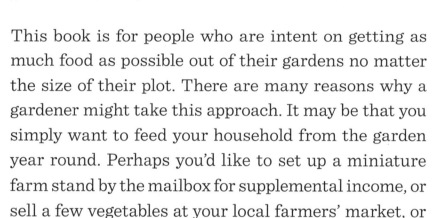

This book is for people who are intent on getting as much food as possible out of their gardens no matter the size of their plot. There are many reasons why a gardener might take this approach. It may be that you simply want to feed your household from the garden year round. Perhaps you'd like to set up a miniature farm stand by the mailbox for supplemental income, or sell a few vegetables at your local farmers' market, or coordinate a community garden.

Drawing from our backgrounds in small- and large-acreage farming, as well as in backyard gardening, we've taken the systems and practices that successful, professional growers use every day and adapted them for use at the scale of a home garden. Using these techniques to manage your garden like a professional small farmer will dramatically increase its yields while maintaining soil fertility and your sanity. We call this approach high-yield vegetable gardening.

THE BASIC TENETS OF HIGH-YIELD GARDENING

Understanding the basics of what makes a garden produce well is the first step toward creating a highly productive garden. Once you've identified these basics, you can then create systems to achieve maximum production. To get the most out of your garden, it's important to do the following:

Select the best site and use it efficiently. Thinking ahead and placing annual and perennial crops in the most appropriate spaces is vital to getting the most from your garden. For most crops and climates, more sun is always better. Lay out your garden to maximize productive space, and find creative solutions for spaces outside of the main vegetable garden. Keeping a productive garden space requires using non-garden spaces in support roles.

Plan well and keep good records. Spend time before each season to make a thorough plan of the garden. Update the plan throughout the season as you make necessary revisions. Maintain an accurate record of these garden tasks, as well as what happens in the garden, and use this information to inform future plans.

Know your plants. To get the most out of your crops, you must develop a deep understanding of the physiology, genetics, and cultural needs of the plants. The more you know about your crops, the easier it will be for you to increase their yields.

Select the best crops. Choose crops and specific cultivars that perform well in your climate and are suited to a given season. You'll want to select varieties that are vigorous, produce well, and taste to your liking.

Grow for a purpose. Take the time to consider the goals of your project. Grow for the tastes you prefer and yields you can use. Make sure to have a use in mind for each crop before it goes in the ground.

Observe and respond. You are the best ongoing source of information about your own garden. Keep track of which varieties perform best and which pests show up. The insights you gain will enable you to customize your project to suit your specific conditions.

Maximize your time and energy. You save time and energy when you develop systems and use tools that maximize efficiency. Time is nearly always the most limited resource of the high-yield gardener, so be sure to make the most of it.

Maintain fertile soil. Successful growers say, "Care for the soil, not the crops." Ongoing and meticulous care of the soil in your garden is essential. Soil amendment should happen several times every year.

Water well. Vegetable plants need consistent and adequate water. Carefully manage watering — by the time you notice signs of water stress, the overall yield potential of your crops will have already been reduced.

Extend the seasons, but also expand them. Create spaces to extend planting and harvest dates earlier and later in the season. Stay organized with succession planting so that you can grow multiple crops in each space throughout the year.

Deal with pests, diseases, and weeds immediately. Closely and frequently monitor your garden for problems. Vigilance allows you to deal with them immediately.

Harvest and store crops smartly. Know the appropriate stage to harvest your crops and understand post-harvest care to ensure maximum quality and storage life.

THINK LIKE A FARMER

In our experience, the most successful growers have a positive way of thinking about their gardens. Although intensive food production is challenging, these growers understand that they are most successful when they find joy in the process itself. They do not allow the inevitable struggles to tarnish their experiences. After all, intensive food production is hard work. It is at times exhausting and frustrating, and at times exhilarating and joyful. Crops will fail, seasons will be unexpectedly hot or cold, and more insects than you imagined possible will eventually cross your path.

To be successful and to improve their growing systems year after year, high-yield gardeners relish the opportunity to learn from their mistakes. Likewise, they actively study the vagaries of nature. Like farmers, they understand that learning how their crops grow and how the plants respond to their care is vital to the success of their livelihood and well-being. It is embracing this interaction and the give-and-take with nature that makes food production so captivating and so rewarding. A successful grower recognizes that highs and lows are part of the agreement to work with nature.

While most everyone would prefer to spend less time weeding and more time harvesting crops that are free from insect damage, it's essential to seek creative ways of overcoming the challenges that weeds, pests, and weather present, and to find joy in the simple pleasure of doing a little better each season.

The Art of High-Yield Gardening

You might say that production gardeners are a bit like artists; the soil is their canvas, plants are their medium, and each onion, apple, and head of lettuce is a work of art. Their work is a constant presence in everything they do.

Like artists, many growers find that their passion increases over time. As you become intimately familiar with your crops and your soil, your techniques will become second nature and you will truly get lost in your work. The most successful growers are those who continue to find new inspiration in their crops and systems. For some, experimenting with new varieties every year helps keep them engaged and motivated. For others, achieving a continual harvest of salad greens or breeding their own variety of winter squash feeds the passion.

Anyone can become an artist in their garden. No matter the size of your plot, you'll find that as your knowledge and experience grow, so will your yields and your passion for food production.

> To be successful and to improve their growing systems year after year, high-yield gardeners relish the opportunity to learn from their mistakes.

HOW TO USE THIS BOOK

This book is not a comprehensive encyclopedia of vegetable production. Rather, it's a guide to help you maximize garden productivity at home. Although we provide useful information for growers at every skill level, we focus on techniques designed to increase yields for the production-minded gardener. We give you the systems, techniques, and knowledge used on small vegetable production farms every day. If you follow the processes detailed throughout the book, you can expect a more productive and educational gardening season.

It will take time for you to develop a system that employs all of the techniques outlined in this book. Even though you will improve your garden productivity from day one, you should approach your project with a long view. We recommend that you apply your new skills as they become appropriate, as you work to develop your own high-yield production garden.

It should be no surprise that professional growers take their work very seriously. They monitor every aspect of their farm: recording when crops are planted, fertilized, irrigated, weeded, thinned, pruned, and harvested. They note which varieties perform best, and they continuously make adjustments to their practices as they develop more efficient and successful ways of caring for their crops. We have outlined these practices and we think that, with time and consideration, you, too, will become a successful high-yield vegetable gardener.

High-Yield Garden Profiles

In this section, we profile high-yield gardeners and their spaces. Throughout the book, we'll come back to these gardens and take a closer look at the crop plans, rotation plans, and irrigation maps of their sites, so you can really see how all the elements of a high-yield garden might come together in one place.

Each of the following profiles is based on a real high-yield garden site that we helped design and implement. We've changed the names of the homeowners, but the rest of the details are true to life. We hope that you'll see similarities to your own site and situation, and that these profiles will help you visualize your own project.

RYAN AND KIWI
Neighborhood: urban
Lot size: 5,000 square feet (approx. ⅛ acre)
Garden size: 400 square feet
Garden goals: maximize production from a limited space

JASON
Neighborhood: suburban
Lot size: 10,000 square feet (approx. ¼ acre)
Garden size: 1,040 square feet
Garden goals: grow lots of tomatoes and peppers!

DAVE AND ERIN
Neighborhood: rural
Lot size: 44,000 square feet (approx. 1 acre)
Garden size: 8,000 square feet
Garden goals: produce vegetables for family consumption and a strawberry U-pick for friends and neighbors

A TYPICAL CITY LOT

Ryan, Kiwi, and their new baby live close to the city in a residential urban neighborhood comprising 5,000-square-foot, rectangular lots organized in a grid pattern. Their house is set smack-dab in the middle of the yard, with a driveway and one-car garage on the northeast side.

Ryan and Kiwi have been living and gardening in the space for a few years, and they've used just about every nook and cranny to create the high-yield garden of their dreams. The total square footage of the annual garden beds is just 400 square feet, but they make the most of it. The garden is broken up into a few different areas to make the best use of the sunniest portions of the property. They've also created a small indoor plant nursery in the laundry room, which has an east-facing window and easy access to the garden and the outdoor hose bib (faucet).

A portion of the garage serves as the tool shed, perennial herbs and berries fill the front yard and surround the back deck, and the shade of the large maple tree in the northeast corner provides an ideal mushroom-growing habitat.

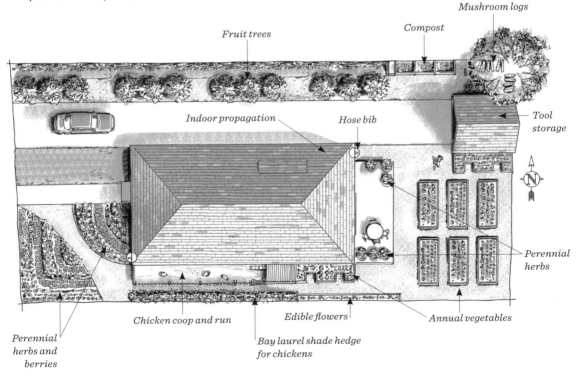

Mushroom logs

Compost

Fruit trees

Indoor propagation

Hose bib

Tool storage

N

Perennial herbs

Chicken coop and run

Edible flowers

Bay laurel shade hedge for chickens

Annual vegetables

Perennial herbs and berries

A QUARTER-ACRE IN THE SUBURBS

Jason lives in a residential neighborhood that's just far enough from the city to have yards that are a little larger and more open. The entire backyard has been transformed into a highly productive raised-bed garden (800 square feet of raised beds and 240 square feet of greenhouse bed space). The whole property receives a full day of sunlight, so he converted every inch of it into workable garden space.

The house came with a south-facing atrium, which he converted into a great propagation nursery. As an extra bonus, there is a small shed and a little area that has an open-air storage area covered by a metal roof that the previous owner used for boat storage. (Jason calls this area "The Lid.") He keeps his mower and other power tools in the shed and keeps garden tools under The Lid. This area also serves as a great outdoor

work space when the weather is uncooperative but he still wants to get some work done outside.

Jason has built a small chicken coop, planted dwarf fruit trees, and set up a pretty big greenhouse (10' × 30') to extend his growing season.

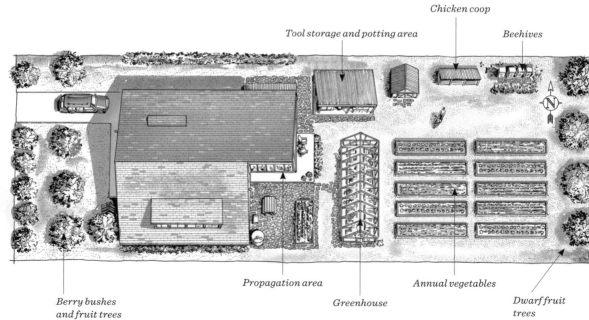

Chicken coop

Beehives

Tool storage and potting area

Propagation area

Greenhouse

Annual vegetables

Dwarf fruit trees

Berry bushes and fruit trees

ONE RURAL ACRE

Dave and Erin live in a rural area where lots can range anywhere from half an acre to 10 acres. They're thrilled with the garden space they have but feel that any more would probably be too much to manage. The lot has a unique shape, and they've decided to leave the "back 40" as a wild area to attract wildlife and create a sound buffer between them and the nearest street.

They have a lot of space to spread out, so even though the garden is very large (approximately 8,000 square feet), it doesn't seem overwhelming in the space. They've set up a small propagation greenhouse near the house, for easy access. The garden sits a bit farther back, where the ground is level and there is ample sunlight.

Native trees and shrubs

Wine grapes

Sport court

Propagation greenhouse

N

Tool storage

Vegetables and strawberries

Berry bushes

PART 1

Planning and Planting What You Need

CHAPTER 1

Making a Site Plan

Before you start digging up your yard, it's a good idea to develop a complete site plan and a detailed strategy for developing your garden. To attain your high-yield goals, it's important to efficiently utilize as much of the yard as possible. Developing a comprehensive site plan will help you meet this goal with a minimum of headaches and backaches.

Creating your site plan can be one of the most creative and fun aspects of the project. It's a way to brainstorm and plan for all the elements you'd ultimately like to see in your garden. This is the time to be open-minded and consider as many variations on the project as possible. Soliciting outside opinions from friends and other gardeners can generate great new ideas and/or confirm your original thoughts.

If you're starting the garden from scratch, creating a detailed map will help you think about your space holistically and place the elements of your garden in the best location possible. If you have an existing garden, this process can help you reorganize or expand your garden and find ways to add new production spaces.

MAPPING YOUR PROPERTY

You can draw your site plan any time of year, but the off season is a great time to get started. Knowing that you have a few months of lead time will make you less likely to rush or cut corners, which you might be prone to do when you are eager to get your plants in the ground. If you already have a garden on your property, the best time to create your map is right after the end of a growing season. Putting the pieces together is often easiest when you're cleaning up your summer crops and the past year's successes and failures are fresh in your mind.

Create a Base Map

To create your site plan, start with a base map of the space you'll be working with. Try to make the representation of your property as accurate as possible, so that different areas are drawn in scale to each other.

In order for areas and elements to appear in scale on the map, you'll need to know how large and how far apart they are in your yard. This will require that you take a lot of measurements. Recruit an assistant, if possible, and use a tape measure to find all possible dimensions of the yard. Measure the edges of your property line, the dimensions of your house, the location of any other notable items (such as the driveway or walkways), existing planting beds, and the placement of hose spigots and dryer vents on the house. Even small, seemingly insignificant details can affect the garden, so try and take note of everything you can. (For example, a dryer vent can blast very warm, drying air outside and coat nearby plants in a film of lint, both of which can result in stress and lower productivity.)

If you're computer savvy, you can use online resources that will make mapping

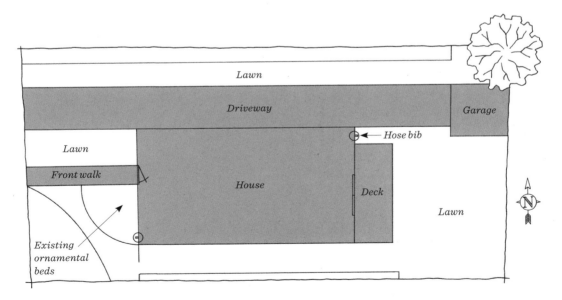

The first step to planning the garden is to create a base map. This one shows existing structures, impermeable surfaces, and landscape elements.

your property much easier. Depending on your location and other variables such as how much tree canopy cover is on your property, you might be able to trace an image of your lot in Google Earth and print the image, or even export it to a computer-drawing program such as SmartDraw, SketchUp, AutoCad, or Inkscape.

You may be able to use a few other shortcuts to create your property map. For example, you may have received a map of the property when you purchased your home. If not, in many municipalities you can request a map of your property from the city or town government. If you have an existing map, scan it into the computer or trace it onto a new sheet of paper for use as a starting point for your garden design. Be sure to draw in elements like utility lines, trees, ornamental landscaping, fences, patios, decks, water sources, streets, alleyways, light poles, and known time capsules.

How Much Garden?

Following are some general guidelines on the needs and potential productivity of different garden sizes. These are only rough estimates: everyone uses a garden differently. Not everyone grows food for the same number of people, and those people will vary in age and dietary preferences. The time needed to manage your space also depends on how tidy and weed-free you like to keep it.

Spend some time considering the number of other time commitments you typically have throughout the year. An honest assessment will really help you determine which garden size may work best for you. The good news is that it's relatively easy to expand or shrink a garden from year to year; you can adjust as needed after a season or two of experience.

100–200 Square Feet

This is an appropriate size for a beginning gardener who wants to try a few different crops and eat consistently from the yard during the peak harvest seasons. Half an hour to an hour a week will be enough to keep up with all garden tasks.

200–400 Square Feet

This is a good size garden for the intermediate gardener with a hectic schedule. It will yield adequate fresh produce for one to four people throughout spring, summer, and fall, with some produce left for putting up. An hour or two of work a week will be sufficient.

400–800 Square Feet

A group of two to six people can expect to eat fresh from the garden during the main growing season and also harvest quite a bit for late fall and winter storage. A space this size will require at least two to three dedicated hours per week for upkeep, harvesting, and processing of crops.

800–1,500 Square Feet

This size garden can feed four to eight people through the growing season and produce enough storage vegetables to supplement your diet through much of the winter. Plan to spend at least four to six hours a week managing the space for maximum production and appearance.

SITING GARDEN SPACE

Once you have a good map of your property, it's time to figure out how your garden fits into it. There are four important questions to ask:

- How big will your annual vegetable garden be?

- Will perennial garden spaces be incorporated into the plan?

- Where will garden spaces be located on your property?

- Where will garden-related elements like toolsheds and compost bins be located?

Once you've identified the general areas you're going to use for garden space, you'll choose the exact location of your garden beds and other elements within the space. Because annual garden spaces are much more time and energy intensive than

1,500–2,000 Square Feet
This is a large-enough garden to feed 6 to 10 people during the season and still distribute small quantities of especially productive crops. With proper planning, it is possible to grow substantial storage crops and cold-season greens. Expect to spend six to eight hours a week keeping up with the garden.

2,000–4,000 Square Feet
This is entering into the realm of a serious undertaking, with a garden that will supply 8 to 15 people with fresh produce through much of the season. Keeping up with this much space will require at least 8 to 12 hours a week. During peak harvest season, you may need to spend several nights a week processing and storing your crops.

4,000–8,000 Square Feet
A very substantial home vegetable garden, this much space will feed up to 20 people and may also provide a few crops for wider distribution. Plan to spend 12 to 15 hours a week, plus extra time for processing and distribution, as needed.

8,000–15,000 Square Feet
The largest home garden we have seen falls in this range. You will have the opportunity to produce great quantities of food year-round for up to 25 people. Plan to spend 15 to 20 hours a week managing your space.

15,000–22,000 Square Feet
Managing this much space will be a part-time job. Expect to spend at least 20 hours per week or more. A garden this

size can feed up to 30 people and can provide many opportunities for storage, processing, and selling of produce.

22,000–44,000 Square Feet
This is an endeavor large enough to require a full-time manager. This range is approximately half an acre to one acre (43,560 square feet is one acre). A garden this size is a serious endeavor and will likely require additional equipment and supplies that are not described in this book. However, the techniques and systems we describe will be very applicable to a project of this size, but you would need to research the equipment necessary to effectively manage such a space.

perennial garden spaces, deciding on the size and location of your annual beds should be the first priority. In general, we recommend against mixing annual and perennial crops in a single planting bed.

Determining Size

Annual beds can be created to fit whatever space you have available. As the garden increases in size, you'll have more opportunities to diversify your crop selection, extend your harvest season, and increase the overall volume of food grown on site. Even the most intensively managed garden space has limits to how much food it can produce, so adding square footage will always add productivity. At the same time, adding space means that you'll need to invest additional time and materials to create and manage your garden.

Let's take a look at the three factors that will help you determine how large a garden you might be ready to manage. You should think in terms of space, time, and priorities.

How Much Space Do You Have?

First, look at your property map and think about the amount of space you can devote to your garden. It may be that you're comfortable opening up your entire property to food production, or you may find that you have a few other competing priorities that you must resolve first. Do you need to preserve some play space, for example, or do you want to retain the large screening hedge that shades the side yard? In addition to the spaces that will be used for growing, you'll also need to identify the areas you have available to help support your garden, including spaces for tool storage and composting.

How Much Time Can You Spend?

Your time commitment and availability is something you'll need to honestly assess before developing your garden plan — this may be even more important than deciding how much of your yard you can commit.

If you create an annual garden that is three times larger than you have time to manage, you will have created a weed propagation site that exponentially adds to the work you have to do. If you plant more crops than you can tend, food may go to waste. It's important to remember that creating a highly productive home farm is a lifestyle choice, and that a portion of your free time will be dedicated to caring for it. If you plan to take long summer vacations, for example, you may miss the harvest of some of your crops.

Fall is an especially busy time of year for the production gardener, as many hours are needed to harvest and preserve your amazing food. Fall evenings and weekends are often needed to complete this work. If you're truly interested in high-yield gardening, you'll most likely take pleasure in these tasks, and probably choose to harvest during the growing season and find time for vacations during the off-season.

> Creating a highly productive home farm is a lifestyle choice . . . a portion of your free time must be dedicated to caring for it.

What Are Your Growing Priorities?

Why are you building a high-yield garden? Do you want to sell tomatoes to the local corner store? Do you want the most diverse range of edible plants possible? It's important to identify your end goals for the project so that you can intelligently lay out the garden and dedicate appropriate amounts of space to each crop.

For example, if you want to grow salad for dinner every night, you will have to determine how much salad your household uses, how many nights per week you eat at home, how long it will take each planting to grow, and how many plantings you'll need to make through the year. This planning process is actually a lot easier than it sounds, and it can be fun to do, as you'll see in the next chapter.

Write down your big-picture priorities as clearly as you can, and use them as a reference during the design process. You will need to keep these goals as your guiding light through the process so that you stay on track and actually get what you want from your project.

Siting Annual Beds for Ideal Production

After determining the size of your annual garden beds, finding the best location for them will most likely be your next priortity. You may want to include lots of other features in your garden, such as tool storage and vegetable washing stations. However, your annual beds will be the most intensively managed and productive space, and will require the most sunlight, so they should be given primary consideration.

You should consider the following few factors when selecting the best spot for your garden beds. Bear in mind that your entire garden doesn't need to be in one spot — it can be dispersed across the space, if that works best on your property.

Full Sun Exposure = Productive Plants

Good sun exposure — a minimum of six hours of direct sunlight per day — should be Rule #1 in the high-yield vegetable gardener's handbook. There is a direct correlation between hours of sunlight and plant productivity, and with few exceptions, more sun is always better. Without adequate light, even a garden with the most amazing soil and meticulous care will produce leggy, stressed crops and minimal harvests. If your yard has many shady areas, reserve them for other uses such as shade-tolerant perennial edibles, mushroom production, tool storage, or a potting area.

Seeking the sun with technology. There are several new technologies that can help you identify sun exposure, and we encourage you to try them out. If you have a smartphone or other mobile device, try an app called Sun Seeker. The paid version of this app allows you to create a 3-D view of your space, including the trajectory of the sun on a given day, and on the winter and summer solstice! There are probably other similar apps on the market, so explore the options and find one that works for you. Technologies such as these will be a quick and invaluable resource when selecting a garden site.

Just look around. Barring the use of such technology, you might have to locate the sunniest spots the old-fashioned way: by looking around. Make note of the sunlight and shadows in your yard at different times of day. You may already know which parts of your property get the most sun, but once you start looking, you may be surprised to find previously overlooked potential garden locations.

Timing the Light

If you have difficulty determining the best spot(s) for your garden, wait for a clear, sunny day and keep an eye on the yard throughout the day. Write down what time a potential garden area starts getting sun and what time it becomes shaded. The sunlight doesn't need to be continuous; a few hours of midday shade is okay, as long as the total sun exposure adds up to at least six hours.

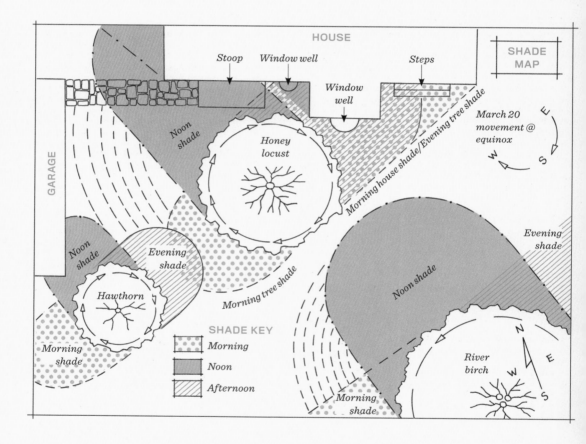

SHADE MAP

HOUSE

Stoop

Window well

Window well

Steps

March 20 movement @ equinox

Noon shade

Honey locust

Morning house shade/Evening tree shade

GARAGE

Noon shade

Evening shade

Morning tree shade

Noon shade

Evening shade

Hawthorn

Morning shade

SHADE KEY

Morning

Noon

Afternoon

River birch

Morning shade

Without adequate sunlight, even a garden with the most amazing soil and meticulous care will produce leggy, stressed crops, and minimal harvests.

Orientation. A sunny area may be on any side of the yard — north, south, east, or west. What's important is the garden space's relationship to your house, nearby trees, fences, neighbor's houses, and other shadow-casting objects. If you want to place a garden to the north of a tall object, assume that the object will cast a shadow equal to its height. For example, if your house has a roof that's 20 feet high, a garden on the north side of it should be at least 20 feet away.

It's also important to think about the light your yard gets in the morning and evening. A space to the east of a large object might be sunny in the morning but completely shaded in the afternoon. Growers in cooler summer climates generally prefer western exposure (plants don't do much growing during cool summer mornings), and growers in hotter summer climates generally prefer eastern exposure (it may be too hot in the afternoon for the plants to do much growing).

Seasonal variation. Depending on your latitude, the amount of sun a space receives can change dramatically from season to season. Unless you live on the equator, the trajectory of the sun changes throughout the year. The arc of the sun is higher in the summer and lower in the winter. Therefore, a location that is shady in December may get plenty of sun in midsummer. If you are analyzing your space in midwinter, keep in mind that deciduous trees will create lots of shade in the summer. During winter, sunlight may be filtering through the exposed branches of trees, so remind yourself that things will look very different in the middle of July, when the tree has fully leafed out (although a spot near a deciduous tree might work well for a shoulder-season fall or spring garden bed).

Identifying Beneficial Microclimates

Every property has a unique set of climatic conditions that contribute to the property's "microclimate." Wind patterns, sun exposure, and the building materials on your property all have significant effects on plant health and productivity. Building materials can have surprisingly large impacts; for example, a concrete driveway will capture and radiate much more heat than a gravel driveway. Similarly, an exposed concrete wall will capture and radiate more heat than a wooden wall.

Keep the following points in mind as you identify microclimates on your site.

- Urban areas are typically warmer than rural areas; as a general rule, the closer to a city you live, the warmer your property will be. Man-made structures tend to absorb heat, so the density of buildings and pavement correlates to a warmer local environment. This is often referred to as the heat-island effect.

- Areas on your property that are adjacent to east-, west-, or south-facing walls often have higher temperatures. The exterior walls of your home, garage, shed, or other outbuildings absorb heat from the sun throughout the day. These walls act as a heat sink, capturing warmth and radiating it back out into the environment when temperatures drop. The heat-sink effect creates higher daytime and nighttime temperatures.

- Ground-level pavement or stonework can also act as a heat sink. Your driveway or patio might be several degrees warmer than a nearby lawn.

- Tall structures and plants can create windbreaks. Wind can cool down crops and dry them out. An area that is relatively protected from prevailing winds may be a better garden location.

- The areas underneath trees and the eaves of buildings may have extremely dry soil.

- Areas at the base of a hill may be cooler than nearby areas. Just as hot air rises, cool air sinks, and cool air pockets can settle at the bottom of a hill. Properties or portions of a property that lie in a valley may experience earlier and later frosts each season than the surrounding areas.

Deep, Rich Soil

In a perfect world, the soil in your yard will be deep, rich, and full of organic matter, primed and ready for vegetable growing. From our experience, this is a very uncommon occurrence. Most likely, you will be spending some time and effort improving the soil on site. (See chapter 5, beginning on page 112.)

Don't worry too much if the soil in your ideal garden location needs help. If you're concerned about contamination (lead, arsenic, or others), then you should get the soil tested. (See chapter 5 for more information on testing for contaminants.) Contamination issues aside, consider soil improvement to be a standard part of your garden-creating process and an ongoing part of your maintenance practices. In other words, don't rule out a space just because it seems to have poor soil.

Good Access

Determine what path you will be taking to and from the garden, and make sure there are no obstacles in the way of efficient garden work. Not every garden can be placed right outside your back door, but you'll want to make accessing the garden as quick and simple as possible. All those wasted minutes running all the way around the house to grab a tool or packet of seeds add up during the course of a season. And you'll want the opportunity to run out to the garden to grab last-minute vegetables while cooking up dinner. Even small inefficiencies, repeated over and over, can become obstacles to effective garden care.

You'll also want to consider access to water when locating your garden beds. No matter what irrigation system you employ, it is essential that watering the garden not be a hassle or an additional burden on your time. Identify all of your available water lines and determine the easiest routes to bring that water to your garden site.

Grade – Less Is More

Consider whether a slope on your property requires additional work or management to be included in your garden project. A very slight slope of 3 percent or less is easily managed in a garden. Greater angles will cause soil erosion and poor water infiltration. In addition, slopes are uncomfortable working spaces. Plan to terrace or regrade garden areas as necessary, or focus your efforts on flatter portions of the yard.

Fencing Needs

If there's a high probability that deer, rabbits, unruly dogs, or other large animals may wreak havoc in the garden, consider preemptive fencing and whether it is feasible in your ideal garden spot. The size and type of fence you need depends on the specific concern, but large animal intrusion is a big enough threat that you should address this issue early on in your planning process.

Shape and Dimension

A garden can take any shape. Traditionally, vegetable gardens have been laid out with square or rectangular beds. These types of gardens are still most common because of their natural space efficiency and ease of use, but there is no rule that dictates the shape of your garden space and beds. Whatever the shape, make sure to create beds that are easy to work in and work around.

Fitting beds into the space that is available to you gives you the best opportunity for maximizing your productivity. For example, if an area tapers significantly at one end, create a triangle-shaped bed so that you are able to use the whole space. Always look for opportunities to increase your plantable square footage.

We recommend that you plan to create planting beds that are no wider than 4 feet wide, so that you can reach into them without stepping into the bed. Wider beds will present management challenges or create dead spaces that you can't reach.

Beds can be any length that works in the space. Make sure you include enough pathways to make movement through the garden comfortable and easy. Paths can be any width that is comfortable — use 2 feet wide as a starting point and adjust to meet your

needs. For larger gardens, consider including a wider access path for wheelbarrows or garden carts.

In most locations, for efficiency of space and ease of use, we prefer 4-foot-wide rectangular beds with 2-foot-wide pathways that are mulched with newspaper and straw, wood chips, or bark mulch.

Siting Additional Elements

After determining the best location for your vegetable beds, it's time to think about the other elements of your space. A few elements that play important roles in a high-yield production garden follow here; we recommend that you read about them in more detail before you finalize your site plan.

- *Propagation and nursery area.* Propagating and growing out your own plants is a fun and money-saving process that extends the gardening season, allows you to manage your garden more intensively, and connects you more closely to the garden. Propagating your own transplants is not absolutely necessary, but doing so is made easier if you have an appropriate space for it.

- *Large composting area.* High-yield gardens produce more food and more plant waste than typical home gardens. Regardless of the composting structure and technique you use, choosing a way to process and manage plant waste is essential. Some plant waste will be easy to compost and some will be pest and disease ridden, so proper technique is crucial (see page 242).

- *Tool storage.* You'll need a space to keep your tools protected from the elements and easily accessible. Possible locations include a garage, a tool shed, a spot under the eaves of the house, inside your propagation area, or under an elevated deck.

PUTTING IT ON PAPER

Now it's time to figure out which garden elements are most important to you and where to place them on your plan. Seeing fully conceptualized plans on paper may help you brainstorm, so as you proceed, refer back to the garden profiles on pages 8–11.

Make a Comprehensive List of All Elements You'd Like to Include

This list should be as specific as possible and should include garden and non-garden-related elements. We strongly believe that an edible garden is most productive when it's a space where you want to spend time and that meets your specific needs. For some people, this means using every square foot of the yard for food production and its supporting activities. Others will want to balance their high-yield garden with other lifestyle and recreational needs. Make a design that accommodates each of your desired elements, so that everything is set in the best possible location.

Write up a first draft of your list and revisit it over several days, adding and crossing off elements as you refine your plans.

Pencil In the Elements You're Certain About

Maybe there's only one part of your yard that's appropriate for an orchard, greenhouse, or other garden element. Marking out the footprints of these elements first will help you assess the remaining available spaces. At this point in the process your goal is to determine the potential of every space in your yard. We strongly believe that virtually every square inch of most any property can be used to further the end goal of high-yield food production. Not every location is appropriate for vegetable beds or nursery propagation, but an awkward, challenging spot may turn out to be perfect for root cellaring, composting, or storing wheelbarrows or extra straw bales. Be open-minded. Walk your property over and over again, considering the potential of every space.

Prioritize Your Elements

Number each element according to priority. Take time to consider the importance of year-round production, ease of care, and aesthetics.

Place Elements on Your Site Plan

Now that you have a map of your property (including the location of your annual garden beds), it's time to put the remaining elements on the map and finalize your site plan. Some items may fit perfectly into a single, obvious spot. Others might take some finagling and compromise to fit them in. Elements should be placed in relation to each other whenever possible. For example, keeping the seed-starting supplies next to the seed propagation area will save you a lot of time in the nursery.

Determine a Timeline for Installation of the Elements

Chances are that you will not be ready to build every portion of your project immediately. Even if you are, it will likely take several weeks or months to accomplish all of the work. Prioritize the most important elements and make a realistic timeline for their installation.

Possible Elements of a High-Yield Landscape

A. Fruit trees (which types and what size — dwarf, semi-dwarf, or full size?)

B. Annual vegetable/herb/flower beds

C. Beehives and mason bee boxes

D. Cistern/water catchment

E. Compost system

F. Fish tank or pond for fish production

G. Greenhouse

H. Habitat plantings, especially for pollinators and other beneficial insects

I. Livestock pens: chickens, ducks, goats, rabbits

J. Mushroom production area

K. Outdoor dining area with firepit

L. Outdoor wash/pack station

M. Perennial herb beds

N. Pest exclusion fences: deer fence, rabbit fences, dog fences

O. Produce stand

P. Propagation area

Q. Shrubs: berries

R. Tool and equipment storage

S. Water feature for ducks, frogs, wild birds

INDOORS: Indoor production area for microgreens and sprouts, kitchen space adequate for food processing, pantry storage, refrigeration/freezing storage, root cellar, seed storage (freezer, fridge, dresser, cabinet, plastic tubs)

CHAPTER 2

Crop Selecting, Scheduling, and Recordkeeping

Your goal as a high-yield gardener is not just to grow a huge amount of food but also to have it be consistently available over the course of the year. It doesn't do you any good to grow 100 pounds of basil in July if you can't eat all of it or store it to eat later!

To maximize production from the garden, you'll need a planting plan — a schedule specific to your garden that tells you which crops you're going to plant and when you're going to plant them. This plan, along with detailed recordkeeping, is what really distinguishes high-yield production gardening from ordinary back-yard gardening. Crop scheduling allows you to make more efficient use of your space. In fact, you may double or triple the harvests you would otherwise expect from a given amount of garden space.

In addition to helping you increase the volume of food your garden produces, your planting plan will also help you avoid waste from over-planting, make the best use of your soil nutrients, and minimize pest and disease problems.

CONSIDER CROP LIFE SPAN WHEN PLANNING

You may already have a very good idea which crops you want to grow, or you may be exploring ways to expand your planting palette. Regardless, knowing more about the life span and growth cycle of your crops will help you make decisions about what to plant, when to plant it, where to plant it, and how much of it to plant.

Make the Most of Annual Crop Space

When most people think of a vegetable garden, they picture annual plants — botanically defined as those that complete their life cycle in one growing season. Typically these plants are started from seed, planted in the garden, produce a harvest, and then perish a few weeks or a few months later. Some annual crops like bush beans die mid-season, right after the edible portions are harvested. Many others, like tomatoes and squash, die as soon as temperatures drop below freezing.

Depending on where they're grown, some plants that are cultivated as annual crops can actually live for more than one season. Some herbs — such as basil, cilantro, dill, and parsley — fall into this category. Peppers and tomatoes can grow as perennials in equatorial South America, but they are almost always grown as annuals in more temperate regions such as the United States and Canada. Artichokes are perennials in moderate climates such as the central coast of California, but must be grown as annual crops in the Northeast and Midwest where winter temperatures are too cold for them to survive.

Annual Plants vs. Annual Crops

It can be a little confusing, but there is a subtle difference between annual plants and annual *crops*. Understanding the distinction is important; it may help you to grow a crop that otherwise would be considered not viable in your climate.

Annual plants are those that, in one growing season, start as seeds and grow roots, stems, leaves, flowers, and fruit; then set seed and die. Annual plants include lettuce, beans, and squash (and many ornamental flowers, which are often just referred to as "annuals").

Annual crops are planted, grown, harvested, and either die on their own or are turned into the soil (or removed from the garden) over the course of one growing season. There are perennial plants that are grown as annual crops in many situations. For example, wild arugula is a perennial plant, but is grown as an annual crop in the northeastern United States because it can't survive the winter there.

Annual Crop Life Span

DIRECT-SEEDED CROPS

Short Season (in Days to Harvest)

Arugula, 30–60
Dill, 40–60*
Lettuce, Baby Mix, 25–40
Mustard Greens, 20–25 (baby)
Mustard Greens, 40–50 (full size)
Radishes, 30–60
Spinach, 30–40*
Turnips, 30–60

Half Season (in Days to Harvest)

Beans, Lima, 60–90
Beans, Snap, 50–60*
Beets, 50–60*
Carrots, 50–80
Cilantro, 50–60
Mâche, 50–65
Peas, Shelling, 50–65*
Peas, Snap, 50–65*
Scallions, 60–70*

Long Season (in Days to Harvest)

Beans, Edible Soy (Edamame), 75–90*
Beans, Fava (Broad), 75–120*
Beans, Shell, 70–85*
Corn, Sweet, 65–85*
Parsley, 70–80*
Parsnips, 100–120
Peanuts, 90–150
Potatoes (from tubers), 70–120
Rutabagas, 90–100
Squash, Pumpkins, 80–120*
Squash, Winter, 80–120*
Watermelon, 70–90 *

Can be planted either from seed or from transplant

TRANSPLANT

Short Season (in Days to Harvest)

Basil, 60
Bok Choy, 45–60 (full size)*
Endive, 45–60*
Lettuce, Head, 30–45*
Raab, 35–45

Half Season (in Days to Harvest)

Broccoli, 60–75
Cabbage, 60–90
Cabbage, Chinese, 50–60
Cauliflower, 50–80
Chard, Swiss, 50–60
Collards, 50–60
Cucumbers, 50–60*
Eggplant, 55–75
Kale, 50–60
Kohlrabi, 40–80
Okra, 50–60
Radicchio, 55–70
Squash, Summer, 45–60*
Tomatillos, 55–75
Tomatoes, 55–85

Long Season (in Days to Harvest)

Brussels Sprouts, 90–120
Celeriac, 90–110
Celery, 75–85
Fennel, 75–85 (bulbing)
Garlic, 210+ (planted from cloves)
Leeks, 70–120
Melon, Cantaloupe, Honeydew, 70–90*
Onions, Bulb, 90–110
Peppers, Hot, 70–120
Peppers, Sweet, 70–120
Squash, Gourds, 90–130*
Sweet Potatoes (from slips), 90–100

When you're planning what to grow, it's important to consider how long each crop will be in the ground, especially if you have limited space for growing annual plants.

Short-season crops can be grown from seed or transplant, and can be ready to harvest in a short period of time (30 to 60 days). Since they have a short growing season, you can plant these crops several times over the course of the year. Examples include arugula, cilantro, lettuce, radishes, and spinach.

Half-season crops take roughly half of a standard growing season to reach maturity (50 to 80 days). You might plant these two to three times over the course of the season: once in the spring, once in early summer, and again in mid- to late summer. Examples include beets, broccoli, cabbage, cauliflower, carrots, and kale.

Long-season crops take a long time to reach maturity (70 to 120 days). You'll plant these early in the season and harvest them toward the end of the season. In many cases, you can do two plantings of long-season crops in the spring, and then harvest them a few weeks apart in the fall. Examples include melons, peppers, tomatillos, tomatoes, and winter squash.

Super-long-season crops are the outliers in the general crop categorization. They are commonly planted in the fall and harvested in the summer of the following season. These crops include garlic, some types of onions, and (in some climates) fava beans.

Plan for Continued Perennial Food Production

You may want to include perennial crops in your garden. These are plants that are expected to live for more than one growing season. Some short-lived perennials, often referred to as biennial crops, typically live for one and a half or two years (parsley, for example). Other perennials might live for two to three years (some types of sage, strawberries), up to 15 years (asparagus), or even 100 years (apple trees).

In general, perennials require less maintenance and care than annuals. Perennials can provide additional food production from spaces that may not be ideal for annuals. (For example, many perennials require less sun exposure and irrigation than the average annual crop.) They can also add year-round beauty to the landscape. On the downside, some perennials spread aggressively over time, taking up valuable space and producing more than you could possibly use. Some perennials can take several years to generate a harvest, so considerable time and space must be dedicated to nurturing them to maturity. In these cases, there is always the additional risk that, once mature, you won't actually like the variety or taste of the crop you have produced! Always take time to thoroughly research and taste perennial crops and varieties before commiting.

Knowing the average life span of each perennial crop is essential when you're planning for continued production over the long term. Some perennials, such as strawberries or lavender, will only produce for a few seasons before losing vigor or becoming

Older Plants = Sooner Harvest

With woody perennial plants, the time between planting and harvest depends on the particular plant and on the size at which it is purchased. For example, if you plant a three-year-old blueberry bush, you'll be able to start harvesting blueberries sooner than if you plant a one-year-old blueberry bush. Mail-order plants are usually young and small, whereas plants from a local nursery may be larger and older (and more expensive). You'll need to decide for yourself whether or not older plants (that will produce sooner) are worth the money.

Try to get perennial plants into the ground early in your garden development plan so that they can become established and grow to maturity as soon as possible. This is why it's so important to have a full site plan in place: you want to ensure that you've already set aside appropriate places for these crops.

Recommendations for Herbs

For most perennial herbs, we recommend initially purchasing plants from a nursery rather than starting your own from seed or cuttings. Purchasing even relatively small, inexpensive plants (for example, a 4-inch pot) should enable you to start harvesting two to three seasons earlier than if you'd propagated your own plants. Purchase larger, longer-lived herb plants (such as bay laurel) in 1-gallon pots or larger.

Once your plants are established and producing harvests, you can propagate new plants from them for future generations of herbs. Many perennial herbs, even if they're still alive, will become overly woody, stemmy, and difficult to keep healthy after several seasons. If you plan to replenish your stock of new young plants every few years, take cuttings from your established herbs and propagate them in your home nursery until they're ready for planting in the garden (see page 167 to learn more about propagation from cuttings).

Dwarfing Rootstocks and Tree Life Span

For many home orchardists, growing dwarf or semi-dwarf fruit trees makes a lot more sense than full-size fruit trees because they're easier to harvest and prune. It's important to know that, generally speaking, a tree on a dwarfing rootstock will start fruiting earlier than a semi-dwarf (and semi-dwarfs fruit earlier than full-size trees), but their life span is shorter. For example, a dwarf apple tree might start fruiting in 3 to 5 years, but will only have a productive life span of 25 to 30 years. A full-size apple might take 10 years to start fruiting, but could have a productive life span of 50 years or longer.

unsightly. Further, they won't produce anything the first year you plant them. For these types of crops, you'll want to make sure to schedule future plantings carefully so as to prevent gaps in production a few years down the road. Other perennials like fruit and nut trees might produce for 30 years or more, but can take anywhere from 3 to 10 years to start producing (depending on the crop, variety, and rootstock, if the plant was grafted).

Staggering Your Fruit Harvest

Most fruit harvests are once-a-year events. Blueberry season is midsummer, for example, and apple season is in the fall. It is a delightful practice to consume as much fresh fruit as possible during these periods, while simultaneously attempting to preserve as much as you can for the rest of the year. However, it is possible to extend the harvest season of many perennial fruits by planting many different varieties with staggered harvest times. For example, planting a mix of early-season, mid-season, and late-season varieties of blueberries will give you a much longer harvest period than if you only plant mid-season varieties. The same principle holds true for plum trees, raspberries, and many other perennial crops.

Plant Perennials Separately

For many reasons, we recommend planting perennial crops in locations that are separate from your annual crops. Many perennials will stay in the garden or landscape for several years with minimal care, and the frequent soil management needed for annual crops can be disruptive for perennials. And

although perennial plants often lend beauty and structure to the overall landscape, they can also grow aggressively and take over larger spaces than you intended, competing with annual crops for water and nutrients.

Take time to understand the mature size and growth habits of perennial crops before placing them in the garden. The array of sizes and habits of perennial crops can be quite stunning. Even though lovage and oregano are both fast-growing perennial herbs, the lovage can grow to 6 feet tall, while the oregano will never reach more than 2 feet. Horseradish, mint, and raspberries are known to spread aggressively, and can quickly become nuisance plants if not contained. Some types of fruit trees (figs and apples, for example) respond amazingly well to heavy pruning and shaping, so you can manipulate them to fit the spaces you have. On the other hand, other species like cherries can grow so vigorously that you might have trouble keeping them in shape. Different species of fruit trees can even have drastically different life spans ranging from 15 to over 100 years. The key here is to adequately research and understand your perennial crop choices before selecting their home in the garden. Refer to the table on page 300 for more information.

Extend the harvest season of many perennial fruits by planting different varieties with staggered harvest times.

PLANNING FOR STORAGE

Growing appropriate amounts of storage crops is the key to enjoying produce from your garden in a steady, consistent supply throughout the growing season and into the winter. So, when you're developing a planting plan, give some thought to how your crops will ultimately be stored and make selections based on your storage capacities and preferences.

Some crop varieties have much better storage lives than others. If you're planning to store a crop for a long period, make sure you choose a variety that stores well. For example, the yellow onion variety 'Copra' will hold much longer than the sweet white onion variety 'Ailsa Craig'. A good seed catalog or some online research will help you determine if a particular variety is well suited for storage.

Fresh crops that must be processed for storage. These include vegetables like tomatoes, peppers, broccoli, summer squash, and snap beans. They are typically grown to be eaten fresh, but can also be canned, frozen, or dehydrated for long-term storage. (See chapter 14, starting on page 270, for more information.)

Single-planting storage crops. This includes bulb onions, garlic, potatoes, and winter squash. These crops are typically planted once per year, harvested, and preserved by holding them at the proper temperature and humidity (in a root cellar, for example). With enough space and proper conditions, you can be eating these delicious crops from your garden well into the winter months or even into the following spring.

Keep in mind that certain varieties will last much longer in storage than others. For example, softneck garlic stores for a longer time than most hardneck types. Similarly, small, yellow onions store longer than big, sweet white or red onions. Plant some varieties for long-term storage and other varieties for shorter-term storage or fresh eating.

Succession planting storage crops. Some crops that are planted in successions throughout the year for fresh eating are also excellent keepers in storage. Classic examples are carrots, beets, and turnips. A typical strategy for these crops is to make multiple small plantings during the growing season for fresh eating, then making a large final planting toward the end of the season for storage. Properly stored root crops can last six months or longer.

Grains and legumes. It is possible to grow and store considerable amounts of carbohydrates and protein via crops like dry beans, peanuts, field corn, and small grains such as wheat or rye. To produce usable yields from these sources, a large space may be necessary. Also, many of these crops become very time intensive to process and store on a small scale without specialized equipment. For these reasons, we don't discuss growing them in this book (other than as cover crops). For more information, consult the resources on page 307.

Perennial storage crops. Many perennial crops produce high yields and can be readily converted into long-term storage foods. Perennial herbs such as oregano and thyme can be cut and dried for year-round use. Fruit trees typically yield once a year but often provide an abundant harvest that can be kept as fresh fruit for several months, while the remainder can be processed into sauce, jam, and other storable items.

CONSIDER LOCAL CONDITIONS

As you might imagine, crops that grow best in one region may not always grow well in another. Local conditions dramatically affect the success of crops and should be taken into account when selecting varieties, determining when to plant, and anticipating potential problems.

Schedule Plantings to Match Your Growing Season

The best time of the season to plant each crop varies by region. It takes experience and local knowledge to really determine ideal dates on a planting schedule. So if you're new to an area or have never grown food in a certain climate, talk to experienced local growers or call an Extension agency to learn their secrets, like how early you can plant tomatoes or what's the latest date you can direct seed bush beans. If you don't have access to local knowledge for all the crops you want to plant, you can build a planting calendar based on your average first and last frost dates. (See page 54.)

USDA Plant Hardiness Zones

Pay special attention to climatic conditions when selecting your perennial crops. Almost any plant will be rated by its hardiness, as determined by the United States Department of Agriculture (USDA) Plant Hardiness Zone Map. The USDA uses climate data to ascertain the average low temperature for different regions of the country. The map was updated in recent years and will likely be continually updated as temperature ranges shift in coming decades. To find your zone, visit the USDA's website (see Resources, page 309).

Winter hardiness is the baseline for your perennial plant selection. Find plants and varieties that are hardy where you garden, but be aware that rare weather events can still damage or kill plants that are technically considered viable in your climate. Another tactic is to use microclimates in your yard to grow crops that are generally considered borderline hardy in your region.

Precipitation and Crop Yield

High-yield growers must know their local precipitation patterns and be prepared to respond as necessary. We believe it's important for all gardeners to have some way to irrigate their crops. This becomes vital if you have to accommodate significant dry spells during your growing season.

For example, although the Pacific Northwest is known for its rainy spells, almost all of this rain comes in the fall, winter, and early spring. Gardeners must be able to irrigate continuously through the dry months of June through September. In contrast, a grower in the Midwest may experience good rainfall throughout the growing season, but will still need to irrigate during dry periods between rain events for maximum yields.

Keep in mind that all precipitation doesn't fall as gentle rain. Heavy precipitation such as thunderstorms or hail can damage crops. If you know that these types of precipitation are common in your climate, be prepared to protect your crops with row cover, and if possible, to time plantings to avoid damage.

Snow cover will also affect your crops. Snow can act as an insulator, protecting overwintering crops. It can also kill tender crops if it comes at an unanticipated time. Growers in regions that are prone to late-spring or early-fall snow events may need to rely on season-extension techniques to protect their crops (see page 252 for more information). Always be prepared for unseasonal weather events. Review the weather forecasts every day and be ready to act accordingly.

Latitude Affects Growth

Your position on the globe can have a surprising effect on crop growth habits. Areas in more northerly latitudes will have longer days during the summer, which cause crops to grow to maturity very quickly. However, these regions have shorter days in fall and winter, which lead to slower growth of fall plantings and slower spring regrowth of hardy greens grown in protective structures.

In southern latitudes, crops may grow to maturity at a slower rate because day length is shorter than in northern regions during the growing season. However, the overall growing season in the southern regions will be longer, meaning that fall and winter production may be more feasible as compared to more northern latitudes.

Knowledge of how plants respond to day length is vital if you're going to maximize your onion production.

STRATEGIES FOR PLANTING

There are many ways of scheduling crops to get the most out of your garden. Some growers live and die by a single method, while others use a combination of all of the following strategies. Examine each type of planting strategy and decide how each can be incorporated into your garden, keeping in mind that certain crops are better suited to certain strategies.

Succession Planting for a Consistent Supply

Succession planting — the practice of planting small quantities of a crop on a regular basis so that they can be harvested at regular intervals — is by far the most essential planting strategy for increasing garden production and maintaining a consistent supply of short-season crops throughout the growing season. For example, many new growers catch spring fever and plant a huge amount of salad greens early in the season, only to wonder what to do with their 75 heads of lettuce come June. A better approach (assuming you're growing lettuce only for your own household use) would be to plant for two heads of lettuce every week, starting as early as weather allows and continue until late in the season. This would allow you to harvest two heads of lettuce a week from April through October, enough for a salad every night of the week.

Some short-season crops are at their peak harvest stage for a very short period, after which they quickly lose their texture and taste. Lettuce, arugula, and cilantro are good examples. These crops need to be planted every one or two weeks to ensure a steady supply of high-quality produce. Crops that can hold their quality a bit longer in the field or have a longer harvest period (beets, carrots, bush beans) might be planted every two to four weeks.

Of course, there are many situations where you might want a large quantity of one crop at one time for canning, freezing,

Onions: A Special Consideration

To maximize yield when growing onions, it's important to understand how different varieties respond in different latitudes. So-called short-day onions start forming a bulb when day length reaches 12 to 13 hours. Intermediate-day (or day-neutral) onions bulb between 13 to 14 hours. Long-day onions bulb when day length reaches 14 hours or more.

Mature bulb size is correlated with the size of the plant when bulbing initiates, so if you have a very tiny onion plant that starts bulbing, you're going to end up with a very tiny onion bulb at the end of the year. If you live at a northerly latitude, you might have 12 or 13 hours of daylight in March or early April, when you've just set out your onion starts. If you set out a short-day onion, it is destined to produce a diminutive onion. If you set out a long-day onion, it might have another month or two of growing time before bulbing occurs. In the south, if you plant a long-day onion, it might never form a mature bulb because bulbing won't initiate until too late in the season for it to fully form.

Clearly, knowledge of this physiological trait is vital if you're going to maximize your onion production. If you're gardening north of 40 degrees north latitude, be sure to choose long-day onions. Gardeners south of 36 degrees north latitude should be growing short-day onions, and those in between should grow day-neutral types. Some onions are listed in catalogs as "widely adapted" and can be grown throughout the United States.

In mild northern climates like the Pacific Northwest, some growers trick short-day onions by direct seeding them in the fall and overwintering them. This creates a larger plant in the spring when bulbing initiates, and is how 'Walla Walla' sweet onions are grown in Washington and Oregon states. You can also try this with day-neutral onions in southern latitudes.

It's vital to start your onions early and to give them optimal care in the spring to make sure the plant is as large as possible when bulbing begins. Here in the north, we start our onion transplants in a green-house in mid-January.

---

or serving at a large party. Just make sure to size each planting of each crop appropriately for its intended end use.

Plant in Succession to Avoid Disease

Some half- and long-season crops can be planted in succession to avoid disease problems and to maintain the longest possible harvest period. For example, many growers in the Midwest plant three to four successions of tomatoes to keep ahead of early blight. Growers in the Pacific Northwest plant two to three successions of summer squash to ensure a prolonged harvest: later season plantings come into maturity just as early plantings succumb to powdery mildew.

Successions, Spacing, and Scheduling

In this table, you'll find information on how far apart to space plants, how much of the growing season each crop will take to grow, and how frequently to plant crops in order to maintain a consistent supply. To determine first and last planting dates for your climate, please see the Planting Dates chart on page 56.

ANNUAL VEGETABLES, FRUITS, AND HERBS

Arugula
Spacing: seed thickly in rows, approx. 30 plants per row foot
Scheduling: short season
Successions: weekly

Basil
Spacing: 6–12"
Scheduling: half season
Successions: 1–3 plantings

Beans, Edible Soy (Edamame)
Spacing: 1.5–2"
Scheduling: long season
Successions: 1–3 plantings

Beans, Fava (Broad)
Spacing: 4–6"
Scheduling: half season
Successions: generally, 1–3 plantings in spring; fall planting is possible in areas with winter lows above 10°F

Beans, Lima
Spacing: 3"
Scheduling: long season
Successions: 1–3 plantings

Beans, Shell
Spacing: 3–4"
Scheduling: half season
Successions: 1–3 plantings

Beans, Snap
Spacing: 2–3"
Scheduling: half season
Successions: every 2–3 weeks

Beets
Spacing: 4"
Scheduling: half season
Successions: every 2–3 weeks

Bok Choy
Spacing: for baby size, 2–4", for full size, 6–12"
Scheduling: short–half season
Successions: every 1–2 weeks

Broccoli
Spacing: 12–18"
Scheduling: half season
Successions: every 2–3 weeks

Brussels Sprouts
Spacing: 18"
Scheduling: long season
Successions: 1–2 plantings in spring

Cabbage
Spacing: 12–18"
Scheduling: half season
Successions: every 2–3 weeks

Cabbage, Chinese
Spacing: 12–18"
Scheduling: half season
Successions: every 2–3 weeks

Carrots
Spacing: 2"
Scheduling: half season
Successions: every 2–3 weeks

Cauliflower
Spacing: 12–18"
Scheduling: half season
Successions: every 2–3 weeks

Celeriac
Spacing: 8"
Scheduling: long season
Successions: 1–2 plantings in spring

Celery
Spacing: 8–12"
Scheduling: long season
Successions: 1–2 plantings in spring

Chard, Swiss
Spacing: 8–12"
Scheduling: half season
Successions: every 4 weeks

Cilantro
Spacing: seed thickly in rows, 12–24 plants per row foot
Scheduling: short season
Successions: weekly

Collards
Spacing: 8–12"
Scheduling: half season
Successions: every 4 weeks

Corn, Sweet
Spacing: 8–12"
Scheduling: half–long season
Successions: weekly

Cucumbers
Spacing: 12" if trellised, 5 sq. ft. per plant if sprawling
Scheduling: half season
Successions: every 4 weeks

Dill
Spacing: 9"
Scheduling: half season for leaf, long season for flowers/seeds
Successions: weekly

Eggplant
Spacing: 12"
Scheduling: long season
Successions: 1–2 plantings in spring

Endive
Spacing: 8–12"
Scheduling: short season
Successions: weekly in spring and fall

Fennel, Bulbing
Spacing: 6–12"
Scheduling: half season
Successions: weekly

Garlic
Spacing: 6–8"
Scheduling: long season
Successions: one planting in fall

Kale
Spacing: 8–12"
Scheduling: half season
Successions: every 4 weeks

Kohlrabi
Spacing: 4–6"
Scheduling: half season
Successions: weekly

Leeks
Spacing: 6"
Scheduling: long season
Successions: 1–2 plantings in spring

Lettuce, Baby Mix
Spacing: thickly seeded in rows, approx. 30 plants per row foot
Scheduling: short season
Successions: weekly

Lettuce, Heads
Spacing: 6–12"
Scheduling: short season
Successions: weekly

Mâche
Spacing: 1"
Scheduling: half season
Successions: every 1–2 weeks in early spring and fall

Melon, Cantaloupe, Honeydew
Spacing: 2–3'
Scheduling: half–long season
Successions: 1–3 plantings

Mustard Greens
Spacing: for baby greens, seed thickly in rows, approx. 30 plants per foot; for full-size greens, space at approx. 1"
Scheduling: short–half season
Successions: every 1–2 weeks

Okra
Spacing: 12–18"
Scheduling: half season
Successions: 1–3 plantings

Onions, Bulb
Spacing: 4–6"
Scheduling: long season
Successions: 1 planting

Parsley
Spacing: 8–12"
Scheduling: half–long season
Successions: 1–3 plantings

Parsnips
Spacing: 2"
Scheduling: long season
Successions: 1 planting

Peanut
Spacing: 10"
Scheduling: long season
Successions: 1 planting

Peas, Shelling
Spacing: 1–2"
Scheduling: half season
Successions: 1–3 plantings in spring, 1–2 in fall

Peas, Snap
Spacing: 1–2"
Scheduling: half season
Successions: 1–3 plantings in spring, 1–2 in fall

Peppers, Hot
Spacing: 12"
Scheduling: long season
Successions: 1–3 plantings

Peppers, Sweet
Spacing: 12"
Scheduling: long season
Successions: 1–3 plantings

Potatoes
Spacing: 12"
Scheduling: long season
Successions: 1 planting

Raab
Spacing: 1–2"
Scheduling: half season
Successions: every 1–2 weeks

Radicchio
Spacing: 10–12"
Scheduling: half season
Successions: every 1–2 weeks in spring and fall

Radishes
Spacing: 1–2"
Scheduling: short season
Successions: weekly

Rutabagas
Spacing: 6–8"
Scheduling: half season
Successions: 1–3 plantings

Savory, Summer
Spacing: 12"
Scheduling: long season
Successions: 1 planting

Scallions
Spacing: ½"
Scheduling: half season
Successions: every 1–2 weeks

Spinach
Spacing: 1–2"
Scheduling: short–half season
Successions: every 1–2 weeks in spring and fall

Squash, Gourds
Spacing: 2–3'
Scheduling: half–long season
Successions: 1–3 plantings

Squash, Pumpkins
Spacing: 2–3'
Scheduling: long season
Successions: 1–3 plantings

Squash, Summer
Spacing: 2–3"
Scheduling: half season
Successions: 1–3 plantings

Squash, Winter
Spacing: 2–3'
Scheduling: long season
Successions: 1–3 plantings

Sweet Potatoes
Spacing: 12–18"
Scheduling: long season
Successions: 1 planting

Tomatillos
Spacing: 18–24"
Scheduling: long season
Successions: 1–3 plantings

Tomatoes
Spacing: 18–24"
Scheduling: long season
Successions: 1–3 plantings

Turnips
Spacing: 4–6"
Scheduling: short season
Successions: every 1–2 weeks

Watermelon
Spacing: 2–3'
Scheduling: long season
Successions: 1–3 plantings

PERENNIAL VEGETABLES

Artichoke
Spacing: 2–3'
Scheduling: perennial

Asparagus
Spacing: 12"
Scheduling: perennial

Cardoon
Spacing: 2–3'
Scheduling: perennial

Jerusalem Artichoke, Sunchoke
Spacing: 12"
Scheduling: perennial

Rhubarb
Spacing: 3–4'
Scheduling: perennial

PERENNIAL GARDEN FRUITS

Blackberries
Spacing: 2–3'
Scheduling: perennial

Blueberries
Spacing: 3–6'
Scheduling: perennial

Raspberries
Spacing: everbearing types: 12", June–bearing types: 2–3'
Scheduling: perennial

Strawberries
Spacing: 12"
Scheduling: perennial

PERENNIAL HERBS

Anise Hyssop
Spacing: 6"
Scheduling: perennial

Bay
Spacing: 2–4'
Scheduling: perennial

Chives
Spacing: 10–12"
Scheduling: perennial

Chives, Garlic
Spacing: 10–12"
Scheduling: perennial

Fennel
Spacing: 3'
Scheduling: perennial

Horseradish
Spacing: 12"
Scheduling: perennial

Lavender
Spacing: 2–3'
Scheduling: perennial

Lemon Balm
Spacing: 12"
Scheduling: perennial

Lemongrass
Spacing: 18–36" (culinary types)
Scheduling: perennial

Lemon Verbena
Spacing: 18"
Scheduling: perennial

Marjoram
Spacing: 8–12"
Scheduling: perennial

Mint
Spacing: 12–18"
Scheduling: perennial

Oregano
Spacing: 12+"
Scheduling: perennial

Purple Coneflower
Spacing: 42"
Scheduling: perennial

Rosemary
Spacing: 18–24"
Scheduling: perennial

Sage
Spacing: 2–3'
Scheduling: perennial

Savory, Winter
Spacing: 12–18"
Scheduling: perennial

Stevia
Spacing: 12"
Scheduling: perennial

Tarragon
Spacing: 18–24"
Scheduling: perennial

Thyme
Spacing: 18–24"
Scheduling: perennial

Valerian
Spacing: 12–18"
Scheduling: perennial

Relay Planting for Efficient Use of Space

Relay planting is the practice of growing two crops in the same bed, or planting a second crop in a bed where a crop is already growing, knowing that you'll harvest the first crop before the second grows too large to compete with it.

This way of planting is a great way to get crops planted earlier if you have a limited amount of space, or if you want to maximize production per square foot. The drawback is that the close spacing of crops can encourage the spread of fungal and bacterial disease. It's best to try relay planting with crops that you don't generally have disease issues with. Following are some ideas to get you started; feel free to experiment and try new ideas out as you gain experience.

Onions across the Seasons

Another kind of succession planting is simply to include many different kinds of related crops that can be used in similar ways. Onions are a good example of this. There's a wide range of onion types that prefer different growing and storage conditions, but have very similar taste and nutritional benefits. In many regions, given enough space and proper planning, there is no reason you couldn't grow and eat onions every day of the year.

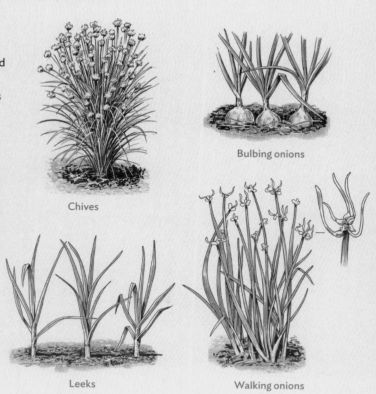

Chives

Bulbing onions

Leeks

Walking onions

Snap peas. If you don't have problems with powdery mildew, try transplanting a row of snap peas along a trellis, then direct seeding a row of peas along the same trellis one week later. The direct-seeded peas should come into production as the transplanted ones are petering out. You can also try planting pole beans along the trellis in May; they'll start climbing over the peas after the peas are done producing.

Carrots and tomatoes. Carrots and tomatoes are a classic companion planting. Try seeding an entire bed of carrots with 6 inches between the rows about six to eight weeks before you transplant your tomatoes. When you're ready to plant the tomatoes, clear 8-inch-diameter holes in the carrot seedlings every 18 inches down the center of the row, and transplant tomatoes into the holes. Carefully harvest the carrots with a

First in Spring

Chives are a hardy perennial green onion, tolerant of a range of conditions. They sprout early in the spring and can be harvested repeatedly throughout the season. Growing more like a grass than a normal vegetable crop, a few bundles of chives planted in the garden can provide almost unlimited green onions for the duration of your growing season. These could be up and growing before your cache of stored onion bulbs has been depleted.

Through the Summer

Bulbing onions are typically long-season crops that are started indoors in late winter, planted in spring, and harvested in midsummer. Depending on the variety,

they will have different storage capacities. Generally, yellow types store longest. If properly cured and stored, it is possible to eat bulbing onions from midsummer through the following spring.

Fall and Winter

Leeks are a very long season crop; they're also very cold hardy. They're typically planted for fall harvest and used through the fall and into the winter. In some regions, the hardier varieties of leeks can also be heavily mulched to survive the winter and be harvested in spring.

Continual Harvest

Scallions grow relatively quickly and can be succession planted many times throughout the growing season. Since they take up little space, these

green onions can fit into your planting plan in small amounts whenever needed.

Shallots are like miniature bulb onions that can be planted numerous times per year. Shallots can be planted in fall for late winter and spring harvest, or they can be planted in spring for summer and fall harvest.

Walking onions are a perennial plant that produces an array of crops — bulbs (similar to shallots), shoots (similar to chives), and a unique "topset" of tiny airborne bulbs. Crops can be harvested spring through fall.

To maximize space efficiency, tomatoes can be relay-planted into a bed of carrots — once the carrots have been pulled, the tomatoes will have room to grow.

trowel when they've sized up. If things go as planned, all the carrots will be harvested before they compete with the roots of the tomatoes. This technique also works well with direct-seeded lettuce mix, arugula, and spring spinach.

Salad greens and long-season transplanted crops. Place a lettuce transplant in between each transplanted pair of tomato, summer or winter squash, cucumber, or brassica. Plan to harvest the lettuce just before it's overwhelmed by the other, larger crop. Direct seeding a row of lettuce mix, arugula, or mustard greens on the outside edges of a tomato or summer squash bed will produce the same results.

Potatoes and short-season crops. Start by planting potatoes at 1-foot spacing in a bed, then direct seed arugula, spinach, or mustard greens in between the rows. You should be able to harvest the greens before the potato foliage fills out and shades the area.

Companion Planting

Companion planting is the practice of growing two different crops together or adjacent to each other to save space, or because the close proximity of the paired-up plants is mutually beneficial. One caution: be careful to give each plant the space it needs to grow well. We've seen a lot of leggy, stressed basil plants overwhelmed by sprawling tomatoes because the two crops were planted nearly on top of each other.

For Saving Space

Carrots and radishes. Start by direct seeding rows of carrots spaced 6 inches apart. Then plant a row of radishes in between each row of carrots. The radishes germinate and grow much more rapidly than the carrots, meaning that you should be harvesting radishes about a week or two after the carrot tops emerge.

Corn and winter squash. Because corn grows vertically and winter squashes have a sprawling habit, the two can be grown together in the same plot to save space. Some growers believe that the scratchy leaves of the squash plants also help discourage raccoons from eating the corn. At the very least, the spreading squash plants reduce the need for weeding around the corn. Make sure the plants are irrigated well and the soil is very fertile because both crops are quite heavy feeders.

Corn and pole beans. Corn stalks can provide a structure for pole beans to climb. Sow two or three pole beans around each corn stalk a few weeks after the corn has emerged from the soil and begun to grow. The beans make an especially great companion for corn because they fix nitrogen into the soil, helping the corn (a very heavy feeding crop) along.

For Deterring Pests

The examples listed here are not necessarily scientifically validated. They have been employed by growers, and anecdotal evidence suggests that these these pairings deter pests. Many growers will agree that experimenting with new crop arrangements is worthwhile even if results are not guaranteed, which is usually the case in food production, even under the best of circumstances.

Onions and carrots. Onions (and other alliums) are believed to repel carrot rust fly. Interplant them with carrots to keep this nasty pest away. Try spacing carrot rows 12 inches apart and planting a row of bulb onions in between the rows, or space the carrot rows 9 inches apart and plant scallions in between rows.

Scallions and brassicas. Interplanting scallions between brassica plants can help repel root maggot flies. Plant a clump of 2 or 3 scallion plants in between brassica plants that are spaced 18 inches apart.

Cilantro and beans. Cilantro is believed to help repel aphids. Seed successions of cilantro near crops that have aphid problems, such as brassicas and beans.

CREATING YOUR PLANTING PLAN AND CALENDAR

Now that you're up to speed on the concepts and techniques that production growers use to maintain a steady harvest, we can describe how to create a planting plan and how one can help you make a high-yield garden happen. Your planting plan will be the backbone of your recordkeeping system — and using a simple recordkeeping process ensures that the experience you gain each season can inform future choices and help improve yields over time.

Making a planting plan can be daunting if you've never done it before, but once you get started, we think you'll find it to be a fun, exciting, and rewarding task. To build your own planting plan, you'll need to make the following decisions in this order:

1. Which crops to grow

2. How much of each crop to plant

3. When/how often to plant them

Once you've made these decisions, you will input all the data into your planting calendar. During each week of the growing season, you should refer to your planting calendar to see how much of which crops to plant during that week. Out in the garden, things never go exactly as you plan, so your planting calendar should have space for you to write down what you actually do. (For example, maybe you decide to plant carrots a week early, or you increase the amount of salad mix you sow each week midway through the season.)

Begin by working through the Crop Amount Worksheet and the Yields of

Annual Vegetables and Herbs chart that follow. This will help you calculate how many pounds you'll need of each crop. Once you've figured this out, you'll need to determine your average last spring frost date and first fall frost date.

Once you've identified these dates, you can then refer to the Planting Dates chart on page 56 to find out your first and last planting date for each crop. Refer back to the succession planting chart on page 36 to determine how frequently to plant each crop.

If you're growing your own transplants, you can figure out when to start the seeds using the chart on page 56. Once your planting calendar is complete, you can decide where to plant the crops in your garden. Include this information on your planting calendar if you so desire. (See page 70.)

Electronic versions of the following spreadsheets are available on Seattle Urban Farm Company's website (see Resources, page 309). We recommend saving an unedited version of each as a basic template, and then creating a new version each season going forward.

Weekly Crop Harvest Goals

What are your harvest goals for the garden? How much of each crop do you want to harvest each week? You can use the following Crop Amount Worksheet as a reference to help guide your thoughts. At this point, you might not know exactly how many pounds of each crop you'll need. If so, just put down your best estimate. You might want to make a detailed plan for every crop you plan to grow, or you might create a plan for one or two important crops and wing it for the rest.

How Much to Plant, Based on Your Needs

Now that you've identified how much you'd like to harvest, you'll need to determine how much to plant so that you can meet that goal. Use the yield chart on page 51, referring back to your calculations on the Crop Amount Worksheet, and enter the numbers for each crop you're planning to grow. Grab a calculator to figure out how many row feet you need to plant to get your desired amount, or download a spreadsheet at Seattle Urban Farm Company's website and use its automatic formulas (see Resources, page 309). Refer back to the succession planting chart on page 36 to determine how frequently to make a planting of a crop.

The 20 Percent Buffer

When determining crop production yield, standard practice is to plant 20 percent more than you think you'll need. Doing so accommodates for low germination rates, pest issues, and other unpredictable occurrences. For example, if your calculations indicate that you should plant 100 row feet of beets for your desired yield, plan to seed 120 row feet to make sure you get the harvest you want.

Crop Amount Worksheet

To determine the number of servings you want to produce per week, consider how many people you will be growing for and how many servings they will eat each week. You can also account for extra amounts for freezing and/or canning in this column. Please note that the weights and volumes in the Average Serving Size column are for raw produce (before cooking). For more on planning for crop storage, see page 32. To determine the number for the Total Weight of Crop column, multiply the number of ounces in the Average Serving Size column with the number you wrote in the Number of Servings column, and then divide by 16 (because there's 16 ounces in a pound).

Download this chart at Seattle Urban Farm Company's website (see Resources, page 309) if you don't want to do the math yourself.

Annual Vegetables	Average Serving Size	Number of Servings You Want to Produce Each Week	Total Weight of Crop Needed per Week in Pounds
ARUGULA	4 ounces		
BASIL	8 leaves or 1 ounce		
BEANS, EDIBLE SOY (EDAMAME)	1 cup or 4 ounces, unshelled		
BEANS, FAVA (BROAD)	8 ounces unshelled beans		
BEANS, LIMA	8 ounces fresh, in pods		
BEANS, SHELL	20 pods		
BEANS, SNAP	1 cup or 3.8 ounces		
BEETS	½ cup or 3 ounces		
BOK CHOY	2 cups or 5 ounces		
BROCCOLI	¾ cup or 2.4 ounces		
BRUSSELS SPROUTS	6 sprouts or about 4 ounces		
CABBAGE	1 cup or 3 ounces		
CABBAGE, CHINESE	1 cup or 3 ounces		
CARROTS	1 medium or 2.2 ounces		
CAULIFLOWER	½ cup or 2 ounces		
CELERIAC	½ cup or 2.5 ounces		
CELERY	½ cup or 2 ounces		
CHARD, SWISS	3 cups raw, chopped or 8 ounces		
CILANTRO	used as spice, about 0.5 ounce		
COLLARDS	3 cups raw, chopped or 8 ounces		

Crop Amount Worksheet CONTINUED

Annual Vegetables	Average Serving Size	Number of Servings You Want to Produce Each Week	Total Weight of Crop Needed per Week in Pounds
CORN, SWEET	1 ear or about 2.2 ounces kernels		
CUCUMBERS	½ cup or 8 ounces		
DILL	used as spice, about 0.5 ounce		
EGGPLANT	1 cup or 3 ounces		
ENDIVE	1 cup or 1.7 ounces		
FENNEL, BULBING	1 cup or 3 ounces		
GARLIC	1 clove or 0.2 ounce		
KALE	3 cups raw, chopped, or 8 ounces		
KOHLRABI	½ bulb or about 4 ounces		
LEEKS	1 cup or 8 ounces		
LETTUCE, BABY MIX	4 ounces		
LETTUCE, HEADS	2 cups or 2 to 4 ounces		
MÂCHE	4 ounces		
MELON, CANTALOUPE, HONEYDEW	½ cup or 3 ounces		
MUSTARD GREENS (FULL SIZE FOR BRAISING)	3 cups raw, chopped, or 8 ounces		
OKRA	10 pods or 3.5 ounces		
ONIONS, BULB	½ cup or 3 ounces		
PARSLEY	used as spice, about 0.5 ounce		
PARSNIPS	4 ounces		
PEANUT	1.5–2 ounces		
PEAS, SHELLING	8 ounces unshelled or ½ cup shelled		
PEAS, SNAP	1 cup or 2.2 ounces		
PEPPERS, HOT	variable, 0.1–1 ounce		
PEPPERS, SWEET	½ cup or 2.6 ounces		
POTATOES	3–4 ounces		
RAAB	¾ cup or 2.4 ounces		
RADICCHIO	1 cup or 1.4 ounces		

Annual Vegetables	Average Serving Size	Number of Servings You Want to Produce Each Week	Total Weight of Crop Needed per Week in Pounds
RADISHES	½ cup sliced or 2 ounces		
RUTABAGAS	6–8 ounces		
SCALLIONS	½ cup or 1.7 ounces		
SPINACH	1 cup or 1.1 ounces		
SQUASH, PUMPKINS	8 ounces		
SQUASH, SUMMER	1 cup or 4 ounces		
SQUASH, WINTER	8 ounces		
SWEET POTATOES	½ cup or 2.5 ounces		
TOMATILLOS	2–4 ounces		
TOMATOES	4 ounces (1 medium-size tomato)		
TURNIPS	6–8 ounces		
WATERMELON	½ cup or 2.7 ounces		

Perennial Vegetables	Average Serving Size	Number of Servings You Want to Produce Each Week	Total Weight of Crop Needed per Week in Pounds
ARTICHOKE	1 artichoke or 4.5 ounces		
ASPARAGUS	1 cup or 4.5 ounces		
CARDOON	2 basal leaves or 4 ounces		
JERUSALEM ARTICHOKE, SUNCHOKE	3–4 ounces		
RHUBARB	1 stalk or 2.5 ounces		

Crop Amount Worksheet CONTINUED

Perennial Garden Fruits	Average Serving Size	Number of Servings You Want to Produce Each Week	Total Weight of Crop Needed per Week in Pounds
BLACKBERRY	½ cup or about 2 ounces		
BLUEBERRY	½ cup or about 2.5 ounces		
CURRANT	½ cup or about 2 ounces		
ELDERBERRY	½ cup or about 2.5 ounces		
GOJI BERRY	¼ cup or about 2 ounces		
GOOSEBERRY	½ cup or about 2 ounces		
HUCKLEBERRY	½ cup or about 2 ounces		
JOSTABERRY	½ cup or about 2 ounces		
LINGONBERRY	1 ounce		
RASPBERRY	½ cup or about 2 ounces		
STRAWBERRY	½ cup or about 3.5 ounces		
WINTERGREEN	not applicable		

Perennial Herbs	Average Serving Size	Number of Servings You Want to Produce Each Week	Total Weight of Crop Needed per Week in Pounds
ANISE HYSSOP	approx. 1 tablespoon or about 0.1–0.2 ounce		
BAY	approx. 1 tablespoon or about 0.1–0.2 ounce		
CHIVES	approx. 1 tablespoon or about 0.1–0.2 ounce		
CHIVES, GARLIC	approx. 1 tablespoon or about 0.1–0.2 ounce		
FENNEL	approx. 1 tablespoon or about 0.1–0.2 ounce		
HORSERADISH	approx. 1 tablespoon or about 0.1–0.2 ounce		
LAVENDER	approx. 1 tablespoon or about 0.1–0.2 ounce		

Perennial Herbs	Average Serving Size	Number of Servings You Want to Produce Each Week	Total Weight of Crop Needed per Week in Pounds
LEMON BALM	approx. 1 tablespoon or about 0.1–0.2 ounce		
LEMONGRASS	approx. 1 tablespoon or about 0.1–0.2 ounce		
LEMON VERBENA	approx. 1 tablespoon or about 0.1–0.2 ounce		
MARJORAM	approx. 1 tablespoon or about 0.1–0.2 ounce		
MINT	approx. 1 tablespoon or about 0.1–0.2 ounce		
OREGANO	approx. 1 tablespoon or about 0.1–0.2 ounce		
PURPLE CONEFLOWER	approx. 1 tablespoon or about 0.1–0.2 ounce		
ROSEMARY	approx. 1 tablespoon or about 0.1–0.2 ounce		
SAFFRON	approx. 1 tablespoon or about 0.1–0.2 ounce		
SAGE	approx. 1 tablespoon or about 0.1–0.2 ounce		
SAVORY, WINTER	approx. 1 tablespoon or about 0.1–0.2 ounce		
SORREL	approx. 1 tablespoon or about 0.1–0.2 ounce		
STEVIA	approx. 1 tablespoon or about 0.1–0.2 ounce		
TARRAGON	approx. 1 tablespoon or about 0.1–0.2 ounce		
TEA, CAMELLIA	approx. 1 tablespoon or about 0.1–0.2 ounce		
THYME	approx. 1 tablespoon or about 0.1–0.2 ounce		
VALERIAN	approx. 1 tablespoon or about 0.1–0.2 ounce		

Fruit and Nut Trees	Average Serving Size	Number of Servings You Want to Produce Each Week	Total Weight of Crop Needed per Week in Pounds
ALMOND	¼ cup or about 1 ounce		
APPLE	1 apple or about 4–6 ounces		
ASIAN PEAR	1 pear or about 4–6 ounces		
CHERRY	2.5–3 ounces		
CITRUS	variable		
EUROPEAN PEAR	1 pear or about 4–6 ounces		
FIG	1 fig or 2–3 ounces		
HAZELNUT	¼ cup or about 1 ounce		
MULBERRY	½ cup or about 2 ounces		
PEACH	1 peach or about 6 ounces		
PLUM	1 plum or about 5–6 ounces		
WALNUT	¼ cup or about 1 ounce		

Vines	Average Serving Size	Number of Servings You Want to Produce Each Week	Total Weight of Crop Needed per Week in Pounds
AKEBIA	2.5 ounces		
GRAPES	1 cup or about 3–4 ounces		
HOPS	not applicable		
KIWI	1 cup or about 6 ounces		

Yields of Annual Vegetables and Herbs

Yields can vary greatly, depending on your climate, soil fertility, which cultivars you select, and many other factors. We strongly suggest you keep your own records and adjust your plantings accordingly in future seasons.

Yields are approximate and calculated per row foot. If you are growing using the square-foot method, you can still easily determine how many row feet of each crop you have. For a given crop, take the length of one side of the square in feet and multiply it times the total number of plants you will be setting out. For example, if you will be growing 8 kohlrabi plants in 6" squares, 0.5' × 8 plants = 4 row feet of kohlrabi.

Arugula
Yield: 0.25 pound
Note: per cutting; expect 1–2 cuttings a week apart

Basil
Yield: 0.1 pound
Note: per week; expect 1–2 harvests per week over the course of the season

Beans, Edible Soy (Edamame)
Yield: 0.2 pound

Beans, Fava (Broad)
Yield: varies
Note: expect to harvest 15–60 total pods over the harvest period (closer to 15 for large-seeded varieties, closer to 60 for small-seeded varieties) per plant

Beans, Lima
Yield: 0.1–0.2 pound

Beans, Shell
Yield: 0.1–0.2 pound

Beans, Snap (bush)
Yield: 0.25 pound
Note: per picking; expect 1–4 pickings about 1 week apart

Beans, Snap (pole)
Yield: 0.25 pound
Note: per picking; expect 6–12 pickings about 0.5–1 week apart

Beets
Yield: 0.5 pound
Note: not including greens
Alternative quantity per row foot: 2–3 roots

Bok Choy
Yield: 1.3 pounds
Note: for full-size types; yield is less for baby size

Broccoli
Yield: 0.4 pound
Note: from cutting of main head; plant will continue to produce smaller quantities of side shoots for 1–4 weeks after main head is cut
Alternative quantity per row foot: 1 head plus side shoots

Brussels Sprouts
Yield: 0.6 pound
Note: you will probably harvest this amount over the course of 2–3 pickings unless you cut the entire stalk at once

Cabbage
Yield: 1.5 pounds
Alternative quantity per row foot: 1 head

Cabbage, Chinese
Yield: 1.5 pounds
Alternative quantity per row foot: 1 head

Carrots
Yield: 1 pound
Alternative quantity per row foot: 4–6 roots

Cauliflower
Yield: 0.75 pound
Alternative quantity per row foot: 1 head

Celeriac
Yield: 0.75 pound
Alternative quantity per row foot: 1–2 roots

Yields of Annual Vegetables and Herbs CONTINUED

Celery
Yield: 0.75 pound
Alternative quantity per row foot: 1 head

Chard, Swiss
Yield: 0.3 pound
Alternative quantity per row foot: ⅓ of a bunch per week

Cilantro
Yield: 0.5 pound
Note: per cutting; expect 1–3 cuttings about a week apart

Collards
Yield: 0.3 pound
Note: per picking; expect about 1 picking per week for 2–5 months
Alternative quantity per row foot: ⅓ of a bunch per week

Corn, Sweet
Yield: 0.5 pound
Alternative quantity per row foot: 1–2 ears

Cucumbers
Yield: 0.75 pound
Note: per picking; expect about 1–2 picking per week for 1–2 months
Alternative quantity per row foot: 1–2 fruits per week

Dill
Yield: 0.5 pound
Note: per cutting; expect about 1 cutting per week for 2–3 weeks

Eggplant
Yield: 0.75 pound
Note: per picking; expect about 1 picking per week for 1–3 months
Alternative quantity per row foot: 1–2 fruits per week

Endive
Yield: 0.75 pound
Alternative quantity per row foot: 1 head

Fennel, Bulbing
Yield: 0.75 pound
Alternative quantity per row foot: 1 bulb

Garlic
Yield: 0.1 pound
Alternative quantity per row foot: 1–2 bulbs

Kale
Yield: 0.3 pound
Note: per picking; expect about 1 picking per week for 2–5 months
Alternative quantity per row foot: ⅓ of a bunch per week

Kohlrabi
Yield: 0.4 pound
Alternative quantity per row foot: 2–3 bulbs

Leeks
Yield: 1 pound
Alternative quantity per row foot: 2–3 leeks

Lettuce, Baby Mix
Yield: 0.15 pound
Note: per cutting, expect 1–4 cuttings about a week apart depending on conditions

Lettuce, Heads
Yield: 0.75 pound
Alternative quantity per row foot: 1 head

Mâche
Yield: 0.1 pound

Melon, Cantaloupe, Honeydew
Yield: 1.5 pounds
Note: expect 5–10 fruits total per plant with 1–3 ready to pick each week at 1 plant per 3 feet of row

Mustard Greens
Yield: 0.7 pound
Note: at large braising size; for baby salad size, see Lettuce, Baby Mix

Okra
Yield: 0.1–0.2 pound
Note: per picking; expect 2–3 pickings per week; yield is lower at first picking and increases later in the season

Onions, Bulb
Yield: 0.8 pound
Alternative quantity per row foot: 2 onions

Parsley
Yield: 0.1–0.2 pound
Note: per picking; expect 1 picking per week, yield increases later in season when plant is larger

Parsnips
Yield: 0.75 pound
Alternative quantity per row foot: 4–6 roots

Peanut
Yield: 0.3 pound, green/ 0.1 pound, dry

Peas, Shelling
Yield: 0.25 pound
Note: total yield including hulls; expect to get this over the course of 2–3 pickings; 1 pound of peas with hulls yields about 1.25 cups shelled peas

Peas, Snap
Yield: 0.1–0.2 pound
Note: per picking; pick 2–3 times per week for about a month

Peppers, Hot
Yield: 0.5–1 pound
Note: per picking; harvestable season varies by variety

Peppers, Sweet
Yield: 0.5–1 pound
Note: per picking; harvestable season varies by variety

Potatoes
Yield: 3 pounds

Radicchio
Yield: 0.75 pound
Alternative quantity per row foot: 1 head

Radishes
Yield: 0.5 pound
Alternative quantity per row foot: 1 bunch

Rutabagas
Yield: 1.5 pounds
Alternative quantity per row foot: 2–3 roots

Scallions
Yield: 0.3 pound

Spinach
Yield: 0.2 pound baby, 0.4 pound full size
Note: per cutting/picking; expect 1 harvest per week over 2–4 weeks

Squash, Pumpkins
Yield: 1–3 pounds
Note: expect 1–5 fruits per plant, depending on the variety

Squash, Summer
Yield: 1 pound
Note: per picking; pick 1–2 times/week for 1–2 months

Squash, Winter
Yield: 1 pound
Note: expect 3–10 fruits per plant, depending on the variety

Sweet Potatoes
Yield: 2 pounds

Tomatillos
Yield: 0.7 pound
Note: per picking; pick 1–2 times per week over 1–2 months

Tomatoes
Yield: 1
Note: per picking; pick 1–2 times per week over 1–2 months

Turnips
Yield: 0.3 pound
Alternative quantity per row foot: 2–3 bulbs

Watermelon
Yield: 2 pounds
Note: expect 1–2 fruits per plant

When to Plant

Every region and microclimate has ideal earliest and latest planting times for each crop. As you develop detailed records and gain years of experience, you will be the best source of your local climatic data. In the meantime, you may have access to an experienced local grower who can assist you in determining target planting dates. If not, you'll have to rely on more generalized information to begin your planting calendar.

A great starting point is to base your planting calendar on your average last and first frost dates as specified by the USDA, NOAA (National Oceanic and Atmospheric Administration), or another reliable data source. Local agricultural Extension agencies will know these dates, but first and last frost dates can also be found online (see Garden Wizards, Resources, page 309 to find yours).

It is important to realize that first and last frost dates are not set in stone. In any

Determining Days to Maturity

Different varieties of a crop may take different amounts of time to reach maturity, or their point of harvest (which may be when the crop is not quite fully mature). For example, 'Bay Meadows' broccoli is ready for harvest in 60 days, and 'Diplomat' is ready in 68 days. You can look up this information in a good seed catalog or online (Johnny's Selected Seeds and Fedco Seeds both have a lot of useful information in their catalogs). This information also appears on commercial seed packets. In some cases, days to maturity is indicated for growing the plant from seed, and in others it is indicated from the time of transplanting. A good catalog will indicate this clearly.

Knowing a variety's days to maturity is useful for many reasons. For example, you may be trying to squeeze in a faster-maturing variety late in the season to make sure it's ready before your first frost, or you may plant slower-maturing varieties to make sure they aren't ready to harvest during a period when you'll be out of town.

Also, you can extend your harvest period from a single planting by using different varieties. If you plant a 50-day, a 58-day, and a 64-day cabbage at the same time, the cabbages will be ready for harvest about a week apart from each other. Perfect! Remember, the stated days to maturity for a variety is usually based on ideal, controlled conditions, meaning that the actual days from planting to harvest in your garden might be different from what is indicated on the package or in the catalog.

zone, frosts can happen before or after the date indicated. Moreoever, not all sources site the same frost dates — much data must be considered to determine these dates and not every organization views the data through the same lens. For example, how deep of a frost is necessary for it to be considered — 32 degrees, 31 degrees, 30 degrees? In a single city, one neighborhood may experience frost on March 15, while another more protected area may not see frost after March 1. Additionally, some frost date assessments are based on different levels of risk. Is there a 10 percent chance that a frost will occur after the date noted, or a 20 percent chance?

Use an online chart as the starting point for your calculations, but do additional research in order to identify a more accurate local figure, or simply use your own observations and records over time to adjust your plantings from season to season. In any event, having even a general sense of the beginning and ending of the outdoor growing season will help you plan a successful garden. Many crops can be planted outside of your frost dates, so the success of your plan is not tied tightly to a precise reading on frost dates.

You can enter your first and last frost dates into the following Planting Dates chart, and then use them to determine earliest and latest planting dates for each crop you want to grow. As you gain experience and talk to other growers in your area, you can adjust the planting dates on your planting calendar.

If you live in a region with a relatively short frost-free period, it's especially important to select crops that grow to maturity quickly. You should also focus on season-extension strategies. Knowing the length of your outdoor growing season allows you to start transplants on time, move crops into the garden when appropriate, and protect crops from inclement weather.

Seed packets often contain useful information such as the number of days it takes a crop to mature.

Planting Dates

Ideal earliest and latest planting dates can vary widely depending on your latitude, local microclimate, and days to maturity of the variety you're growing. These dates assume you're not using season-extension infrastructure (if you're using a high tunnel or row covers, earlier first plantings and later last plantings are possible). The dates here are general guidelines; check with other growers in your area and don't be afraid to experiment to fine-tune your planting dates.

Perennial herbs can be planted in spring and early summer in colder climates, and in the fall in areas with mild winters (USDA Zones 7 or 8 or higher). In general, perennial garden fruits can be planted in spring and early summer in colder climates, and in the fall in areas with mild winters (Zones 7 or 8 or higher). The exception is strawberries, which can be planted in spring or fall in a variety of climates. Fruit and nut trees can be planted in spring and early summer in colder climates, and in the fall in areas with mild winters (Zones 7 or 8 or higher). And generally, perennial vines can be planted in spring and early summer in colder climates, and in the fall in areas with mild winters (Zones 7 or 8 or higher).

MY LAST FROST DATE IS:

MY FIRST FROST DATE IS:

ANNUAL VEGETABLES AND HERBS

Arugula
- *Recommended first outdoor transplanting:* not recommended
- *Recommended first outdoor direct seeding:* 4 weeks before last frost
MY DATE IS:

- *Recommended last planting date:* 3–4 weeks before first frost (direct seed)
MY DATE IS:

- *Soil temperature range for germination (°F):* 45–82
- *Optimum germination temperature (°F):* 67
- *Starts grown from seed are ready for transplanting outdoors in:* N/A
- *Notes:* easy and efficient to direct seed

Basil
- *Recommended first outdoor transplanting:* 3 weeks after last frost
MY DATE IS:

- *Recommended first outdoor direct seeding:* 3 weeks after last frost
MY DATE IS:

- *Recommended last planting date:* 10–12 weeks before first frost
MY DATE IS:

- *Soil temperature range for germination (°F):* 70–90
- *Optimum germination temperature (°F):* 80
- *Starts grown from seed are ready for transplanting outdoors in:* 6–8 weeks
- *Notes:* transplanting preferred in most climates

Beans, Edible Soy (Edamame)

- *Recommended first outdoor transplanting:* 2–8 weeks after last frost date
  MY DATE IS:

- *Recommended first outdoor direct seeding:* on last frost date
  MY DATE IS:

- *Recommended last planting date:* 12–16 weeks before first frost (direct seed)
  MY DATE IS:

- *Soil temperature range for germination (°F):* 50–95
- *Optimum germination temperature (°F):* 85
- *Starts grown from seed are ready for transplanting outdoors in:* 2–4 weeks
- *Notes:* direct seeding preferred

Beans, Fava (Broad)

- *Recommended first outdoor transplanting:* 2–8 weeks after last frost date
  MY DATE IS:

- *Recommended first outdoor direct seeding:* 10 weeks before last frost
  MY DATE IS:

- *Recommended last planting date:* varies with climate
  MY DATE IS:

- *Soil temperature range for germination (°F):* 40–75

- *Optimum germination temperature (°F):* 68
- *Starts grown from seed are ready for transplanting outdoors in:* 2–3 weeks
- *Notes:* direct seeding preferred

Beans, Lima

- *Recommended first outdoor transplanting:* 2–8 weeks after last frost date
  MY DATE IS:

- *Recommended first outdoor direct seeding:* when soil temperature is 75°F or above
  MY DATE IS:

- *Recommended last planting date:* 10 weeks before first frost (direct seed)
  MY DATE IS:

- *Soil temperature range for germination (°F):* 75–95
- *Optimum germination temperature (°F):* 85
- *Starts grown from seed are ready for transplanting outdoors in:* 2–3 weeks
- *Notes:* direct seeding preferred

Beans, Shell

- *Recommended first outdoor transplanting:* 2–8 weeks after last frost date
  MY DATE IS:

- *Recommended first outdoor direct seeding:* on last frost date
  MY DATE IS:

- *Recommended last planting date:* 10 weeks before first frost (direct seed)
  MY DATE IS:

- *Soil temperature range for germination (°F):* 60–95
- *Optimum germination temperature (°F):* 80
- *Starts grown from seed are ready for transplanting outdoors in:* 2–3 weeks
- *Notes:* direct seeding preferred

Beans, Snap

- *Recommended first outdoor transplanting:* 2–8 weeks after last frost date
  MY DATE IS:

- *Recommended first outdoor direct seeding:* on last frost date
  MY DATE IS:

- *Recommended last planting date:* 10 weeks before first frost (direct seed)
  MY DATE IS:

- *Soil temperature range for germination (°F):* 60–95
- *Optimum germination temperature (°F):* 80
- *Starts grown from seed are ready for transplanting outdoors in:* 2–3 weeks
- *Notes:* direct seeding preferred

Beets

- *Recommended first outdoor transplanting:* not recommended

Planting Dates CONTINUED

- *Recommended first outdoor direct seeding:* on last frost date
  MY DATE IS:

- *Recommended last planting date:* 12 weeks before first frost (direct seed)
  MY DATE IS:

- *Soil temperature range for germination (°F):* 50–80
- *Optimum germination temperature (°F):* 77
- *Starts grown from seed are ready for transplanting outdoors in:* 4–6 weeks
- *Notes:* transplanting adversely effects growth

Bok Choy

- *Recommended first outdoor transplanting:* on last frost date
  MY DATE IS:

- *Recommended first outdoor direct seeding:* on last frost date
  MY DATE IS:

- *Recommended last planting date:* 4–8 weeks before first frost (direct seed or transplant)
  MY DATE IS:

- *Soil temperature range for germination (°F):* 45–85
- *Optimum germination temperature (°F):* 75

- *Starts grown from seed are ready for transplanting outdoors in:* 3–4 weeks
- *Notes:* transplant or direct seed

Broccoli

- *Recommended first outdoor transplanting:* 2 weeks before last frost
  MY DATE IS:

- *Recommended first outdoor direct seeding:* 2 weeks after last frost
  MY DATE IS:

- *Recommended last planting date:* 10–12 weeks before first frost (transplant)
  MY DATE IS:

- *Soil temperature range for germination (°F):* 45–90
- *Optimum germination temperature (°F):* 85
- *Starts grown from seed are ready for transplanting outdoors in:* 4 weeks
- *Notes:* transplanting preferred in most climates

Brussels Sprouts

- *Recommended first outdoor transplanting:* on last frost date
  MY DATE IS:

- *Recommended first outdoor direct seeding:* 2 weeks after last frost
  MY DATE IS:

- *Recommended last planting date:* 12 weeks before first frost (transplant)
  MY DATE IS:

- *Soil temperature range for germination (°F):* 50–90
- *Optimum germination temperature (°F):* 86
- *Starts grown from seed are ready for transplanting outdoors in:* 4 weeks
- *Notes:* transplanting preferred in most climates

Cabbage

- *Recommended first outdoor transplanting:* 2 weeks before last frost
  MY DATE IS:

- *Recommended first outdoor direct seeding:* 2 weeks before last frost
  MY DATE IS:

- *Recommended last planting date:* 12 weeks before first frost (transplant)
  MY DATE IS:

- *Soil temperature range for germination (°F):* 50–95
- *Optimum germination temperature (°F):* 88
- *Starts grown from seed are ready for transplanting outdoors in:* 4 weeks
- *Notes:* transplanting preferred in most climates

Cabbage, Chinese

- *Recommended first outdoor transplanting:* on last frost date
  MY DATE IS:

- *Recommended first outdoor direct seeding:* 2 weeks before last frost
  MY DATE IS:

- *Recommended last planting date:* 6–8 weeks before first frost (transplant)
  MY DATE IS:

- *Soil temperature range for germination (°F):* 52–95
- *Optimum germination temperature (°F):* 87
- *Starts grown from seed are ready for transplanting outdoors in:* 4 weeks
- *Notes:* transplanting preferred in most climates

Carrots

- *Recommended first outdoor transplanting:* not recommended
- *Recommended first outdoor direct seeding:* 4–6 weeks before last frost
  MY DATE IS:

- *Recommended last planting date:* 12–18 weeks before first frost (direct seed)
  MY DATE IS:

- *Soil temperature range for germination (°F):* 41–98

- *Optimum germination temperature (°F):* 77
- *Starts grown from seed are ready for transplanting outdoors in:* N/A
- *Notes:* direct seeding preferred; transplanting generally produces poor yields

Cauliflower

- *Recommended first outdoor transplanting:* 2 weeks before last frost
  MY DATE IS:

- *Recommended first outdoor direct seeding:* 2 weeks before last frost
  MY DATE IS:

- *Recommended last planting date:* 12 weeks before first frost (transplant)
  MY DATE IS:

- *Soil temperature range for germination (°F):* 45–90
- *Optimum germination temperature (°F):* 85
- *Starts grown from seed are ready for transplanting outdoors in:* 4–6 weeks
- *Notes:* transplanting preferred in most climates

Celeriac

- *Recommended first outdoor transplanting:* 2 weeks after last frost
  MY DATE IS:

- *Recommended first outdoor direct seeding:* 2 weeks before last frost

MY DATE IS:

- *Recommended last planting date:* 16 weeks before first frost (transplant)
  MY DATE IS:

- *Soil temperature range for germination (°F):* 41–100
- *Optimum germination temperature (°F):* 75
- *Starts grown from seed are ready for transplanting outdoors in:* 10–12 weeks
- *Notes:* transplanting preferred in most climates

Celery

- *Recommended first outdoor transplanting:* 2 weeks after last frost
  MY DATE IS:

- *Recommended first outdoor direct seeding:* 2 weeks after last frost
  MY DATE IS:

- *Recommended last planting date:* 16 weeks before first frost (transplant)
  MY DATE IS:

- *Soil temperature range for germination (°F):* 41–100
- *Optimum germination temperature (°F):* 75
- *Starts grown from seed are ready for transplanting outdoors in:* 10–12 weeks
- *Notes:* transplanting preferred in most climates

Planting Dates CONTINUED

Chard, Swiss
- *Recommended first outdoor transplanting:* 2 weeks before last frost
  MY DATE IS:

- *Recommended first outdoor direct seeding:* on last frost date
  MY DATE IS:

- *Recommended last planting date:* 8 weeks before first frost (transplant)
  MY DATE IS:

- *Soil temperature range for germination (°F):* 41–95
- *Optimum germination temperature (°F):* 86
- *Starts grown from seed are ready for transplanting outdoors in:* 5–6 weeks
- *Notes:* transplanting preferred in most climates

Cilantro
- *Recommended first outdoor transplanting:* not recommended
- *Recommended first outdoor direct seeding:* on last frost date
  MY DATE IS:

- *Recommended last planting date:* 4–6 weeks before first frost (direct seed)
  MY DATE IS:

- *Soil temperature range for germination (°F):* 50–80
- *Optimum germination temperature (°F):* 70

- *Starts grown from seed are ready for transplanting outdoors in:* N/A
- *Notes:* direct seeding preferred; transplanted cilantro is prone to bolting

Collards
- *Recommended first outdoor transplanting:* 2–4 weeks before last frost
  MY DATE IS:

- *Recommended first outdoor direct seeding:* 4 weeks before last frost
  MY DATE IS:

- *Recommended last planting date:* 8 weeks before first frost (transplant)
  MY DATE IS:

- *Soil temperature range for germination (°F):* 55–95
- *Optimum germination temperature (°F):* 88
- *Starts grown from seed are ready for transplanting outdoors in:* 4–6 weeks
- *Notes:* transplanting preferred in most climates

Corn, Sweet
- *Recommended first outdoor transplanting:* 2 weeks after last frost
  MY DATE IS:

- *Recommended first outdoor direct seeding:* when soil temperature is above 65°F
  MY DATE IS:

- *Recommended last planting date:* varies with climate; generally, early summer
  MY DATE IS:

- *Soil temperature range for germination (°F):* 60–100
- *Optimum germination temperature (°F):* 86
- *Starts grown from seed are ready for transplanting outdoors in:* 2–4 weeks
- *Notes:* commonly direct seeded, but transplanting is very effective for small plots

Cucumbers
- *Recommended first outdoor transplanting:* 4 weeks after last frost
  MY DATE IS:

- *Recommended first outdoor direct seeding:* 3–4 weeks after last frost
  MY DATE IS:

- *Recommended last planting date:* 12 weeks before first frost (transplant)
  MY DATE IS:

- *Soil temperature range for germination (°F):* 60–95
- *Optimum germination temperature (°F):* 86
- *Starts grown from seed are ready for transplanting outdoors in:* 3–4 weeks
- *Notes:* transplanting is best for early crops; direct seeding is effective when soil has warmed in early summer

Dill

- *Recommended first outdoor transplanting:* on last frost date
  MY DATE IS:

- *Recommended first outdoor direct seeding:* on last frost date
  MY DATE IS:

- *Recommended last planting date:* 4–6 weeks before first frost for leaf harvest (direct seed)
  MY DATE IS:

- *Soil temperature range for germination (°F):* 50–80
- *Optimum germination temperature (°F):* 70
- *Starts grown from seed are ready for transplanting outdoors in:* 4–6 weeks
- *Notes:* most efficient to direct seed

Eggplant

- *Recommended first outdoor transplanting:* 4 weeks after last frost
  MY DATE IS:

- *Recommended first outdoor direct seeding:* 4 weeks after last frost
  MY DATE IS:

- *Recommended last planting date:* 16 weeks before first frost (transplant)
  MY DATE IS:

- *Soil temperature range for germination (°F):* 65–100
- *Optimum germination temperature (°F):* 90
- *Starts grown from seed are ready for transplanting outdoors in:* 8–10 weeks
- *Notes:* transplanting preferred in most climates

Endive

- *Recommended first outdoor transplanting:* 2–4 weeks before last frost
  MY DATE IS:

- *Recommended first outdoor direct seeding:* on last frost date
  MY DATE IS:

- *Recommended last planting date:* 4–6 weeks before first frost (transplant)
  MY DATE IS:

- *Soil temperature range for germination (°F):* 41–85
- *Optimum germination temperature (°F):* 68
- *Starts grown from seed are ready for transplanting outdoors in:* 3–4 weeks
- *Notes:* transplant or direct seed

Fennel, Bulbing

- *Recommended first outdoor transplanting:* 2 weeks before last frost
  MY DATE IS:

- *Recommended first outdoor direct seeding:* 2–4 weeks after last frost
  MY DATE IS:

- *Recommended last planting date:* 12 weeks before first frost (transplant)
  MY DATE IS:

- *Soil temperature range for germination (°F):* 50–100
- *Optimum germination temperature (°F):* 77
- *Starts grown from seed are ready for transplanting outdoors in:* 4–6 weeks
- *Notes:* transplanting preferred in most climates

Garlic

- *Recommended first outdoor transplanting:* N/A
  MY DATE IS:

- *Recommended first outdoor direct seeding:* N/A
  MY DATE IS:

- *Recommended last planting date:* one planting
  MY DATE IS:

- *Soil temperature range for germination (°F):* N/A
- *Optimum germination temperature (°F):* N/A
- *Starts grown from seed are ready for transplanting outdoors in:* N/A
- *Notes:* plant cloves in late fall (October–November in most of the country) for harvest the following summer

Kale

- *Recommended first outdoor transplanting:* 2–4 weeks before last frost
  MY DATE IS:

- *Recommended first outdoor direct seeding:* 2 weeks before last frost
  MY DATE IS:

- *Recommended last planting date:* 8 weeks before first frost (transplant)
  MY DATE IS:

- *Soil temperature range for germination (°F):* 52–100
- *Optimum germination temperature (°F):* 90
- *Starts grown from seed are ready for transplanting outdoors in:* 4–6 weeks
- *Notes:* transplanting preferred in most climates

Kohlrabi

- *Recommended first outdoor transplanting:* 2 weeks before last frost
  MY DATE IS:

- *Recommended first outdoor direct seeding:* 2 weeks before last frost
  MY DATE IS:

- *Recommended last planting date:* 8 weeks before first frost (transplant or direct seed)
  MY DATE IS:

MY DATE IS:

- *Soil temperature range for germination (°F):* 48–86
- *Optimum germination temperature (°F):* 77
- *Starts grown from seed are ready for transplanting outdoors in:* 3–4 weeks
- *Notes:* transplant or direct seed

Leeks

- *Recommended first outdoor transplanting:* on last frost date
  MY DATE IS:

- *Recommended first outdoor direct seeding:* 2 weeks before last frost
  MY DATE IS:

- *Recommended last planting date:* 12–16 weeks before first frost (transplant)
  MY DATE IS:

- *Soil temperature range for germination (°F):* 42–94
- *Optimum germination temperature (°F):* 77
- *Starts grown from seed are ready for transplanting outdoors in:* 6–8 weeks
- *Notes:* transplanting preferred in most climates

Lettuce, Baby Mix

- *Recommended first outdoor transplanting:* N/A
  MY DATE IS:

- *Recommended first outdoor direct seeding:* 2–4 weeks before last frost
  MY DATE IS:

- *Recommended last planting date:* 4 weeks before first frost (direct seed)
  MY DATE IS:

- *Soil temperature range for germination (°F):* 41–85
- *Optimum germination temperature (°F):* 68
- *Starts grown from seed are ready for transplanting outdoors in:* N/A
- *Notes:* direct seed

Lettuce, Heads

- *Recommended first outdoor transplanting:* 2–4 weeks before last frost
  MY DATE IS:

- *Recommended first outdoor direct seeding:* 2–4 weeks before last frost
  MY DATE IS:

- *Recommended last planting date:* 4 weeks before first frost (transplant)
  MY DATE IS:

- *Soil temperature range for germination (°F):* 41–85
- *Optimum germination temperature (°F):* 68

- *Starts grown from seed are ready for transplanting outdoors in:* 3–4 weeks
- *Notes:* transplanting preferred in most climates

Mâche

- *Recommended first outdoor transplanting:* as early as soil can be worked

  MY DATE IS:

- *Recommended first outdoor direct seeding:* as early as soil can be worked

  MY DATE IS:

- *Recommended last planting date:* 2–4 weeks before first frost (direct seed or transplant)

  MY DATE IS:

- *Soil temperature range for germination (°F):* 41–68
- *Optimum germination temperature (°F):* 63
- *Starts grown from seed are ready for transplanting outdoors in:* 4–6 weeks
- *Notes:* transplant or direct seed

Melon, Cantaloupe, Honeydew

- *Recommended first outdoor transplanting:* 4 weeks after last frost

  MY DATE IS:

- *Recommended first outdoor direct seeding:* when soil temperature reaches 70°F

  MY DATE IS:

- *Recommended last planting date:* 16 weeks before first frost (transplant)

  MY DATE IS:

- *Soil temperature range for germination (°F):* 68–100
- *Optimum germination temperature (°F):* 90
- *Starts grown from seed are ready for transplanting outdoors in:* 3–4 weeks
- *Notes:* transplanting is best for early crops; direct seeding is effective when soil has warmed in early summer

Mustard Greens

- *Recommended first outdoor transplanting:* 4 weeks before last frost

  MY DATE IS:

- *Recommended first outdoor direct seeding:* 4 weeks before last frost

  MY DATE IS:

- *Recommended last planting date:* 2–4 weeks before first frost (direct seed or transplant)

  MY DATE IS:

- *Soil temperature range for germination (°F):* 45–86
- *Optimum germination temperature (°F):* 77
- *Starts grown from seed are ready for transplanting outdoors in:* 3–4 weeks
- *Notes:* most efficient to direct seed

Okra

- *Recommended first outdoor transplanting:* 4–6 weeks after last frost date

  MY DATE IS:

- *Recommended first outdoor direct seeding:* when soil temperature reaches 65°F

  MY DATE IS:

- *Recommended last planting date:* 12–16 weeks before first frost (transplant)

  MY DATE IS:

- *Soil temperature range for germination (°F):* 60–95
- *Optimum germination temperature (°F):* 85
- *Starts grown from seed are ready for transplanting outdoors in:* 4–5 weeks
- *Notes:* transplanting preferred in most climates; is a heat lover and grows best in warm climates

Planting Dates CONTINUED

Onions, Bulb
- *Recommended first outdoor transplanting:* 2 weeks before last frost
  MY DATE IS:

- *Recommended first outdoor direct seeding:* 6 weeks before last frost
  MY DATE IS:

- *Recommended last planting date:* variable depending on type
  MY DATE IS:

- *Soil temperature range for germination (°F):* 45–95
- *Optimum germination temperature (°F):* 77–86
- *Starts grown from seed are ready for transplanting outdoors in:* 8–10 weeks
- *Notes:* transplanting preferred in most climates

Parsley
- *Recommended first outdoor transplanting:* 2 weeks before last frost
  MY DATE IS:

- *Recommended first outdoor direct seeding:* 2 weeks before last frost
  MY DATE IS:

- *Recommended last planting date:* 8–12 weeks before first frost (transplant or direct seed)
  MY DATE IS:

- *Soil temperature range for germination (°F):* 50–85
- *Optimum germination temperature (°F):* 75
- *Starts grown from seed are ready for transplanting outdoors in:* 6–8 weeks
- *Notes:* transplants are easier to manage due to slow germination

Parsnips
- *Recommended first outdoor transplanting:* not recommended
- *Recommended first outdoor direct seeding:* as early as soil can be worked
  MY DATE IS:

- *Recommended last planting date:* 20–24 weeks before first frost
  MY DATE IS:

- *Soil temperature range for germination (°F):* 40–80
- *Optimum germination temperature (°F):* 65
- *Starts grown from seed are ready for transplanting outdoors in:* N/A
- *Notes:* direct seed

Peanut
- *Recommended first outdoor transplanting:* when soil temperature reaches 65+°F
  MY DATE IS:

- *Recommended first outdoor direct seeding:* when soil temperature reaches 65+°F
  MY DATE IS:

- *Recommended last planting date:* 16–20 weeks before first frost
  MY DATE IS:

- *Soil temperature range for germination (°F):* 65–100
- *Optimum germination temperature (°F):* 86–91
- *Starts grown from seed are ready for transplanting outdoors in:* 4–6 weeks

Peas, Shelling
- *Recommended first outdoor transplanting:* 4 weeks before last frost
  MY DATE IS:

- *Recommended first outdoor direct seeding:* as early as soil can be worked
  MY DATE IS:

- *Recommended last planting date:* generally, plant in early–mid spring; fall crops are possible; direct seed about 8 weeks before first frost
  MY DATE IS:

- *Soil temperature range for germination (°F):* 40–75
- *Optimum germination temperature (°F):* 75
- *Starts grown from seed are ready for transplanting outdoors in:* 2–3 weeks
- *Notes:* transplant or direct seed

Peas, Snap

- *Recommended first outdoor transplanting:* 4 weeks before last frost
  MY DATE IS:

- *Recommended first outdoor direct seeding:* as early as soil can be worked
  MY DATE IS:

- *Recommended last planting date:* generally, plant in early–mid spring; fall crops are possible; direct seed about 8 weeks before first frost
  MY DATE IS:

- *Soil temperature range for germination (°F):* 40–75
- *Optimum germination temperature (°F):* 75
- *Starts grown from seed are ready for transplanting outdoors in:* 2–3 weeks
- *Notes:* transplant or direct seed

Peppers, Hot

- *Recommended first outdoor transplanting:* 2 weeks after last frost
  MY DATE IS:

- *Recommended first outdoor direct seeding:* not recommended
- *Recommended last planting date:* 16 weeks before first frost (transplant)
  MY DATE IS:

- *Soil temperature range for germination (°F):* 68–95
- *Optimum germination temperature (°F):* 85
- *Starts grown from seed are ready for transplanting outdoors in:* 6–8 weeks
- *Notes:* transplanting preferred in most climates

Peppers, Sweet

- *Recommended first outdoor transplanting:* 2 weeks after last frost
  MY DATE IS:

- *Recommended first outdoor direct seeding:* not recommended
- *Recommended last planting date:* 16 weeks before first frost (transplant)
  MY DATE IS:

- *Soil temperature range for germination (°F):* 68–95
- *Optimum germination temperature (°F):* 85
- *Starts grown from seed are ready for transplanting outdoors in:* 6–8 weeks
- *Notes:* transplanting preferred in most climates

Potatoes

- *Recommended first outdoor transplanting:* N/A
  MY DATE IS:

- *Recommended first outdoor direct seeding:* 4 weeks before last frost
  MY DATE IS:

- *Recommended last planting date:* N/A; one planting in spring
  MY DATE IS:

- *Soil temperature range for germination (°F):* N/A
- *Optimum germination temperature (°F):* N/A
- *Starts grown from seed are ready for transplanting outdoors in:* N/A
- *Notes:* plant tubers in early spring

Raab

- *Recommended first outdoor transplanting:* 2 weeks before last frost
  MY DATE IS:

- *Recommended first outdoor direct seeding:* 2 weeks before last frost
  MY DATE IS:

- *Recommended last planting date:* 4–6 weeks before first frost (transplant)
  MY DATE IS:

- *Soil temperature range for germination (°F):* 45–85
- *Optimum germination temperature (°F):* 77
- *Starts grown from seed are ready for transplanting outdoors in:* 3–4 weeks
- *Notes:* transplant or direct seed

Radicchio
- *Recommended first outdoor transplanting:* 2 weeks before last frost
  MY DATE IS:

- *Recommended first outdoor direct seeding:* 2 weeks before last frost
  MY DATE IS:

- *Recommended last planting date:* variable; generally, plant in early spring and late summer for fall production
  MY DATE IS:

- *Soil temperature range for germination (°F):* 40–85
- *Optimum germination temperature (°F):* 75
- *Starts grown from seed are ready for transplanting outdoors in:* 3–4 weeks
- *Notes:* transplant or direct seed

Radishes
- *Recommended first outdoor transplanting:* not recommended
- *Recommended first outdoor direct seeding:* 4 weeks before last frost
  MY DATE IS:

- *Recommended last planting date:* 4 weeks before first frost (direct seed)
  MY DATE IS:

- *Soil temperature range for germination (°F):* 45–90
- *Optimum germination temperature (°F):* 85
- *Starts grown from seed are ready for transplanting outdoors in:* N/A
- *Notes:* direct seed

Rutabagas
- *Recommended first outdoor transplanting:* not recommended
- *Recommended first outdoor direct seeding:* 12–14 weeks before first frost
  MY DATE IS:

- *Recommended last planting date:* 12–14 weeks before first frost
  MY DATE IS:

- *Soil temperature range for germination (°F):* 65–85
- *Optimum germination temperature (°F):* 77
- *Starts grown from seed are ready for transplanting outdoors in:* N/A
- *Notes:* direct seed

Scallions
- *Recommended first outdoor transplanting:* 6 weeks before last frost
  MY DATE IS:

- *Recommended first outdoor direct seeding:* 6 weeks before last frost
  MY DATE IS:

- *Recommended last planting date:* 8 weeks before first frost (transplant or direct seed)
  MY DATE IS:

- *Soil temperature range for germination (°F):* 45–95
- *Optimum germination temperature (°F):* 75
- *Starts grown from seed are ready for transplanting outdoors in:* 6–8 weeks
- *Notes:* transplant or direct seed

Spinach
- *Recommended first outdoor transplanting:* 4 weeks before last frost
  MY DATE IS:

- *Recommended first outdoor direct seeding:* as early as soil can be worked
  MY DATE IS:

- *Recommended last planting date:* 2–4 weeks before first frost (direct seed or transplant)
  MY DATE IS:

- *Soil temperature range for germination (°F):* 45–75
- *Optimum germination temperature (°F):* 70
- *Starts grown from seed are ready for transplanting outdoors in:* 3–4 weeks
- *Notes:* transplant or direct seed

Squash, Gourds

- *Recommended first outdoor transplanting:* 2 weeks after last frost

  MY DATE IS:

- *Recommended first outdoor direct seeding:* when soil temperature has reached 70°F

  MY DATE IS:

- *Recommended last planting date:* variable depending on type

  MY DATE IS:

- *Soil temperature range for germination (°F):* 60–95
- *Optimum germination temperature (°F):* 86
- *Starts grown from seed are ready for transplanting outdoors in:* 3–4 weeks
- *Notes:* transplanting is best for early crops; direct seeding is effective when soil has warmed in early summer

Squash, Pumpkins

- *Recommended first outdoor transplanting:* 2 weeks after last frost

  MY DATE IS:

- *Recommended first outdoor direct seeding:* when soil temperature has reached 70°F

MY DATE IS:

- *Recommended last planting date:* variable depending on type

  MY DATE IS:

- *Soil temperature range for germination (°F):* 60–95
- *Optimum germination temperature (°F):* 86
- *Starts grown from seed are ready for transplanting outdoors in:* 3–4 weeks
- *Notes:* transplanting is best for early crops; direct seeding is effective when soil has warmed in early summer

Squash, Summer

- *Recommended first outdoor transplanting:* 2 weeks after last frost

  MY DATE IS:

- *Recommended first outdoor direct seeding:* when soil temperature has reached 70°F

  MY DATE IS:

- *Recommended last planting date:* 12 weeks before first frost (transplant)

  MY DATE IS:

- *Soil temperature range for germination (°F):* 60–95

- *Optimum germination temperature (°F):* 86
- *Starts grown from seed are ready for transplanting outdoors in:* 3–4 weeks
- *Notes:* transplanting is best for early crops; direct seeding is effective when soil has warmed in early summer

Squash, Winter

- *Recommended first outdoor transplanting:* 2 weeks after last frost

  MY DATE IS:

- *Recommended first outdoor direct seeding:* when soil temperature has reached 70°F

  MY DATE IS:

- *Recommended last planting date:* variable depending on type

  MY DATE IS:

- *Soil temperature range for germination (°F):* 60–95
- *Optimum germination temperature (°F):* 86
- *Starts grown from seed are ready for transplanting outdoors in:* 3–4 weeks
- *Notes:* transplanting is best for early crops; direct seeding is effective when soil has warmed in early summer

Sweet Potatoes

- *Recommended first outdoor transplanting:* after last frost, when soil temperature is above 60 degrees
  MY DATE IS:

- *Recommended first outdoor direct seeding:* N/A
  MY DATE IS:

- *Recommended last planting date:* N/A
  MY DATE IS:

- *Soil temperature range for germination (°F):* N/A
- *Optimum germination temperature (°F):* N/A
- *Starts grown from seed are ready for transplanting outdoors in:* N/A
- *Notes:* sweet potatoes are usually grown from slips, or bare-root transplants propagated from the tubers of the plant

Tomatillos

- *Recommended first outdoor transplanting:* 2 weeks after last frost
  MY DATE IS:

- *Recommended first outdoor direct seeding:* not recommended
- *Recommended last planting date:* variable; generally, 12–16 weeks before first frost
  MY DATE IS:

- *Soil temperature range for germination (°F):* 60–90
- *Optimum germination temperature (°F):* 85
- *Starts grown from seed are ready for transplanting outdoors in:* 4–5 weeks
- *Notes:* transplanting preferred in most climates

Tomatoes

- *Recommended first outdoor transplanting:* 2 weeks after last frost
  MY DATE IS:

- *Recommended first outdoor direct seeding:* not recommended
- *Recommended last planting date:* variable depending on type
  MY DATE IS:

- *Soil temperature range for germination (°F):* 60–90
- *Optimum germination temperature (°F):* 85
- *Starts grown from seed are ready for transplanting outdoors in:* 6–8 weeks
- *Notes:* transplanting preferred in most climates

Turnips

- *Recommended first outdoor transplanting:* not recommended
- *Recommended first outdoor direct seeding:* 2 weeks before last frost
  MY DATE IS:

- *Recommended last planting date:* 6–8 weeks before first frost (direct seed)
  MY DATE IS:

- *Soil temperature range for germination (°F):* 50–86
- *Optimum germination temperature (°F):* 77
- *Starts grown from seed are ready for transplanting outdoors in:* N/A
- *Notes:* direct seed

Watermelon

- *Recommended first outdoor transplanting:* 4 weeks after last frost
  MY DATE IS:

- *Recommended first outdoor direct seeding:* when soil temperature has reached 70°F
  MY DATE IS:

- *Recommended last planting date:* variable; generally, 16 weeks before first frost
  MY DATE IS:

- *Soil temperature range for germination (°F):* 68–100
- *Optimum germination temperature (°F):* 95
- *Starts grown from seed are ready for transplanting outdoors in:* 4 weeks
- *Notes:* transplanting is best for early crops; direct seeding is effective when soil has warmed in early summer

PERENNIAL VEGETABLES

Artichoke
- *Recommended first outdoor transplanting:* 2 weeks after last frost

  MY DATE IS:

Asparagus
- *Recommended first outdoor transplanting:* spring

  MY DATE IS:

- *Notes:* use transplants or crowns

Cardoon
- *Recommended first outdoor transplanting:* spring

  MY DATE IS:

- *Notes:* use transplants or root pieces

Jerusalem Artichoke, Sunchoke
- *Recommended first outdoor transplanting:* fall

  MY DATE IS:

- *Notes:* grow from tubers

Rhubarb
- *Recommended first outdoor transplanting:* spring or fall

  MY DATE IS:

- *Notes:* use transplants or root pieces

MAKING YOUR OWN PLANTING CALENDAR

Here's where it all comes together. A planting calendar is just what it sounds like: something you can look at each week to determine how much of each crop to plant. The calendar is there to help you control impulse decisions. For example, after a hard winter you might have the urge to run outside in early May and plant your entire garden in spinach. Instead, you check the planting calendar at the beginning of each week, and then go out to the garden and calmly plant exactly according to plan. Here are three general formats you might use to build your planting calendar.

Print Calendar/Online Calendar

These are great because you can quickly see what's coming up next week or next month. Online calendars are helpful because you can make one entry and set it to repeat for succession plantings. Google, Yahoo, Microsoft, and other online email services provide digital calendars to their users. Although these calendars are easy to use, they may not have a lot of extra space for taking notes or keeping track of other details.

Spreadsheet Calendar

You can make your own calendar in the form of a spreadsheet, which will allow you to keep track of many different types of information. You can do this by hand if you like, but a computer-generated spreadsheet program (such as Microsoft Excel or Google Sheets) is much more efficient. We generate planting calendars this way for every growing space, ranging from 200-square-foot backyard gardens to 20-acre production farms, and it works great.

Use the Planting Calendar Worksheet to get started (see page 72). You can also download the Planning Calendar Worksheet template from Seattle Urban Farm Company's website (see Resources, page 309).

Cloud-Based Farm Recordkeeping

You can create a planting calendar using online software specifically designed for farms, such as AgSquared or COG Pro (see Online Farm Recordkeeping, Resources, page 307). These programs allow for very advanced and detailed recordkeeping, and are suitable for managing organic certification records and/or running a professional production farm. They can work well for intensive home growers, too. A yearly fee is charged for these programs.

WHAT YOU'LL WRITE ON THE CALENDAR

At a bare minimum, you'll want to note each crop you intend to plant, how much you need to plant, and the week or date that you'll be actually doing the planting. This might be tracked in the number of row feet for direct-seeded crops, or in the number of plants when transplanting. You'll also need a blank space to note the date that you actually do the planting (in case it's not the same date you originally planned), and how many row feet you actually seed or actual number of transplants you set out. Here are a few other items that are useful to note:

- crop variety
- exact location in the garden
- weather conditions
- fertilization application quantities and dates

Some growers also leave space on the calendar to note their harvest data:

• harvest date(s)
• crop yield
• taste characteristics
• how the variety or crop performed

Other growers like to use a separate log for harvest information. There will be more to come on recordkeeping in chapter 3.

If you plan to grow your own transplants, you can use the calendar to note when to start the seeds indoors so that the transplants can be ready to go out to the garden when the time is right. If you grow a lot of transplants, you might make two calendars: a greenhouse seeding calendar and a planting calendar for the garden. If you have a greenhouse or are interested in season extension, make sure to read the chapter on season extension (starting on page 252) before making your planting plan.

Following is a sample planting calendar worksheet that was originally made using an Excel spreadsheet. A calendar like this could work for everyone, from the smallest scale high-yield gardener to a professional vegetable farm manager.

Experiment with Planting Dates

Many variables can affect planting dates for outdoor crops (primarily your local climate and microclimate). For example, in the Pacific Northwest, it is possible to harvest broccoli side shoots from the field all winter because of the mild weather. But in order to do this, the plant must have reached maturity by mid-September. This means that the planting date for this crop is extremely important (in many regions, the same broccoli would be killed at the onset of winter).

Use the Planting Dates chart (see page 56) as a starting point, but continue to consult with other local growers and do your own experimentation (don't forget to keep records). Finesse the calendar accordingly to find the ideal dates.

Planting Calendar Worksheet

Each row on page 73 has directions for completion, based on the information found in this chapter. You can download and print blank calendar templates and a spreadsheet with built-in formulas at Seattle Urban Farm Company's website (see Resources, page 309).

Rows 1 and 2: Fill out the first two rows with the crops you've selected from the Crop Amount Worksheet (page 45) and the varieties you think will be best suited to your climate or taste preferences.

Row 3: Use the number of row feet you calculated on the yield chart (page 51) to fill out this row. For transplants, you can convert row feet to the number of plants, if you like. Consult the spacing column on the succession planting chart on page 36. Divide your desired number of row feet by the plant spacing in feet. This will give you the number of plants to set out. For example, you calculate you need 20 row feet of broccoli. The spacing for broccoli is 1 foot. Twenty row feet ÷ 1-foot spacing = 20 plants. Here's a quick reference for spacing plants less than a foot apart: 8 inches = 0.67 foot, 6 inches = 0.5 foot, 4 inches = 0.33 foot, 3 inches = 0.25 foot, 2 inches = 0.17 foot.

Row 4: Use your average first and last frost dates and the Planting Dates chart (page 56) to determine your planting date. Consult the succession planting chart on page 36 to help decide how many plantings to make and how many weeks apart to space the plantings.

Row 5: Specify in this row whether you'll be transplanting or direct seeding the crop.

Rows 6 and 7: These rows apply only if you'll be growing your own transplants. In Row 6: If you're growing your own transplants, note the date to start the seeds here. Consult the chart on page 56. Subtract the number of weeks listed for your crop from the planting date you specified in this chart. This is the date you should seed the crop in your propagation area. In Row 7: Add 20% to the number of plants you specified in Row 3. This is the number of seeds you should start in your propagation area.

Row 8: Indicate when you actually planted the crop.

Row 9: Indicate how many row feet of the crop you actually planted.

Rows 10 and 11: Note when harvest occurred and how much was harvested.

1	**CROP**	
2	**VARIETY**	
3	**QUANTITY**	
4	**EXPECTED PLANTING DATE**	
5	**TRANSPLANT OR DIRECT SEED?**	
6	**SEED STARTING DATE**	
7	**NUMBER OF TRANSPLANTS**	
8	**ACTUAL PLANTING DATE**	
9	**ROW FEET PLANTED**	
10	**HARVEST DATE**	
11	**HARVEST AMOUNT**	
12	**NOTES**	

NONSTOP ARUGULA

Ryan loves arugula. This year, he decides that he'll grow enough arugula so that he and Kiwi can eat a fresh salad every day from his garden, and also put some on their almond-butter sandwiches at lunch. He guesses this will be about 1 pound per week based on his grocery store purchases.

First, Ryan checks the yield chart (page 51) to see how much he should plant. He then consults the Successions, Spacing, and Scheduling chart (see page 36) to see how often he should plant. Four row feet will yield about a pound, and the succession chart tells him he should plant once a week.

Next, he figures out his earliest and latest planting dates for arugula using the Planting Dates chart (see page 56). Ryan and Kiwi's frost dates are approximately March 1st and September 15th.

Therefore, Ryan plans to plant 4 row feet of arugula each week starting the week of March 1st and ending on the week of September 15th. Every Monday from March 1st to September 15th, he writes on the calendar hanging on his refrigerator, "Seed 4 row feet of arugula, variety 'Roquette'."

March

SUNDAY	MONDAY	TUESDAY	WEDNESDAY	THURSDAY	FRIDAY	SATURDAY
1	2 SOW 4 ROW FEET OF ARUGULA ('ROQUETTE')	3	4	5	6	7
8	9 SOW 4 ROW FEET OF ARUGULA ('ROQUETTE')	10	11	12	13	14
15	16 SOW 4 ROW FEET OF ARUGULA ('ROQUETTE')	17	18	19	20	21
22	23 SOW 4 ROW FEET OF ARUGULA ('ROQUETTE')	24	25	26	27	28
29	30 SOW 4 ROW FEET OF ARUGULA ('ROQUETTE')	31				

JASON

TOMATOES FOR CANNING AND FRESH EATING

Jason is a fiend for fresh garden tomatoes. His favorite variety is 'Sun Gold', an orange cherry tomato, but he also loves 'San Marzano' (a classic Roma) for canning. This year, he decided to set up a 12' × 30' greenhouse. He will be growing starts inside his atrium and transplanting them into the greenhouse in mid-spring. He knows he uses about 50 pounds of Romas a week during the canning season, and he likes to eat 3 pints (about 2¼ pounds) of cherry tomatoes each week.

First he checks the yield chart and calculates that he'll need 3 'Sun Gold' plants (3 row feet at 18-inch spacing) and 33 'San Marzano' plants (50 row feet at 18-inch spacing) to produce the yield he wants. Next, he checks the Planting Dates chart (see page 56) and sees that he can set out his tomato transplants on May 15th. He knows the greenhouse will provide extra protection, so he decides to get a jump on the season by planting the tomatoes 4 weeks before he would normally plant them outside (around April 15th).

Finally, he checks the "Starts grown from seed are ready for transplanting outdoors" line of the Planting Dates chart, which tells him it should take about 6 weeks from seed for the tomatoes to reach the proper stage for transplanting.

Jason loves spreadsheets, so he uses Excel to create a seeding schedule for growing his starts and a planting schedule for planting crops in the garden.

On March 1st on the seeding schedule, he notes, "Seed 5 'Sun Gold' plants and 45 'San Marzano' plants." (Note that he's seeded more tomato plants than he actually needs to make sure he has enough. See chapter 8, beginning on page 164, for more information.) On his planting schedule spreadsheet, he notes on the week of April 15th, "Transplant 3 'Sun Gold' and 33 'San Marzano' plants from the greenhouse."

Jason's Planting Schedule

Date	Crop	Variety	Transplant or Direct Seed?	Quantity	Location	Date Completed
1–Apr	Kale	'Red Russian'	TP	35	Garden Bed 1, 5	
1–Apr	Lettuce Mix	'Freedom'	DS	10 row feet	Garden Bed 2	
15–Apr	Tomato	'Sun Gold'	TP	3	Greenhouse Bed 1	
15–Apr	Tomato	'San Marzano'	TP	33	Greenhouse Bed 1	
15–Apr	Lettuce Mix	'Freedom'	DS	10 row feet	Garden Bed 2	

CARROTS FOR A WEDDING

Dave and Erin's son is getting married on August 19th, and they want to grow all the carrots for the wedding dinner in their garden. The caterer tells them they need 25 pounds to make the dinner happen. They check the yield chart and see they'll need to seed about 25 row feet to get 25 pounds. They increase this to 35 row feet to make sure there will be enough.

It's already early June, so they choose 'Nelson', a 56-day variety that is known to grow well during warm summer temperatures. If they get the seeds planted by June 15th, they should have just enough time to be ready (allowing for germination time and a few extra days, should the the carrots grow a little more slowly than the stated days to maturity). They note in their online calendar for June 15th, "Plant 35 row feet of 'Nelson' carrots."

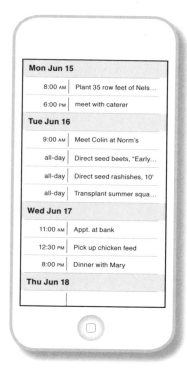

Mon Jun 15	
8:00 AM	Plant 35 row feet of Nels…
6:00 PM	meet with caterer
Tue Jun 16	
9:00 AM	Meet Colin at Norm's
all-day	Direct seed beets, "Early…
all-day	Direct seed rashishes, 10'
all-day	Transplant summer squa…
Wed Jun 17	
11:00 AM	Appt. at bank
12:30 PM	Pick up chicken feed
8:00 PM	Dinner with Mary
Thu Jun 18	

Garden Mapping and Crop Rotation

After you've determined when and how much of each crop to plant, the next step is to decide where to plant those crops in the garden. Both short-term and long-term planning are necessary for creating a successful high-yield garden. Garden mapping enables you to keep track of what happened in the past and project the best ways to use the garden in the future. Your garden map will become a key element in your record-keeping, and allows you to fine-tune your crop rotation plans in the future.

So that you can reach your harvest goals, you should develop your plan ahead of time. Doing so will allow you to make efficient use of your space, anticipate when space will open up for plantings later in the season, and ensure that you allot enough space for each crop. In any given season, you'll have to make decisions about where a crop is planted in the garden and in which particular bed. Garden mapping lets you make these decisions with forethought and mental clarity before the craze of planting time comes.

MAPPING THE CROPS IN YOUR GARDEN

The first thing you need to do when preparing to map your crops is enlarge the annual garden portion of your site plan. By drawing the garden on a larger scale, you can note details about how you will use the space. This lets you keep track of where everything will go, and where you planted each crop in past seasons, if that is the case.

If you're handy on the computer, you can make a map using free software such as SketchUp (see chapter 1, Making a Site Plan, for more information). A digital map allows you to easily record any expansions or changes that you make to your garden layout. Drawing by hand works fine, too, though. We recommend making copies of your map and using a new one each year so that you have a quick visual record of where you've planted crops each season.

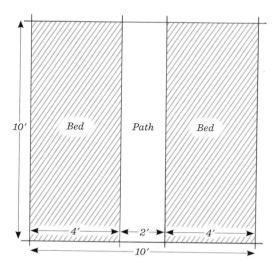

A 10' × 10' space can be divided into two permanent 4' × 10' beds and a 2'-wide path.

This is a good time to discuss a few more layout and organization concepts before you fill in your garden map .

Setting Up Beds

We recommend that you divide up your garden space into separate, permanent beds. The old way of planting a home garden was to till up a squarish patch of soil (say 20 × 20 feet), spread on a bunch of compost and organic fertilizer, and plant all your crops in rows in that big patch. At the end of the season you'd clear everything out, and the following spring you'd repeat the process.

The problem with this method is that when you walk between two rows, you'll probably be walking where you will be planting in a following year. Walking on the soil compacts it; and if you compact the soil this way, you'll need to spend extra time loosening it up prior to your next planting. Also, when you add soil amendments over the entire area, you end up spreading them both in your planting spaces (where they're needed) and in your walking paths (where they won't do any good). Further, by creating permanent beds you'll also be creating permanent pathways. Keeping pathways untilled and mulched will keep latent weed seeds suppressed and reduce your overall workload.

Create Permanent Paths and Efficient Beds
We suggest laying out specific planting beds in the garden space where you always grow food from year to year. You should also establish permanent paths where you always walk. This means you will add soil amendments only to the spaces where you actually need them, and can mulch your pathways to prevent weeds from growing.

The bed system makes it easier to develop a crop rotation plan. It is also easier to conceptualize planting by the square foot when using this system. We still like to plant direct-seeded crops in rows, but we evenly space the rows across the bed as appropriate for the crop. For example, we might plant seven rows of carrots spaced 6 inches apart across a 4-foot bed, or plant three rows of beans spaced 18 inches apart.

As we mentioned in chapter 1 (page 14), 4 feet is a good bed width. This size allows for the middle to be easily reached from either side of the bed. Some people prefer 3-foot-wide beds, or narrower because they prefer an even shorter reach. A good width for a path is 1 to 2 feet, depending on how agile you are. If you have a large garden, consider creating an extra-wide centrally located pathway (3 feet or wider) to accommodate a wheelbarrow or harvest cart.

Consider making a standardized bed size for your entire annual garden space, or at least for as much of the garden as possible. Standardized bed sizes allow you to reuse materials in different beds without any modification. For example, if all of your garden beds are 4 × 10 feet, then you can reuse a piece of row cover, bird netting, or irrigation tubing on any bed from season to season.

ROTATE CROPS FROM YEAR TO YEAR

You must do more than decide where to plant crops in a given season; you must also plan where to plant them from year to year. Crop rotation — the practice of planting annual crops in different spaces each year to avoid pest and disease problems, and to use soil nutrients efficiently — can help you create a productive garden for the long-term. Moving the planting location of each crop from year to year allows you to avoid overly taxing the soil. Crop rotation also disrupts pest and disease life cycles.

When you plant super-long-season crops like garlic, make sure they won't be in the way of crops you'll be planting in the space the following season.

Plant taller crops (in this case, tomatoes) to the north of shorter plants (such as broccoli) to prevent the taller crop from shading the shorter one. A 60-day broccoli planted in mid-spring will allow for a follow-up planting of another half-season crop.

Group and Rotate Annual Crops by Family

In order to effectively rotate crops, it's very helpful to group related crops together. This is especially important for controlling pest and disease issues, and for accommodating particular cultural needs or growth habits.

To successfully rotate crops, you must understand how crops are related. A crop family is part of the Linnaean classification system, which you may remember from high school biology. You may have learned "Kings Play Cards On Fat Green Stools" or "Kids Prefer Candy Over Fancy Green Salad" (which we hope isn't completely accurate, but probably is) to help you remember Kingdom-Phylum-Class-Order-Family-Genus-Species.

Separate Space for Perennial Vegetables

Perennial edible crops — such as rhubarb, asparagus, artichokes, and sunchokes — have different growth habits and space requirements than annual edible crops. Perennials live in one place for multiple years and have different management needs than annuals, so mixing the two together can complicate your crop management. Perennial garden beds typically do not require yearly overhauling in the same way annual beds do. Because the crops will remain in the same location from year to year, the soil is not aerated and prepared for new plantings each season. In addition, perennial crops are often less needy, so smaller applications of compost, organic fertilizers, and other soil amendments will keep them healthy and productive.

Many perennial crops tend to spread out over time, taking up more and more space, unless you manage them so that they remain in a restricted area. To keep perennials from spreading, it might be necessary to root prune the edges of your plantings each season, dig up and divide the base of the plant, or mow them down. Management techniques will vary by crop. Some perennials like mint and horseradish are aggressive enough that they should be planted in rigidly contained areas like pots, wood-framed raised beds, or spaces with existing frameworks such as a bed surrounded by concrete pathways.

The good thing is that perennial crops can be incorporated into many different kinds of spaces throughout the yard. Fruit trees can be trained to grow as espaliers along fence lines or property lines, dwarf fruit trees can be grown in tight corners, and an array of perennials can be combined to form a dynamic edible landscape, replacing traditional ornamental plants.

If you are interested in growing perennial edibles, take the time to fully understand their life spans, growth habits, and space requirements before placing them on the garden map (and into the garden). Also refer to resources on page 307 for recommendations on caring for perennial edibles.

This classification system indicates how a specific plant is related to all other plants (and animals). For example, a cabbage plant might be classified as follows:

Kingdom: Plantae (plants)
Phylum: Tracheophyta
Class: Angiospermae
Order: Dicotyledonae
Family: Brassicaceae*
Genus: *Brassica**
Species: *Brassica oleracea**

*These are the key designations to consider.

Some families hold a great number of standard garden crops, so it's easy to group them together for the purposes of crop rotation. Others are on their own within a family, so you may need to group them with other families when developing your rotation plan.

Plant Families That Require Frequent Rotation

Brassicaceae
Other names: Brassicas, cole crops, cruciferous crops, or crucifers
Common crops: Broccoli, Brussels sprouts, cauliflower, cabbage, collards, kale, bok choy, radishes, and mustard greens
Rotation notes: Broccoli, Brussels sprouts, cabbage, cauliflower, and kale all have similar spacing and nutrient needs, and share many nasty soil-borne pests and diseases. For this reason, we believe that these brassicas are the most important crops to rotate. We're less concerned about rotating some of the smaller brassicas like bok choy, radishes, and mustards, and often group them in with other crops in our rotation plans.

Solanaceae
Other names: Nightshades, solanums
Common crops: Tomatoes, peppers, eggplant, tomatillos, and potatoes
Rotation notes: These crops can share soil-borne diseases such as verticillium wilt and should be rotated. Though we eat their fruits and tubers, they all have mildly toxic foliage. They are all heavy feeders.

Cucurbitaceae
Other names: Cucurbits
Common crops: Summer squash, winter squash, pumpkins, cucumbers, and gourds
Rotation notes: These crops have similar cultural requirements and share insect and disease problems. Most of their issues are not soil borne, but we still recommend planting them together and rotating them.

Plant Families That Require Less-Frequent Rotation
These crops are family groups, but they have either fewer problems that can be addressed by crop rotation or very different cultural requirements and disease issues within one family.

Apiaceae
Other names: Umbelliferae, umbellifers
Common crops: Carrots, celery, chervil, cilantro, dill, fennel, parsley, and parsnips
Rotation notes: If you have problems with the carrot rust fly, it's good to move these crops from place to place each year to avoid overwintering larvae. Otherwise, these crops don't have a strong need for rotation.

The characteristic flower structure of this family (which looks like an upside-down umbrella) is very attractive to beneficial insects. Many growers will let mid-season plantings of cilantro or dill go to flower to help draw these creatures into the garden.

Asteraceae
Other names: Daisy family

Common crops: Lettuce, artichokes, and sunflowers

Rotation notes: Lettuce is usually clumped in with other crops in rotations, but it is important to move it each year to avoid lettuce root aphids.

Some non-edible members of this family attract beneficial insects: calendula, cosmos, daisies, dahlias and zinnias, echinacea, and yarrow. Others help repel pests: chrysanthemums (a source of pyrethrin, an organic insecticide) and marigolds.

Amaranthaceae (a.k.a. Chenopodiaceae)
Other names: Amaranth family

Common crops: Beets, spinach, and chard; also includes the grains amaranth and quinoa, and the edible weeds lamb's-quarter and pigweed

Rotation notes: Beets, chard, and spinach have different cultural requirements, but they share pest and disease problems (most notably downy mildew and leaf miners). In farming circles, these crops are known for having a deleterious effect on the crop that follows them in rotation.

Poaceae
Other names: Grass family

Common crops: Corn, wheat, rice, rye, barley, and millet

Rotation notes: Other than sweet corn, there are no common annual vegetables in this family. This makes small grains very useful as cover crops because they don't share diseases with most vegetable crops.

Amaryllidaceae
Other names: Alliums (when referring to onion relatives)

Common crops: Onions, leeks, garlic, scallions, and chives

Rotation notes: Alliums are generally light feeders and don't have many disease issues, so are not major concerns in our rotation scheme. They can be susceptible to root maggots, however, so moving them every year is still a good idea. Alliums are generally considered to be beneficial to the crops that follow them in rotations.

Fabaceae (a.k.a. Leguminosae)
Other names: Legumes

Common crops: Peas, beans, and peanuts

Rotation notes: The crops in this family are all able to fix nitrogen from the air into the soil. These are easy to include in rotations because they have few soil-borne diseases, and they supply nitrogen to the following crop. Because of this, they're often used as cover crops; clover, hairy vetch, and field peas are the most common leguminous cover crops.

Length of Crop Rotation
The longer you extend the length of the crop rotation — the number of seasons you wait before replanting a crop in the same space — the more effective you will be at helping to keep diseases at bay. For example, growing corn in one garden plot and beans in another and then switching them every year constitutes a two-year rotation of corn and beans. If you grow cabbage once every four years in

a plot, you have a four-year rotation. Pretty simple, right?

For the best chances of avoiding vegetable diseases, a rotation of four years or more is ideal, especially with brassicas. Some very skilled organic growers have up to 10-year rotation plans.

In a home garden setting, though, perfect crop placement and rotation can be elusive. In many cases, total garden square footage is a limiting factor in terms of maximizing yield. In these situations, it is usually undesirable to take portions of the garden out of rotation to allow for cover cropping and fallow seasons because this will simply reduce the number and size of your yearly plantings. Also, it's difficult to perfectly adapt a large-scale rotation plan for a limited number of beds that typically grow a diverse selection of crops. Given all that, apply the concept of rotation as best you can to your particular garden.

Grouping Crops by Fertility Needs

Because grouping crops by family in a small production garden can be difficult (you simply may not grow enough crops in a family for them to balance out a different family in the rotation), you might instead choose to group crops by their fertility needs. For example, if you grow lots of tomatoes (nightshades) and only one winter squash (cucurbit), you might group the two together in a rotation because they're both heavy feeders. This will make it easier to apply appropriate amounts of fertilizer to the bed throughout the season. Rotating heavy feeders, light feeders, and legumes (nitrogen fixers) is a common rotation plan.

The Spring vs. Fall Brassica Conundrum

One difficult choice small-scale production gardeners have to make is where to plant fall brassicas. If you're a brassica lover and you plant them in both the spring and fall, you may not have enough room to plant them in two different spaces in your garden in the same year and also maintain a three- or four-year rotation.

Gardeners in this situation have two choices: plant fall brassicas in a different space than spring brassicas, and maintain only a two-year rotation; or plant fall brassicas in the same space as spring brassicas (basically, clearing the ones from the spring when they're finished producing and immediately replanting for the fall).

The second option seems like it's breaking a lot of rules, but we actually prefer it because it makes conceptualizing and keeping track of crop rotation much easier. Go this route only if you don't have problems with soil-borne diseases, and be sure to apply compost and organic fertilizer between plantings.

Crop Height, Life Span, and Fertility Needs

ANNUAL VEGETABLES AND HERBS	MATURE HEIGHT	LIFE SPAN*	FERTILITY NEEDS
ARUGULA	6–8"	short	low
BASIL	24"	medium	low
BEANS, EDIBLE SOY (EDAMAME)	24"	medium	low
BEANS, FAVA (BROAD)	36"	long	low
BEANS, LIMA	24"	medium	low
BEANS, SHELL	24" bush / 6' pole	long	low
BEANS, SNAP	24" bush / 6' pole	medium	low
BEETS	6–8"	medium	high
BOK CHOY	12–18"	short	low
BROCCOLI	24"	medium	high
BRUSSELS SPROUTS	36–42"	long	high
CABBAGE	12"	medium	high
CABBAGE, CHINESE	12"	medium	high
CARROTS	6–8"	medium	high
CAULIFLOWER	12–16"	medium	high
CELERIAC	6–8"	long	medium
CELERY	12–16"	long	medium
CHARD, SWISS	24–36"	medium	medium
CILANTRO	6–8"	short	low
COLLARDS	36–42"	medium	high
CORN, SWEET	5–8'	medium	high
CUCUMBERS	sprawling or 5–8' on trellis	long	high
DILL	4–5'	medium	low
EGGPLANT	36"	long	high
ENDIVE	12"	short	low
FENNEL, BULBING	12"	medium	low
GARLIC	12–16"	long	medium
KALE	36–42"	medium	high
KOHLRABI	12"	short	low

ANNUAL VEGETABLES AND HERBS	MATURE HEIGHT	LIFE SPAN*	FERTILITY NEEDS
LEEKS	12–24"	long	medium
LETTUCE, BABY MIX	6–8"	short	low
LETTUCE, HEADS	8–12"	short	low
MÂCHE	6"	medium	low
MELON, CANTALOUPE, HONEYDEW	sprawling or 6–10' on trellis	long	high
MUSTARD GREENS	6–18"	short	low
OKRA	36"	long	high
ONIONS, BULB	12–18"	long	medium
PARSLEY	12"	long	low
PARSNIPS	6–8"	long	medium
PEANUT	12–18"	medium	high
PEAS, SHELLING	24" bush / 6' pole	long	low
PEAS, SNAP	24" bush / 6' pole	medium	low
PEPPERS, HOT	24–36"	long	high
PEPPERS, SWEET	24–36"	long	high
POTATOES	12–24"	medium	high
RAAB	24–36"	medium	high
RADICCHIO	12"	medium	medium
RADISHES	6"	short	low
RUTABAGAS	12–18"	short	medium
SCALLIONS	12"	short	low
SPINACH	6–12"	short	low
SQUASH, GOURDS	sprawling or 6–10' on trellis	long	high
SQUASH, PUMPKINS	sprawling or 6–10' on trellis	long	high
SQUASH, SUMMER	36"	medium	high
SQUASH, WINTER	sprawling or 6–10' on trellis	long	high
SWEET POTATOES	12"	long	high
TOMATILLOS	36"	long	high
TOMATOES	36" determinate / 6–10' indeterminate	long	high
TURNIPS	12"	short	medium
WATERMELON	sprawling or 6–10' on trellis	long	high

*Short = 1–3 months; medium= 3–5 months; long= 6–12 months

Crop Rotation Profiles

Following are a few examples of different rotation plans that have worked for gardeners with varying crop needs and garden spaces. You'll see that they all break some of the "rules" of crop rotation, but each plan works well for the given situation.

ROTATION AND MICROCLIMATE

Eggplant and peppers are Kiwi's favorite crops. She's found that in her cool Pacific Northwest climate they grow best when planted right up next to the house and garage (a great microclimate because of the southern exposure). She's never had any soil-borne disease problems with these solanaceous crops, but she is dedicated to crop rotation, and so she rotates them between the two beds each season. One season, she plants the eggplant and pepper at the house and uses the garage bed for pole beans and onions; the next year she switches them. She also plants a few basil plants in the very southern edges of the keyhole beds in both areas because she knows they love the extra heat.

She splits the remainder of her favorite crops into a three-year rotation: brassicas, cucurbits, and miscellaneous other crops (lettuce, beets, radishes, dill, bush beans). She has six beds to work with, so has labeled them 1A, 1B, 2A, 2B, 3A, and 3B to make the three-year rotation easy to visualize. She uses relay planting to squeeze in early carrots and salad greens around the squash and brassicas. She can't quite grow everything she wants, but is able to eat fresh arugula salads from the garden almost every week of the year (see page 74), and has plenty of jalapeños, beans, broccoli, and cabbage during the growing season.

YEAR 1

1A: Brassicas

1B: Brassicas

2A: Cucurbits

2B: Cucurbits

3A: Miscellaneous
(lettuce, beets, etc.)

3B: Miscellaneous
(lettuce, beets, etc.)

4: Eggplants and peppers

5: Pole beans and onions

YEAR 2

1A: Miscellaneous
(lettuce, beets, etc.)

1B: Miscellaneous
(lettuce, beets, etc.)

2A: Brassicas

2B: Brassicas

3A: Cucurbits

3B: Cucurbits

4: Pole beans and onions

5: Eggplants and peppers

YEAR 3

1A: Cucurbits

1B: Cucurbits

2A: Miscellaneous
(lettuce, beets, etc.)

2B: Miscellaneous
(lettuce, beets, etc.)

3A: Brassicas

3B: Brassicas

4: Eggplants and peppers

5: Pole beans and onions

JASON

GREENHOUSE ROTATION FOR TOMATOES AND PEPPERS

Jason loves growing tomatoes and 'Czech Black' hot peppers. He knows his productivity and yield will increase if he grows these crops in his greenhouse. He loves setting up his lounge chair in the greenhouse for early-spring naps, so he starts by establishing a 4-foot-wide path down the middle so he has room to stretch out. This leaves space for a 3-foot-wide bed on each side of the structure. On April 15th (four weeks ahead of his suggested outdoor planting dates for tomatoes and peppers) he plants tomatoes in one bed and 'Czech Black' in the other. He plans to rotate the tomatoes with the peppers each year. He knows they're both solanums so it's not a great rotation, but he doesn't really eat many other vegetables so figures he'll have to make it work. After he clears the summer crops in late September, he squeezes in a planting of mustard greens to harvest over the winter and help keep diseases out of the soil (mustard greens produce glucosinolates in their roots, which naturally suppress many plant diseases when they come in contact with moisture in the soil). He harvests mustard right into April of the following season, so he relay-plants the tomatoes and peppers into it. He then clears the mustard a few weeks later so it doesn't compete with the summer crops.

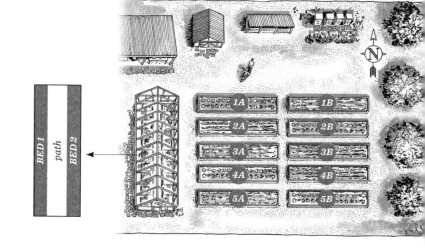

YEAR 1

BED 1: Tomatoes

BED 2: Peppers

YEAR 2

BED 1: Peppers

BED 2: Tomatoes

OUTDOOR BED ROTATIONS

In his outdoor garden, Jason likes to change things up every year. Two years ago, he was way into garlic and planted half his garden with it. Last year, it was cabbage for sauerkraut. This year, he wants lots of tomatoes and kale for his signature massaged-kale salad. He knows the importance of crop rotation, but needs to do it spontaneously each year because his cravings change so much. He has 10 beds, but treats each east and west pair as one bed to make rotation simpler. Fortunately, he keeps excellent records. Every spring he pulls out his garden map from the last few years, his planting plan, and a new blank map, and sits down to decide where things will go in the upcoming season.

He wants four beds of tomatoes, so plants them in beds 3A, 3B, 4A, and 4B. (The onions, kale, and lettuce from last year are light feeders and beans are a nitrogen fixer, so heavy-feeding potatoes should be a good following crop in those beds. Cabbage is a heavy feeder and Jason doesn't want to follow tomatoes with tomatoes, so beds 1, 2, and 5 aren't great choices for this crop.)

He plants his miscellaneous light-feeding crops in bed 2 to follow the heavy-feeding cabbage. Kale will go into beds 1A, 1B, 5A, and 5B. In bed 1, he's following a brassica with a brassica, but he decides it's worth the risk since kale is a lighter feeder than cabbage and he hasn't seen any soil-borne diseases. After all of this planning, he's ready for planting!

2 YEARS AGO	LAST YEAR	THIS YEAR
1A: Garlic	*1A:* Cabbage	*1A:* Kale
1B: Garlic	*1B:* Cabbage	*1B:* Kale
2A: Garlic	*2A:* Cabbage	*2A:* Onions
2B: Garlic	*2B:* Cabbage	*2B:* Lettuce and Beans
3A: Garlic	*3A:* Kale	*3A:* Tomatoes
3B: Garlic	*3B:* Kale	*3B:* Tomatoes
4A: Tomatoes	*4A:* Onions	*4A:* Tomatoes
4B: Tomatoes	*4B:* Lettuce and Beans	*4B:* Tomatoes
5A: Kale and Broccoli	*5A:* Tomatoes	*5A:* Kale
5B: Lettuce and Beans	*5B:* Tomatoes	*5B:* Kale

STRAWBERRY U-PICK

Dave and Erin love growing food. That's a good thing because they have 8,000 square feet of garden space to manage! They use the annual garden for their own use, but also want to set up a small U-pick strawberry operation for their family and neighbors. The field is a slightly awkward shape, but they divide it into four roughly equal parts (approximately 2,000 square feet each).

Strawberries are perennials, but they plan to manage each patch of strawberries for two years before clearing it (a common practice with larger-scale growers). Because strawberries don't produce much during their first year, Dave and Erin need to have a new patch ready for harvest each season. During the first spring, they plant 1,200 square feet of Field 1 in strawberries, and the remaining 800 into their annual vegetable garden. They plant Fields 2, 3, and 4 as grass and clover pasture where they graze a small flock of chickens and two goats.

In year two, they start picking strawberries in Field 1 and plant a cover crop over the 800 square feet that was the vegetable plot. They till up Field 2 and put in a new planting of strawberries along with annual vegetables. In year three, they are picking the strawberries from Field 2 and tilling and planting vegetables and new strawberries in Field 3. They also clear the strawberries in Field 1 and plant it back into a grass and clover pasture. The pattern continues into year four, and the cycle repeats itself in year five.

In this way, they have a full four-year rotation for all of their annual vegetables, have new strawberries to pick every year, and always have a pasture for their animals.

YEAR 1

FIELD 1: Strawberries and vegetables

FIELD 2: Clover and grass

FIELD 3: Clover and grass

FIELD 4: Clover and grass

YEAR 2

FIELD 1: Strawberries (2nd year)

FIELD 2: Strawberries (1st year) and vegetables

FIELD 3: Clover/grass

FIELD 4: Clover/grass

YEAR 3

FIELD 1: Clover/grass

FIELD 2: Strawberries (2nd year)

FIELD 3: Strawberries (1st year) and vegetables

FIELD 4: Clover/grass

YEAR 4

FIELD 1: Clover/grass

FIELD 2: Clover/grass

FIELD 3: Strawberries (2nd year)

FIELD 4: Strawberries (1st year) and vegetables

FILLING IN
YOUR GARDEN MAP

Now you should be ready to start filling in your garden map and working out a rotation plan. Grab your crop checklist, a few blank copies of your garden map, and a stiff drink (whiskey or strong chamomile tea, depending on your preference).

If your garden is new this year, you will have a blank canvas. Start by filling in locations where the long-season crops will go. Make sure tall crops won't be shading shorter crops. Next, write in where the half-season crops will go. You can write in which crops will replace them later in the season; alternatively, you can use two maps per season (one for spring planting and one for midsummer/fall planting). Finally, add the short-season crops. Remember, planting small amounts of these crops in succession is preferable to planting one big patch (and having more ready than you can use).

If it feels weird to leave space open in your garden during spring planting, just think of the lettuce and cilantro you'll be seeding next week and the week after and the week after! Don't forget to use relay planting to fit in early plantings around many long-season crops.

The level of detail you provide on the garden map can vary. You might draw a garden map to scale and note exactly where every plant will go. Such a drawing might look like the image below.

Lots of detail is great, but not absolutely necessary. Many growers will make a general map of where the major crop families or specific crops will go, and work out the details on planting days. A simple garden map can work very well, provided that the finer level of planting information is captured in your planting log.

If you have an existing garden that has been in use for several years, the process is the same as with a new garden. However, you'll want to consider where crops were planted the previous year so you can get a rotation started. If you have past records, great! If not, this is the year to start keeping them.

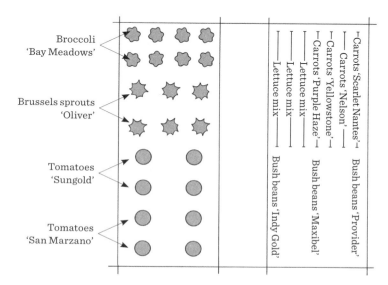

Broccoli 'Bay Meadows'

Brussels sprouts 'Oliver'

Tomatoes 'Sungold'

Tomatoes 'San Marzano'

Lettuce mix Lettuce mix Lettuce mix Lettuce mix Carrots 'Purple Haze' Carrots 'Yellowstone' Carrots 'Nelson' Carrots 'Scarlet Nantes'

Bush beans 'Indy Gold' Bush beans 'Maxibel' Bush beans 'Provider'

This kind of garden map serves as a detailed record of crop amounts, varieties, and their planting locations.

As you're working through the process, a long-term rotation plan might begin to make more sense. If so, you can fill out future garden maps now, noting where crop families will be placed for the next several seasons. If you are unsure of how to complete future maps, that's okay. After a few seasons of practice, a long-term plan might become apparent as you continue to rotate on a year-by-year basis.

KEEPING ADDITIONAL RECORDS

Keeping accurate records is a powerful way to expand your knowledge and improve your growing practices. Good records can help you improve your yields from one year to the next. If you keep good records, you can easily look back through the years and see which soil amendments improved yield and which had no effect, which varieties of beans performed best, which pest control practices actually worked, and how many pounds of spinach you really harvested from that 8-foot row. Keeping track of time between planting and harvest helps you determine the best time of year to plant crops in your specific climate.

Your style of recordkeeping could take any form. Develop a system that works for you, and choose a format that you can (and will) actually maintain. Some people write some or all of their records on their garden maps. Some people keep all their records right on their planting calendar. Some people prefer a regular old notebook and write everything down in it. Some prefer building spreadsheets on a computer, and some might use cloud-based recordkeeping applications.

The basic garden and crop information that we recommend you keep in your records includes:

- Date of harvest for each planting.

- Size of the planting (how many row feet or numbers of transplants).

- Location of planting: the specific field, bed, or part of bed that a crop was planted.

- Yield (how many pounds you harvested).

- Flavor (was it worse than, as good as, or better than expected?).

- Relative performance of different varieties. If certain varieties do not produce well in your garden, you'll want to note this and remove them from your planting plan the following season. If a variety has standout yields, superior pest resistance, or flavor, you'll want to grow more of it next season.

- The soil amendments and organic fertilizers you used, and in what quantities.

- Any pest or disease problems and the control methods you used (and whether or not they were effective).

- General observations throughout the season. This might include information like, "'Red Russian' kale definitely had the best flavor of all the varieties I tried this year," or "The beans I seeded on August 5th didn't have time to mature; I'm going to put my last planting in a little earlier next year."

We also recommend that you keep track of a few other items:

- Lists of seed suppliers, and varieties and quantities you order. This will help you put together next season's seed order. (See chapter 4, beginning on page 96, for more information.)

- A record of suppliers for tools, amendments, and organic pest and disease control materials. If you're interested in tracking costs, keep receipts for these supplies.

- If you use municipal water for irrigation, you might keep a record of your water bills so you can track how much water you use in the garden each season. Similarly, if you use electricity for grow lights or greenhouse heat, keep track of the correlated utility bills.

Visual Recordkeeping

Many growers like to keep track of plantings directly on their garden map. This is a good way for visual thinkers to see what's happened in a particular bed or field over the years. If you want to keep track of a lot of information, this method may be limiting because you only have so much space on your map to write things down.

Bed-Specific Log

A way to have more space to write things down (without using your map to keep the records) is to dedicate a page in your notebook or an individual sheet in your spreadsheet for each bed or field in your garden. A bed-specific log such as this will allow you to easily look back at past seasons to recall what you planted in each bed and when it was harvested. You can also note days to maturity and other information that varies by location.

Individual Logs

Some growers like to use an individual log for different activities. For example, you might have a harvest log, a soil amendment log, a pest and disease control log (see below), and a planting calendar. Going this route means that you have more logs to maintain, but such a system is useful for larger-scale growers who have a lot of information to track. (Note that this is the style of recordkeeping that many inspectors prefer if you are planning to be certified organic.) Moreover, with such a system you can quickly and easily gather information on a specific activity ("what was my earliest harvest of lettuce this spring?" or "what did I spray for powdery mildew last year?").

Individual logs for specific activities in the garden are a great way to record and access detailed information about that activity.

				Pest and Disease Control Log		
Date	Pest/Disease Observed	Location	Crop Affected	Management Applied	Result
13-Jul	imported cabbage worms	east field	broccoli	spray spinosad	7/22: damage appears to have stopped
16-Sep	slugs	northeast plot	spinach	spread diatomaceous earth	9/18: rain washed off DE; repeat application

All in One

Small-scale gardeners might keep track of everything in one general log. On the upside, this keeps things simple because you have fewer logs to maintain. On the downside, you will probably have a little more difficulty finding specific information because individual activities will not be differentiated.

Seattle Urban Farm Company Garden Log

Date	Hours Spent in Garden	Weather Conditions	Planting Log	Fertilization Log	Pest/Disease Log	Harvest Chart	To Do	General Notes and Observations
15-Jun	1	cloudy	direct seed carrots, bed 3; beets, bed 4; transplant lettuce mix, bed 7	mix in 3-3-3 pre-planting for all crops	spray spinosad	harvest spinach from bed 1		
21-Jun	0.25	sunny			weed beds 18 and 19; spray neem and soap for aphids on brassicas in bed 12	9/18: rain washed off DE; repeat application	harvest kale from bed 2	

It's harder to look up specific information in an all-in-one garden log, but it keeps things simple by recording all your garden information in a single document.

Weather-Resistant Notebooks

If you plan to keep any of your records on paper (instead of on a computer), we recommend a book that is designed to withstand moisture and sun exposure. These books typically have thicker paper and a water-wicking cover, and will comfortably put you in the small cadre of notekeeping nerds that includes birders and herpetologists.

CHAPTER 4

Selecting Seeds

Choosing seed varieties and quantities is a great way to begin the season. Many growers enjoy flipping through seed catalogs during the slow winter months, imagining how fabulous their gardens will be in the coming season. Your seeds are the foundation of your annual garden system. Learning to navigate the universe of seeds is a major step toward creating a high-yield garden.

Selecting your seeds early will ensure that your actual seed library matches your expected garden plan. Ordering early also means you'll have the first crack at the most desirable varieties, which often sell out by late spring. Start researching early and try to place your seed order as soon as possible; buying your seeds in December or January will ensure that you have the seeds you want on hand when the season starts.

Growing from seed can dramatically increase your opportunities for better yields. Keeping a well-stocked seed library allows you to take advantage of production opportunities on your own schedule throughout the season. You'll also be able to replant failed crops or squeeze in unexpected successions when weather conditions shift.

SOURCING SEEDS

We recommend that you become accustomed to ordering seeds directly from suppliers whenever possible. This method requires more foresight, since there is a necessary delay between the seed order and delivery of the seed. But seeds purchased this way will be much less expensive, and you will have more options when selecting varieties and quantities. Even when you're buying seeds directly from the company, it still helps to know which local stores carry high-quality seeds in case you run out of a particular seed mid-season and want to do a quick succession planting.

Choosing a Supplier

We encourage you to choose your suppliers based on your location and gardening priorities. Good regional seed companies often carry varieties that are well suited to your climate. It's worth checking in with local suppliers to see what they recommend. Remember not to trust their advice blindly — some "local" seed companies operate with very little gardening knowledge and are happy to sell you a variety that will perform miserably in your climate. Make sure the seed suppliers you choose have a good reputation.

PREPARING YOUR SEED ORDER

We recommend working through the catalog and websites of your preferred seed vendors as early as October or November, while the current season's successes and failures are still fresh in your mind. (Hopefully you have also documented these successes and failures in your records! See page 93 for more information on good recordkeeping practices.)

Try to place your seed order no later than the end of January (we place our orders before the end of each December). The only drawback to a super-early purchase is that you might find out about a new variety of seed after you have placed your order. Of course, you can always add on to your seed order if this happens, but you might incur extra shipping fees or small-order fees.

Organic Seed Stock

Organic crop production does not require that all seeds are certified organic. Organic regulations state that a grower should determine the desired variety of crop and try to find a source of organic seed from at least three suppliers. If certified seed is not available, it is okay to purchase non-organic seed and start the organic production process at your own garden. Certain seed suppliers (such as High Mowing Organic Seeds) only sell certified organic seeds, whereas other suppliers sell both organic and non-organic varieties. Organic seeds typically cost more than other types, but are worth buying when possible to support the expansion of organic seed production.

Seed Order Worksheet

We recommend making a seed order spreadsheet for each gardening year and updating it in the fall for the upcoming season. (Don't copy over old records; it is great to be able to look back at past years to see the quantities and types of seeds you ordered.) It is also possible to include perennial plants and seeds in your seed-ordering spreadsheet. Some perennials can be grown from seed, but many are purchased as plants, roots, or bulbs. Some of these can be easily ordered from seed vendors or other online retailers. Download this spreadsheet at Seattle Urban Farm Company's website (see Resources, page 309) and use the blank rows to insert additional annual and perennial crops you purchase that are not included here.

Crop	Variety Name	Vendor	

Item Number	Quantity/Volume of Seed: Ounces, Pounds or # of Seeds	Price per Unit	Total Price

SELECTING YOUR VARIETIES

The moment you pick up a seed catalog or search a seed supplier's website, you will probably realize that the crops you're looking for come in seemingly endless varieties. This makes the process of seed selecting more exciting, but also more challenging. Some plants are bred or selected to produce the highest yields or the best flavor; others are bred for unique colors, adaptability to a particular climate, or disease resistance. Typically, a vegetable variety offered today has a blend of desirable qualities that makes it adaptable to various situations.

In catalogs and websites, seed suppliers will regale you with tales of success and wonder for their seeds. While it may be that each variety does in fact grow well in some climates with a certain set of circumstances, not all of them will grow well in *your* garden. Be sure to read the catalog descriptions carefully; the best seed companies tell you the conditions for which a variety is best suited. Sometimes, the name of the variety serves as an indicator for the conditions it likes best. For example, 'Winter Density' lettuce grows well in cool temperatures, and 'Summerfest Komatsuna' has been bred to tolerate hot weather.

> Eliminating varieties that do not perform well in your garden is an important step in increasing your garden's productivity.

Your fellow local gardeners and farmers can be good sources for seed recommendations. Websites and online forums can provide some useful insight, too, but Internet research will take some sleuthing. Very targeted searches can help you, though it's important to keep in mind that no single online source can identify the best crops and varieties for your area. As you gain experience, you should rely on your own observations to make these selections for your garden. Choosing the crops and varieties that are best adapted to your growing conditions will make your garden much more productive and successful.

Here are a couple of tactics for refining your variety selection from year to year:

Grow several different varieties of each crop. This way, you'll be able to compare them and determine which are most productive in your climate and in your garden. Furthermore, some varieties are best suited for early-season planting and some for late-season planting. One variety might be best for winter storage while another is ideal for fresh eating. Planting multiple varieties also increases the genetic diversity in the garden. Some varieties are more resistant to disease, drought, or extreme temperatures than others, so planting different types can act as a form of crop insurance. Be sure to keep good records of how your varieties fare, to inform future seed purchasing decisions.

Ditch the duds. Eliminate varieties that do not perform well in your garden. This is an important step in increasing your garden's productivity. Just because a variety is considered tried-and-true by many gardeners doesn't mean it's the right one for your climate or particular garden. Each season, we recommend that you experiment with a few new varieties, pick some of your reliable favorites, and strike the low perfomers from the list.

Seed Definitions

In catalogs, seeds are categorized based on how they were bred. It is important to understand the differences between these categories so that you can make informed choices when selecting your seeds.

Open-Pollinated

Often referred to as OP, open-pollinated seeds are those that "breed true from seed" — meaning that seeds collected from the plants will produce a plant similar to the parent, thus allowing the option of seed saving. Keep in mind that cross-pollination between varieties of the same crop (or even different crops with the same scientific name) will change the genetic makeup of open-pollinated seeds, leading to changes in subsequent generations. For example, if you save seed from a 'Dill's Atlantic Giant' pumpkin and/or a 'New England Pie' pumpkin that were grown in the same garden, that seed could lead to a medium-size pumpkin that tastes like tires.

Heirloom

Heirloom plants are simply old-time, open-pollinated varieties. There is not a defined age a variety must be before it can be considered an heirloom. It is often cited as being somewhere between 10,000 and 50 years old.

Hybrid

Plant breeders sometimes produce hybrid (F_1) varieties by crossing two distinct "pure" genetic lines. Each of these pure lines exhibit one spectacular trait: one of the lines may produce high yields, while the other may produce resistance to a common plant disease. The crossing of the two lines creates a plant with both high yields and a resistance to the disease. This has obvious benefits for the high-yield grower. The downside of hybrid seeds is that they don't "breed true", so you cannot save your own seed.

Genetically Modified (GM)

GM plants have been genetically manipulated. Genetic engineers can insert genes that come from other plants, bacteria, or animals in order to increase a plant's vigor, improve disease resistance, resist herbicides, or last longer in storage. Genetic engineering of agricultural crops is controversial and may have negative effects on the quality and purity of existing genetic material in our ecosystem. Genetically modified seeds are not permitted in organic production, and we don't recommend using them. If you want to make sure you're not buying GM seed, buy from a supplier that has pledged not to source them and/or use certified organic seed.

Hybrid or Open-Pollinated?

One of the options you'll be faced with, when deciding which varieties to choose, is that of open-pollinated or hybrid. For a number of reasons, we feel that it's important to use a combination of both.

What Hybrids Offer

Many hybrid varieties are bred to be resistant to pests and diseases, so they're well suited to organic production methods. Additionally, many hybrids grow more quickly than their heirloom cousins, meaning they are well suited for challenging climates. Hybrids that have been bred for conditions that match yours can be much healthier and more productive than open-pollinated crops. This, in turn, leads to higher yields, lower mortality rates, and easier overall garden management.

For example, most open-pollinated peppers have a difficult time ripening in the cool nights of the Pacific Northwest. Hybrid varieties of peppers can be much more productive in this climate. Similarly, downy mildew can be a terrible problem for spinach growers in wet climates, but by selecting a downy mildew–resistant hybrid variety, it is possible to grow a delicious crop of spinach without using fungicides.

The Benefits of Open-Pollinated and Heirloom Varieties

Open-pollinated and heirloom varieties have a number of positive attributes working in their favor. The primary case for growing open-pollinated crops is that you can collect and use the seed they produce. Open-pollinated crops will "breed true to seed," meaning that subsequent generations will share the same traits as your original seed stock. Older open-pollinated types are often called heirlooms, and these are often thought to be better tasting than new varieties or hybrids, and sometimes they really are. It's important to note, though, that heirloom varieties aren't *inherently* better tasting than hybrids or newer open-pollinated types — it's just that heirloom varieties were often selected for taste rather than other genetic attributes. In addition, some heirloom varieties have been selected for their excellent disease resistance. On the flip side, some heirloom varieties may be more difficult to grow, less tolerant of adverse growing conditions, and may produce lower yields than hybrid or newer open-pollinated varieties. It's important to do your research!

Whatever their attributes or drawbacks, we feel it's vitally important to grow heirlooms simply for the sake of protecting the biodiversity of our food crops. The best way to protect and preserve heirlooms is to grow them, eat them, and save their seeds for replanting. We also feel it's important to support responsible seed companies and the plant-breeding work they do. For these reasons, we recommend that you grow a mixture of open-pollinated varieties, heirlooms, and hybrid crops. Over time, you should continue to select new and different varieties based on your preferences and on the demands of your local conditions.

Selecting Varieties for Seasonality

Seed descriptions will indicate if a variety was bred to tolerate specific weather conditions. This may be included in the variety name, as in 'Black Summer' bok choy. Alternatively, this information may be nestled into the larger description of the crop, which might say "great summer variety" or "best when planted for spring production." A description may even call out a certain region of the country in which the variety does best, such as "great for northern regions" or "adapted for fall planting in the South."

All of these indications are crucial because they tell you when and where to seed the crop for best performance. For example, you've probably noticed that there are hundreds of varieties of head lettuce. Lettuce is well known for its intolerance of hot weather. Summer heat makes it bitter and causes bolting (premature flowering). Because this is such an issue for growers, breeders have worked to develop varieties that perform better in midsummer conditions. The names and descriptions of the lettuce varieties tell you whether the seeds should be planted early in the season, in the middle of the season, or late in the season.

If you want a consistent supply of head lettuce, you will need to use different varieties through the season, changing the type as the weather progresses. For example, 'Winter Density' is a romaine type that grows best in cool temperatures; and 'Jericho' is able to tolerate warmer summer weather. Knowing this, you may want to plant 'Winter Density' in spring and fall, but plant 'Jericho' all summer long.

Choosing Crops for Climate

Certain crops are suited for particular climates. Crops that evolved from wild plants in tropical regions will always be more challenging to grow in cool climates. For example, tomatoes, peppers, and eggplants are heat-loving crops that will produce for incredibly long seasons in southern regions of the United States, but very short seasons in the Northeast and Pacific Northwest.

There are some crops like peanuts, sweet potatoes, watermelons, and okra that require so much heat that they are not even appropriate to plant in cool climates. Similarly, there are crops like spinach and broccoli that perform better and produce greater yields in cooler climates. You're likely to choose crops from all regions of the world, but be sure to match your planting plan and your variety selections to your local climate.

Disease Resistance

Plant breeders have worked hard to create varieties that are resistant to disease. Indications of disease resistance are usually noted in a catalog's crop description. In fact, because these traits are so desirable, disease resistance is usually advertised prominently. This disease resistance is often indicated in written in notation. For

'Winter Density'

'Jericho'

'Jericho' lettuce performs well in summer heat, while 'Winter Density' is very tolerant of cold temperatures.

example, "PM" refers to powdery mildew and "CMV" refers to cucumber mosaic virus.

Before you purchase a disease-resistant variety, however, you should know which diseases are prevalent in your region. Selecting a variety specifically for its resistance to CMV will not be helpful if this disease isn't a problem in your garden to begin with. It's not generally a *problem* to plant a variety that's resistant to a disease your garden doesn't experience, but sometimes varieties bred for disease resistance have other, less desirable traits. For example, such a plant may produce lower yields or smaller fruit than another variety.

Harvest Window and Storage Capacity

Even closely related varieties will show differences in their ability to hold quality in the field and in the pantry. For crops that have the tendency to bolt, look for varieties described as "slow to bolt." Take note of variety names and descriptions to ensure that if you intend to store potatoes through the winter, you're planting a variety that is specifically indicated to be a storage potato. Similarly, other root crops like carrots, for example, can have widely varying storage lives. Keep in mind what your particular goals are for the crop and make sure to order types that will meet that goal.

Plant for Taste

You must often strike a balance to find varieties that meet all of your selection standards. But there is no doubt that your gardening experience will be much more satisfying if you produce crops that you (and the other benefactors of your garden) like to eat. Since catalog descriptions can only do so much to relate the flavors of crops, it will take some time to identify the varieties you like best. You can accelerate this progress by talking with other gardeners in your area and asking for variety names at the farmers' market when you're purchasing vegetables.

HOW MUCH SEED TO ORDER

After you've chosen the specific varieties of crops you'd like to order, you'll need to determine the quantities of seed to order.

Fewer May Be Plenty

The quantity of seed you'll need varies depending on the crop, the number of plants you're planning on growing, and whether or not you'll be seeding in succession plantings. If you're growing a single row of tomato plants, for example, you can probably get away with ordering the smallest quantity available of any tomato variety (usually called a packet). However, if you hope to grow enough for your own garden *and* sell several hundred tomato transplants in the spring, you'll obviously need to scale up.

Other long-season crops that need a lot of space, such as winter squash and tomatillos, might fall into a similar category; a small packet of seeds should be plenty for most growers. Likewise, it's a good practice to order by the packet if you're trying out a new variety but don't yet know if it will perform well in your area or if you'll like the taste (say you want to experiment with watermelon radishes). If the crop performs well and you like what it produces, you can simply reorder either for later in the season or for the following season.

Choosing the Right Carrot for Your Goals

For the most part, carrots are long, narrow, and orange (or purple). However, upon closer examination, carrots have a variety of subtle shape, color, flavor, texture, and storage variations. You should select varieties that best suit your purposes and growing conditions. These differences can be classified by the type of carrot:

Chantenay: Shorter (5–6 inches), conical shape with a blunt tip and wider shoulders (the top part of the root). Handles heavy soil better than other types. Many varieties are excellent for fresh eating and cooking. *Stores well.*

Danvers: Mid-length (6–7 inches), conical shape with wide "shoulders." Usually best cooked. *Stores well.*

Imperator: Long (up to 10 inches), gently tapering shape. Very high yields when grown in loose, sandy soil. Often more fibrous and less sweet than other types, so are best for cooking (some varieties do have excellent raw eating quality). *Stores well.*

Kuroda: Shorter conical type similar to Chantenay, but with less pronounced shoulders. Commonly grown in Asia. *Stores well.*

Nantes: Mid-length, slender, cylindrical shape. Most varieties have excellent raw eating and cooking quality. *Doesn't store as well as other types.*

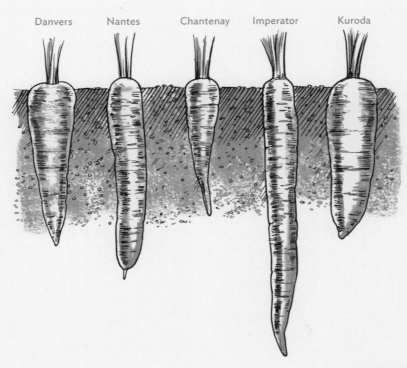

Danvers   Nantes   Chantenay   Imperator   Kuroda

Not all seeds store equally well. The seeds of some crops, like tomatoes and lettuce, maintain viability for five to six years or more; while alliums and parsnips have very limited viability and may only keep for a single year. (See the Seed Life Span chart on page 108 for more information.)

Enough for Several Sowings

If you're planning for multiple successions of short-season crops like a lettuce mix or radishes, you will likely need to order significant quantities of seed. Most good seed catalogs will have information to help you determine how much seed to order for these types of crops. For each one, it will indicate how many seeds to sow per row foot for direct-seeded crops, or how many are needed to produce transplants for X number of row feet. A good catalog may also tell you how many seeds are in an ounce or a pound. We have found the Johnny's Selected Seeds catalog to be one of the best resources

available for this type of information (see Resources, page 307).

Using information from the planting plan you created, you can determine how many row feet or number of transplants for each crop you'll be growing. A bit of quick math will give you the number or quantity of seeds you need to purchase. Plan to order at least 20 percent more seeds than you calculate to compensate for low germination and other variables. Most seeds will remain viable for two to three years, so you can always use extra the following season (see Storing Seeds at right).

Even with the best planning, though, you'll likely run out of (or over-order) certain seeds. Don't worry! With good recordkeeping, your seed-ordering skills will improve with every season. In the meantime, you can download the spreadsheet at Seattle Urban Farm Company's website (see Resources, page 309). This is what we use for calculating seed quantities when seed ordering.

SEED FOR RYAN'S ARUGULA

On page 74, we mentioned that Ryan would like to plant 4 row feet of arugula every week for about 26 weeks (a total of 104 row feet). His seed catalog tells him that 1 ounce of arugula seed will sow 500 feet, so he needs about ¼ ounce of seed to sow 104 feet (plus 20 percent). The only sizes in the catalog are a packet, 1 ounce, and ¼ pound. He knows the packet size won't be enough, so he orders the full ounce (it's only $6, and he can use the extra during the next couple of years, or share those seeds with his friends).

STORING SEEDS

The lifetime of a dormant seed can be anywhere from one season to 10 years, and beyond. Most vegetable seeds have the potential to remain viable for at least two or three years, but this viability is hugely dependent on how a seed is stored. Seeds are often packaged in paper envelopes; they can be stored this way indefinitely so long as they are kept dry and cool at all times.

Most seeds will keep longest if they're placed in a resealable plastic bag or airtight container and stored in a refrigerator or freezer. This is especially true for seeds that have a particularly short storage life. If you'd like to keep allium seeds for more than one season, for example, be sure to put them in the freezer. Keep in mind that every time you move a seed packet from the refrigerator to a warm room, moisture will condense on it (which could limit the storage life of the seed). In light of this, we recommend room-temperature storage for seeds that will be succession planted frequently throughout the year.

In fact, because fridge space is often at a premium, you might store *all* of your seeds at room temperature in an area that remains consistently dark and dry (such as a closet, cabinet, or dresser in a room without south-facing windows). A garage or tool shed is not a great location because of the wide variability in temperature and humidity throughout the year.

As seasons pass, use up your existing store of seed before opening a new package. If you notice germination rates declining, simply plant more seeds to compensate. If plants fail to come up at all, compost the seeds and remember to order less next time or to use them more quickly!

To increase the storage life of short-lived seeds like onions, store them in a resealable plastic bag in the freezer. Most other seeds can simply be stored at room temperature.

Seed Life Span

If you're considering buying large quantities of seed for a particular crop, you should first determine if the excess seed will store well. It can be preferable to purchase relatively small amounts of seeds each year, especially when you're still selecting your preferred varieties. Once you find some tried-and-true varieties for your garden, you can order larger quantities to save on cost.

VEGETABLES AND HERBS

Approx. Seed Storage Life Span (years)

Artichoke, 5
Arugula, 3
Basil, 3
Beans, Edible soy
   (Edamame), 3
Beans, Fava
   (Broad), 3
Beans, Lima, 3
Beans, Shell, 3
Beans, Snap, 3
Beets, 4
Bok choy, 4
Broccoli, 3
Brussels sprouts, 4
Cabbage, 4
Cabbage, Chinese, 4
Carrots, 3

Cauliflower, 4
Celeriac, 5
Celery, 5
Chard, Swiss, 4
Cilantro, 2
Collards, 5
Corn, Sweet, 2
Cucumbers, 5
Dill, 3
Eggplant, 4
Endive, 5
Fennel, Bulbing, 4
Garlic, 1
Kale, 4
Kohlrabi, 4
Leeks, 1
Lettuce, Baby Mix, 5

Lettuce, Heads, 5
Mâche, 5
Melon, Cantaloupe,
   Honeydew, 5
Mustard greens, 4
Okra, 2
Onions, Bulb, 1
Parsley, 1
Parsnips, 1
Peanuts, 1
Peas, Shelling, 3
Peas, Snap, 3
Peppers, Hot, 2
Peppers, Sweet, 2
Potatoes, 1
Raab, 4
Radicchio, 4

Radishes, 5
Rutabagas, 5
Scallions, 1
Spinach, 2
Squash, Gourds, 4
Squash, Pumpkins, 4
Squash, Summer, 4
Squash, Winter, 4
Sweet Potatoes, N/A
Tomatillos, 4
Tomatoes, 4
Turnips, 5
Watermelon, 4

PERENNIAL HERBS

Approx. Seed Storage Life Span (years)

Anise hyssop, 3
Bay, 2
Chervil, 2
Chives, 1
Chives, Garlic, 1
Fennel, 3

Horseradish, N/A
Lavender, 2
Lemon balm, 3
Lemon verbena, 2
Lemongrass, 2
Marjoram, 2

Mint, 3
Oregano, 4
Purple coneflower, 5
Rosemary, 3
Sage, 4
Savory, 2

Stevia, 1
Tarragon, N/A
Thyme, 3
Valerian, 2

Seed Treatments That Improve Yield

Some seed will benefit from special treatments before or at planting time to ensure their success. These treatments may or may not be necessary depending on the crop and the treatment, but it is good to know how they work so you can include them in your tool kit of seeding techniques.

Bacterial or Fungal Inoculation

In the context of gardening, "inoculation" refers to introducing a microbiological agent to your growing system for the benefit of the crop. Common garden inoculants are bacteria or fungi that are intentionally added to the soil or seed to promote a healthier plant. By adding certain microbes directly to the soil, you can help create an especially robust soil ecosystem in your garden.

Rhizobium. The most common garden inoculant is a kind of bacteria known as rhizobium (often sold simply as "garden inoculant"). It is added to the seeds of legume crops at planting time. The most common garden legumes are peas and beans, which are supported by the same strain of bacteria. Additional strains exist for soybeans, peanuts, and leguminous cover crops. The bacteria form a symbiotic relationship with the root nodules of legume crops. It allows the plants to absorb nitrogen from the air, use it for growth, and deposit it into the soil.

Legume plants and crops are unique in this ability (called "nitrogen fixation"). Even though the air we breathe is 78 percent nitrogen (N_2), plants can't use it in this form. N_2 must be converted into ammonium nitrogen (NH_4^+) or nitrate nitrogen (NO_3^-) before plants can absorb it and use it for growth. Rhizobium bacteria allow the legumes to convert N_2 from the air into NH_4. This is helpful for the legume crop, but also leaves behind a store of NH_4 in the soil for the next plants in the garden to use.

Inoculate the seeds just prior to planting by making a "slurry." Separate out the seeds you need for that round of planting, pour them into a plastic or ceramic container, sprinkle inoculant onto the seeds, add a few drops of water, and stir until the powder sticks to the seeds and coats them lightly. The packaging will include an application rate, but the exact proportion of powder to seed is not crucial. A little bit goes a long way, and there are no adverse effects if you use a bit too much.

Mycorrhizal fungi. Another, less commonly used but effective inoculant is made with mycorrhizal fungi. Mycorrhizae are soil-dwelling fungi that have been shown to help a wide range of plants build more robust and healthy root systems. Similar to the bacterial relationship described with rhizobium, these fungi symbiotically colonize plants' root systems. In exchange for carbohydrates from the plant, the fungi expand the plant's underground network, helping the root system absorb water and nutrients from the further reaches of the soil. Mycorrhizal fungi are naturally present in the soil, especially in a well-managed organic garden. However, the addition of extra fungi can boost plant growth, especially in new or poor garden soil that has not developed a robust soil ecosystem.

These fungi can be purchased in liquid, powder, or granular form. Fungi that are appropriate for use in the garden will be referred to as endomycorrhiza (in contrast to ectomycorrhiza, which live on the roots of woody plants). Powdered or granular forms are easy to apply when transplanting crops. Simply add the material to the planting hole as you would with a granular fertilizer. Liquid forms can be easily applied over direct-seeded crops when disturbing the root system is undesirable or impossible.

Other Seed Treatments

Certain seeds benefit from some kind of physical treatment. The two most common types of treatment for annual vegetable crops are scarification and soaking.

Scarification. This refers to the abrasion of the seed coat in order to prepare the seed for germination. It's applicable to seeds with particularly thick seed coats. Common techniques include rubbing with sandpaper and cracking with a hammer. Although not necessary for edible crops, scarification can speed up germination times for large seeds like beans and squash.

Seed soaking. Some seeds will sprout more quickly if soaked in water prior to seeding. This technique is particularly effective for cucurbits, peas, and beans. It can also be effective for slow germinating crops like carrots, parsnips, and parsley. Soak seeds in lukewarm or cool water for up to 12 hours. Some growers add liquid kelp to their seed-soaking water at ¼ teaspoon per quart of water, which is reported to speed up the germination process even further.

PART 2

Growing for Maximum Yield

CHAPTER 5

Prepping Soil for Production

No matter how well you plan, how carefully you site your garden, and how selective you are with your seed purchasing and starting, if you don't have good soil, you'll have a tough time growing big yields. Crops growing in well-balanced soil are amazing to behold: they grow rapidly, have rich coloration, and have huge yields per square foot; their flavor is excellent, too. Good soil is a combination of many factors: the right amount of organic matter for good structure and water retention, a balance of plant nutrients and minerals, and a thriving community of beneficial soil life.

Taking the time to consider all these factors and putting the work in to make sure they're present in your soil will put you solidly on the path to high-yield production, minimizing disease and maximizing nutrition in your produce. Whether you're expanding your growing area with new beds or improving the beds you already have, it's important to understand the process of creating healthy, productive garden soil.

EXPANDING PRODUCTION WITH NEW BEDS

Before you can start setting up new garden beds, you'll first need to eliminate the competition. There are two basic approaches — you can either clear the site completely or you can incorporate existing materials into the soil. Each has its pros and cons.

Clearing the Site

If your garden site is full of undesirable plants, such as invasive weeds or large shrubs, clearing the entire area should be your first task. Removing large plants, random debris, grass sod, rocks, invasive weeds, and ground covers will create a clean slate. Site clearing also provides a great opportunity to regrade and level the space as needed to prevent erosion and improve accessability. Once the site is clean and the space is level, you can work the earth and determine how much soil amending is necessary.

Loosen the Soil

After clearing the site, loosen the soil with a sod fork, shovel, or broadfork. It's not necessary to turn the soil over; simply lift the

Sourcing Quality Bulk Materials

As you expand your production, you're likely to need larger quantities of amendments. Anticipating the materials you'll need during the course of a season will help you prepare for the sourcing, pickup, or delivery of any given material before it's required. Let's take a look at some of the most common soil materials and how to go about acquiring them:

Soil

Do your research and try to locate a seller that has a good reputation and understands the needs of an organic vegetable gardener (you'd be surprised how many don't!). If you're buying new soil for your garden beds, ask for two-way soil mix made of compost and sand; or three-way soil mix made from compost, sand, and topsoil. Soil purveyors will often carry other useful products like compost, gravel, and mulch.

Manure

With some searching you may find sources of manure that are available for free. Make sure the manure is fully (and appropriately) composted before adding it to your garden beds. Fresh, uncomposted manure may be easier to find, but can add pathogens and weed seeds to your garden.

Soil Amendments and Fertilizers

You may need a variety of soil amendments for your garden (see page 125 for more details). If you have the capacity to purchase and store these materials in large quantities, you can save quite a lot of money. Often a 50-pound bag of a basic soil amendment from a distributor costs little more than a 5-pound bag from a garden center. Look for wholesale distributors or local businesses that are willing or able to deal with larger volumes, and consider splitting orders with other local gardeners.

soil and shake it a bit to break up clods. This will typically reveal more roots and rocks that should be removed from the soil. After thoroughly loosening the soil, decide where the annual and perennial beds will be, and where the paths will run. When ready, stake them out.

Amend the Soil

In most home sites, the existing soil will need additional compost or garden-quality soil to create a desirable structure, nutrient base, and depth for annual vegetable crop production. Some perennial edibles are less demanding than annual vegetables, but in our experience, perennials grow best in well-amended soil. The perennial edibles that benefit most from soil amendment are asparagus, artichokes, rhubarb, blueberries, raspberries, and strawberries.

Less demanding perennials, such as fruit trees, most herbs, and sunchokes, can be grown with little additional soil amending. Some growers suggest that planting these perennials in native soils without amendment allows them to adapt better to local conditions and thrive (you'll still need to loosen the soil and remove roots and rocks). This technique won't work if you have extremely sandy, clayey, or otherwise low-quality soil, however. If your existing soil is very poor, prepare perennial beds in the same way you prepare your annual beds, as the following details describe.

Start by spreading a 4- to 6-inch layer of high-quality compost or vegetable garden–quality soil mix onto the beds. Mix this into the existing soil with a shovel or garden fork to create an entirely new soil structure. After adding the new compost or soil, take a soil sample for professional pH testing to determine what other amendments should be added. You can also test the soil pH yourself (see page 117 for more information on soil pH and testing).

Incorporating the Materials on Site

If your new garden site is currently grass lawn or small weeds or a non-aggressive ground cover, you might simply till the existing plants into the soil. Incorporating these plants will help increase nutrient levels and build organic matter content, and will eliminate the need to haul materials off-site.

When incorporating materials into the site, start the process at least four weeks (ideally eight or more) before planting time. Your goal is to give the plants you're tilling in or smothering time to decompose before the crops go in the ground. Planting in the garden too early will be awkward and

A tiller is a great tool for killing sod and cover crops, and for mixing in soil amendments. Because repeated use of the tiller can create a hardpan, however, we recommend using it judiciously and in combination with a sod fork or broadfork to break up the hardpan.

inefficient (because of large clumps in the soil) and will result in poor productivity (soil nutrients will be unavailable because of the decomposing residue). Weeds or ground covers with a woody stem should be removed, not tilled in; they will take far too long to decompose.

The Right Tool for Tilling

The right tool for the job will depend on the scale of the project and your gusto for manual labor. Annual weeds are relatively easy to break up; grass sod is extremely difficult. A sod fork or shovel works for very small spaces. For turning in large areas of grass sod, we strongly recommend using a hydraulic rear-tine rototiller. It might sound intense, but this machine is easy to use and can be rented from most equipment rental stores. To make your job easier, be sure to mow the grass/weeds as short as possible before turning them in.

Chances are, you'll need to work the soil two to three times (or more), especially when trying to break down heavy grass sod. Till everything in, wait two to three weeks, and then till again and wait a few more weeks. If the plants have broken down well and there is no residue, proceed with building your garden. If not, wait longer or turn again. If the soil is dry while the residue is breaking down, water it to promote decomposition.

Smothering Existing Plants

Another method of incorporation is commonly called "layer" or "lasagna" gardening. The idea is that with the addition of enough organic matter (typically layers of compost, organic mulch, and soil), you can smother the existing plants and create new beds directly on top of them. If the new beds are topped with a thick enough layer of soil and compost (6–12 inches), you can plant right away while the underlayers continue to decompose. After you've added the soil and compost, be sure to test the pH or professionally test the soil to determine if any other amendments are needed. For more details on this method, check out the resources section on page 307.

Multiple layers of compost, new soil, and organic mulches can effectively smother grass and weeds.

Mulch Your Pathways

Whether you're starting new beds or improving old ones, we recommend you mulch your pathways. Doing so will reduce erosion and the time you'll spend weeding (plus your shoes and pants will stay cleaner). There are any number of mulch materials you could use. What you choose depends on your preferences and on what's availability. Here are a few ideas to get you started.

Instead of using non-living materials, some growers plant their pathways with a cover crop. It is a kind of "living mulch." If you go this route, be sure to mow the cover crop before it sets seed or it will become a weed problem unto itself. And unless you have timber-framed or other tall, enclosed raised beds, avoid using perennial grasses for living pathway mulch, as the grass will spread by its rhizomes into your garden beds. See page 245 for more information on cover crops.

Recommended

Bark mulch: Must be replenished each year to suppress weeds effectively. In addition to smothering weeds, bark mulch often contains hydroxylated aromatic compounds, naturally occurring chemicals that have an allelopathic effect on weeds (discourages their growth).

Wood chips: Must be replenished each year to suppress weeds effectively. In addition to smothering weeds, some wood chips (such as cedar) contain natural chemicals that help discourage weed growth.

Straw: Must be replenished each year to suppress weeds effectively. Consider using with an underlayer of newspaper or cardboard.

Heavy landscape fabric: Look for a "20 year" rating. Can be rolled up in winter for better longevity. Can be difficult to weed around if weeds get out of control.

Recommended with Reservations

Gravel: Long lasting, but weeds grow through it quickly and are difficult to remove. Best used when applied on top of an underlayer of newspaper, cardboard, or heavy landscape fabric.

Newspaper: Breaks down quickly, presents a tripping hazard, unsightly. Best used as an underlayer, topped with bark mulch, wood chips, or straw.

Cardboard: Effective at blocking weeds, but is annoying to walk on, can acidify soil as it breaks down, and not appropriate for certified organic gardens. Best used as an underlayer, topped with bark mulch, wood chips, or straw.

Not Recommended

Light landscape fabric: Breaks down too quickly, wastes time, money, and resources. Weed roots can grow into the fabric, making it difficult to remove.

Plastic: Tears apart, creates garbage, and is unsightly.

IMPROVING EXISTING BEDS

If you have an existing garden that has not been managed with an eye toward ongoing soil management, you likely have depleted some (or most) of the essential nutrients and could have an overly acidic or basic pH. Plants take up significant quantities of nutrients from the soil each year, and unless you are actively replacing these nutrients, plant vigor and yield will decrease over time. Fortunately, it's never too late to begin rebuilding garden soil, and significant improvements can be made relatively quickly.

Start with a Soil Test

Soil testing might sound intense, but it's really very straightforward and provides a great learning opportunity. Experienced growers might be able to manage their soil without testing, but this comes from years of watching crops respond to their applications of soil amendments, then making adjustments accordingly. Similarly, other gardeners might get by just fine with not professionally testing their soil if they add compost, use organic fertilizers, and are sure that their soil pH is in a reasonable range (between 6 and 7 for most plants).

However, if your goal is to increase your yields using organic methods, a professional soil test will help you discover if your nutrient and pH levels are optimum. Such a test will also help you identify any trouble spots before they become a problem. Different soils can have incredibly different latent nutrient bases, and the lack of a single micro- or macronutrient can dramatically affect the productivity of your garden. Plants do show visible signs of nutrient stress, but these deficiencies can be difficult to correctly identify, especially when you are dealing with micronutrient issues. Identifying your specific soil conditions can be a critical step toward preventive garden health.

When to Test Your Soil

Fall is a great time to test your soil because it gives you time to make changes before spring planting. Early spring is also a good time for the test.

If you're building a new garden, we recommend testing your soil after you've added new soil or compost, as this can change pH and nutrient levels. If you test before you've added compost and soil, your test results will not reflect the changes you've made and may guide you to add more fertilizer and amendments than necessary.

If you have added organic fertilizer or rock powders to your soil, avoid testing for six to eight weeks because nutrient levels will be artificially and temporarily altered.

Take a Sample

First, select a lab to send your samples to. We like the University of Massachusetts Soil and Plant Tissue Testing Lab and A&L Eastern Laboratories because they provide a high-quality, low-cost test (see Resources, page 307). Once you've chosen a lab, read the guidelines for collecting your sample. When taking soil for this test, select many small samples from all over your garden (between 8 and 10 different spots).

For each sample, use a trowel or spade shovel to dig a small hole about 6 inches deep. Take a slice of soil from the edge of the hole and put it in a plastic bucket. The slice should represent the entire depth of the hole (i.e., you're getting bits of soil from 1 inch down, 2 inches down, all the way down to 6 inches). Remove any plant fragments or large chunks of organic matter from the sample. Place all samples into a clean plastic bucket and mix them thoroughly. Remove 1 cup's worth, and then bag, label, and send to the lab, per their specifications. When you send it in, make sure you specify that you'd like recommendations for organic management and that you are growing vegetable crops. This will ensure the test result information is tailored to your needs.

If you have several garden plots that you've been managing differently or have different soil types, you will want to test each plot individually. Similarly, if there's one part of your garden that's having issues, such as plant discoloration or stunted growth, sample it separately from the rest of the garden. For most small production gardens without major issues, one test for the whole plot will yield plenty of information.

Interpreting Soil Test Results

Ah, here's the fun part. A few weeks after you send your soil sample in, you'll get a confusing sheet in your email inbox. You decide you need a PhD to interpret it, and move it into the trash . . . no, wait! It's actually pretty easy to figure things out. Featured in the sample that follows are the results of an actual soil test we took for a small production farm (½ acre) with three different planting areas (labeled North Main, South Main, and East).

Always remember to take soil test results with a grain of salt; sampling errors can yield strange results, and labs can make mistakes. If a soil test shows results that don't correlate to the behavior of your plants, consider doing a second test or trying a different lab. For example, if a test result indicates that your soil pH is extremely low but your plants are growing fine (and a test from the previous year showed the pH of your soil to be in a normal range), consider sending in a new sample to be tested.

1. Recommendations
This is where the lab tells you what to add to the soil so crops thrive.

2. NPK
Nitrogen (N) is responsible for early vegetative growth in plants. Phosphorus (P) is crucial for photosynthesis, early root growth, and flowering. Potassium (K) helps with photosynthesis, fruit formation, and disease resistance. The lab has provided a convenient scale so it is easy to tell if your soil is deficient in any of these key nutrients. The recommendations section (1) provides amounts of these nutrients to add in pounds per acre.

An important item to note is that available nitrogen can vary on a month-to-month and week-to-week basis depending on soil temperatures and precipitation, so what you see in the test may not be what's actually happening in the soil on the day you receive the test. Nitrogen testing is an add-on for this lab, so you may decide not to test for it, as we chose not to do.

3. Calcium and magnesium
An important item to note is that calcium and magnesium should exist together at a ratio of around 5:1 to 7:1 (Ca:Mg). If the ratio gets out of whack, both nutrients can become difficult for plants to absorb. The lab should know this and should reflect it in their recommendations, but it's good to be able to check on your own. To do so, check that the number given for calcium is about

A&L Eastern Laboratories

7621 Whitepine Road Richmond, Virginia 23237 (804) 743-9401 Fax (804) 271-6446
www.aleastern.com

Send To: SEATTLE URBAN FARM COMPANY
11550 NORTH PARK AVE N
SEATTLE WA 98133

Grower:
SEATTLE URBAN FARM COMPAI

Submitted By: BRAD HALM
Farm ID:

SOIL ANALYSIS REPORT

Analytical Method(s): Mehlich 3

Date Received: 01/24/2014   Date Of Analysis: /2014   Date ort: 01/27/2014

Sample ID Field ID	Lab Number	Organic Matter %	Rate	ENR lbs/A	Phosphorus Mehlich 3 ppm	Rate	Reserve ppm	Rate	Potassium K ppm	Rate	Magnesium Mg ppm	Rate	Calcium Ca ppm	Rate	Sodium Na ppm	Rate	pH Soil pH	Buffer Index	Acidity H meq/100g	C.E.C meq/100g
NORTH MAIN	22540	6.3	H	150	19	L			115	M	190	M	1295	M	43	VL	5.6	6.67	2.6	11.1
SOUTH MAIN	22541	6.7	H	150	56	H			94	M	180	H	1148	M	49	VL	5.8	6.75	1.8	9.5
EAST	22542	6.0	H	150	130	VH			149	H	219	M	1703	M	63	VL	6.3		1.3	12.3

Sample ID Field ID	Percent Base Saturation K %	Mg %	Ca %	Na %	H %	Nitrate NO₃N ppm	Rate	Sulfur S ppm	Rate	Zinc Zn ppm	Rate	Manganese Mn ppm	Rate	Iron Fe ppm	Rate	Copper Cu ppm	Rate	Boron B ppm	Rate	Soluble Salts SS ms/cm	Rate	Chloride Cl ppm	Rate	Aluminum Al ppm
NORTH MAIN	3.0	14.0	58.0	2.0	23.0			17	M	2.0	L	7	L	400	VH	3.4	VH	0.6	M					
SOUTH MAIN	3.0	16.0	60.0	2.0	19.0			14	L	2.0	L	9	L	411	VH	3.0	H	0.1	VL					
EAST	3.0	15.0	69.0	2.0	11.0			17	M	6.7	H	24	H	376	VH	2.2	H	0.2	VL					

Values on this report represent the plant available nutrients in the soil. Rating after each value: VL (Very Low), L (Low), M (Medium), H (High), VH (Very High). ENR - Estimated Nitrogen Release. C.E.C. - Cation Exchange Capacity.

Explanation of symbols: % (percent), ppm (parts per million), lbs/A (pounds per acre), ms/cm (milli-mhos per centimeter), meq/100g (milli-equivalent per 100 grams). Conversions: ppm x 2 = lbs/A, Soluble Salts ms/cm x 640 = ppm.

This report applies to sample(s) tested. Samples are retained a maximum of thirty days after testing.

Analysis prepared by: A&L Eastern Laboratories, Inc.

by: Pauric Mc Groary

Pauric McGroary

A&L Eastern Laboratories

7621 Whitepine Road Richmond, Virginia 23237 (804) 743-9401 Fax (804) 271-6446
www.aleastern.com

Send To: SEATTLE URBAN FARM COMPANY
11550 NORTH PARK AVE N
SEATTLE WA 98133

Grower:
SEATTLE URBAN FARM COMPAI

Submitted By: BRAD HALM
Farm ID:

Date Received: 01/24/2014
Date Of Report: 01/27/2014

SOIL FERTILITY RECOMMENDATIONS

Sample ID Field ID	Intended Crop	Yield Goal	Lime Tons/A	Nitrogen N lb/A	Phosphate P₂O₅ lb/A	Potash K₂O lb/A	Magnesium Mg lb/A	Sulfur S lb/A	Zinc Zn lb/A	Manganese Mn lb/A	Iron Fe lb/A	Copper Cu lb/A	Boron B lb/A
NORTH MAIN	Garden, Market	0	1.5	60	200	200	0	27	3.0	3	0	0	2.5
SOUTH MAIN	Garden, Market	0	1.0	60	50	250	0	31	3.0	3	0	0	3.0
EAST	Garden, Market	0	0.0	60	40	118	0	27	0.7	0	0	0	3.0

Comments:

Sample(s) : SOUTH MAIN, EAST Crop: Garden, Market

On market garden apply an additional 40-100# of N per acre sidedress using higher rates for green, leafy vegetables, peppers, tomatoes, sweet corn, etc. and lower rates for peas, beans, melons, cucumbers, carrots, root crops, etc. On tomatoes do not apply additonal N until fruit set are the size of a golf ball.

"The recommendations are based on research data and experience, but NO GUARANTEE or WARRANTY expressed or implied, concerning crop performance is made."

Pauric Mc Groary

Pauric McGroary

five to seven times greater than the number given for magnesium. (Calcium and magnesium levels look good for all the plots in this sample test.)

4. Sulfur, sodium, manganese, iron, copper, boron, and chloride

These are micronutrients, and are important for plant growth but only in very small amounts. Typically you won't need to be concerned about these nutrients unless there is a noticeable deficiency in the test results.

One exception is that brassica crops are known to be susceptible to sulfur and boron deficiencies, so keep an eye on these levels if you grow a lot of brassicas. In this sample test, our sulfur, manganese, zinc, and boron levels look low, so we'll want to boost them (see page 121).

5. Organic matter

In a large-scale agricultural setting, 5 percent organic matter is a great number, and 3 to 4 percent is not bad. Expect a higher percentage of organic matter in clay soils, and lower in sandy soils. If you are growing in intensively managed raised beds or in compost-based potting soil, you might see numbers in the 20 to 30 percent range. As long as you're at 5 percent or higher, you don't need to be concerned about this specific number; organic matter is always breaking down and needs to be replenished regularly using compost or cover cropping techniques. Organic matter levels look great in this sample test.

6. pH and buffer pH

Vegetables like a narrow pH range; 6.3–6.8 is ideal. Buffer pH is an artificial number the lab created so that we can calculate how much lime or sulfur to add to effectively change the pH. In this test, the actual pH is a little low, but the buffer pH is in a good range. The lab suggests adding lime in the recommendations, so we'll go with what they say.

7. CEC (Cation Exchange Capacity)

This is a measure of the soil's ability to both store nutrients (specifically cation nutrients) and make them available to our crops. The higher the number, the higher the storage capacity of the soil, but the more difficult it is for the soil to make the nutrients available (also, the more of an amendment you'll need to add to make a change). The lab knows this and should reflect it in the recommendations.

Generally, as you add compost to the soil, the CEC will rise. Well-composted soils are often in the 15 to 25 range. Clay soils also have a very high CEC (25 to 50), but will still benefit from the addition of compost. You don't need to worry too much about this number unless it's below 10, which probably means you have a very sandy soil that would benefit from the addition of a healthy amount of compost. Numbers on this sample test look good.

8. Percent base, nutrient, or cation saturation

This number tells us how "filled" our particular soil is with certain nutrients. Using these numbers to make recommendations is beyond the scope of this book; suffice it to say you don't need to be too concerned about them. If you want to learn more, check out the resources section (page 307) for further reading.

Other Items You Might See on a Soil Test

Soluble salts. Over-application of fertilizer (either synthetic or organic) can cause salt toxicity in some plants. Look for a range of 0.08 to 0.5 dS/m. Over 0.6 dS/m can cause problems such as poor germination, browning leaf margins, yellowing, and stunted growth.

Lead/aluminum/arsenic/heavy metals. These are elements that can be toxic to humans or plants if levels are too high. Lead and arsenic can be especially important to test for if you're farming in an urban area because there are many potential sources of these contaminants. See Soil Solutions, page 122, for more information on dealing with lead and arsenic.

How We Took Action

Nitrogen, phosphorus, and potassium. Because we always add balanced organic fertilizer to our soil just prior to planting and side-dress heavy-feeding crops (see page 204 for more information), we don't usually worry too much about these numbers. We could spread rock phosphate in the North Main field because the phosphorus tested quite low, but we would still use organic fertilizer at planting time. See Soil Solutions on page 122 for more information on dealing with specific issues like these.

pH: We spread lime in the North and South Main fields at 1.5 tons and 1 ton per acre respectively. Using the information in the Conversions for Amendment Application Rates table (see page 126), we determined this to be about 75 and 50 pounds per 1,000 square feet (0.75 and 0.5 pound per 100 square feet).

Sulfur: We could use elemental sulfur, but that would also cause the pH to drop (we're already trying to raise it). We could use gypsum, which would also add calcium. A little extra calcium is always good as long as we don't throw off the Ca:Mg ratio. However, we're already adding calcium with our lime application. We ultimately decided to use sulfate of potash (langbeinite), since the recommendations call for adding potassium as well. Sulfate of potash (SOP) also contains magnesium, which we don't need any more of, but we'll be adding only a relatively small amount. The additional calcium from the lime should keep everything in balance.

We do some math and find that we need to apply sulfate of potash at about 140 pounds per acre (SOP is about 22 percent sulfur, so that would supply around 31 pounds of it). This comes out to about 3 pounds per 1,000 square feet, or 0.3 pound for 100 square feet. The bag of sulfate of potash says we can apply up to 1 to 2 pounds per 100 square feet, so we know we're in a safe range. See page 126 for tips on spreading small amounts of a soil amendment over a large area.

Boron. We decide to use Granubor, an organically certified boron fertilizer. (Granubor, which is 14 percent boron, is produced by the same company that makes Borax, an all-natural laundry additive. Borax also works well as a soil amendment, and is easier to source for small-scale growers.) We definitely don't want to overdo it with the boron because it can be toxic to plants if the concentration gets too high, so we carefully apply it at 18 pounds per acre, or 0.4 pound per 1,000 square feet.

Zinc and manganese. These two micronutrients are not commonly applied as single nutrient amendments (most growers don't worry about them at all). The good news is that we use kelp meal in our organic fertilizer mix, and kelp contains trace amounts of zinc and manganese. We decide to call that good. Liquid kelp is a great foliar feed, so we may also use that on our plants during the growing season (see page 204 for more information on foliar feeding).

SOIL SOLUTIONS

The test results we shared and interpreted for you on pages 118–20 were specific to that site. Obviously, you'll have to come up with your own solutions for your own garden, based on your own conditions. To help you do that, here's a look at the steps you can take to remedy many common soil composition problems.

One thing to be aware of when testing soil is to avoid a "one nutrient" focus when solving problems. Remember that changing one nutrient level in the soil may affect the availability of other nutrients. Thus, your soil management approach should always be holistic and balanced, and should begin by supplying adequate organic matter with compost. Making minor micronutrient adjustments is a futile exercise if you don't have good overall soil structure to start with.

Adjusting pH

Soil pH in and of itself does not directly affect plants; rather it affects the availability of many nutrients, which in turn affects how well plants grow. We want our soil pH to be between 6.3 and 6.8 to keep nutrient availability in the optimum range for vegetables.

Add Lime to Raise pH

The two kinds commonly used are agricultural lime (also supplies calcium) and dolomitic lime (also supplies calcium and extra magnesium). Only use dolomitic lime if you have a magnesium deficiency, or you might cause an artificial calcium deficiency.

Calcium and magnesium should be present in the soil at a 5:1 to 7:1 ratio to each other. If magnesium levels get too high, the soil can lose pore space and become more prone to compaction.

Lime application rate: Fifty pounds per 1,000 square feet (1 cup per 10 square feet) will raise pH by a level of 0.5. One cup equals about half a pound. Avoid using more than double this rate during the course of a season (i.e., don't spread more than 100 pounds per 1,000 square feet in a season).

Add Elemental Sulfur to Lower pH

Elemental sulfur is an organically approved soil amendment produced when sulfur impurities are extracted from chemicals during industrial processes. It is often sold in pelleted form, which looks like lentils, and is relatively slow acting in the soil. Depending on temperature and soil conditions, it can take several months to effectively adjust soil pH levels downward.

Sulfur application rate: Ten pounds per 1,000 square feet (1/4 cup per 12 square feet) will lower pH by a level of 0.5. One cup equals about half a pound.

To apply lime or sulfur, sprinkle the desired amount over the surface of the soil, and then turn it in to the top 6 inches of soil with a spade shovel or fork. These amendments take a few months to actually make a difference, so they're best added in the fall after you've cleaned up your summer crops.

Dealing with Lead and Arsenic Contamination

If you're gardening in an urban area, chances are you might be dealing with contaminated soil.

High Lead Levels

Lead is toxic to humans, so it's obviously not something you want in your garden soil. The main problem with lead is not that the plants will absorb it from the soil (plants will not take up lead unless they're extremely water or nutrient stressed), but that the lead-contaminated dust from the soil will get on your hands and on the crops, and eventually end up in your mouth through these channels.

Lead contamination is usually the result of past industrial activity, or from lead paint on an old house or shed. Lead paint was outlawed for household use in 1978, so if you're building a garden adjacent to a building built before this date, you should send in a test for lead before getting started. Similarly, if you know the land has a history of industrial use, you should also send in a test. Not all labs offer lead testing, or they may offer it only as an add-on to a normal soil test, so check first before sending in a sample (University of Massachusetts and A&L Eastern both offer tests for lead).

If your soil test shows high levels of lead, don't worry — you can still have a safe and successful garden. In most situations, it will make sense to build your garden up to avoid contact with the contaminated soil. Build raised beds at least 16 inches deep, and fill them with purchased soil. Cover the surrounding paths with a thick layer of mulch to keep dust off of your feet, hands, and garden beds. Wash your crops well before eating (this is a good practice anyway).

Arsenic Contamination

Similar to lead, arsenic contamination can be a problem in areas with an industrial history (especially paper mills and smelting), areas that were orchards prior to the 1960s (because of the use of lead arsenate as a pesticide), or underneath structures built with treated lumber manufactured prior to 2003 (decks, play structures, etc.). If you have reason to suspect arsenic contamination, we recommend testing prior to constructing your garden.

Not all labs offer arsenic testing, so check first before sending in a sample (A&L Eastern offers a test for arsenic). You can also test for arsenic using a home test kit (turn to the resources section on page 307 for more information). As with lead, the main problem with arsenic is not that your plants will take it up from the soil, but that the contaminated soil particles will end up on your hands or on plant foliage. If you determine that your soil is contaminated with arsenic, you can take the same steps as those noted for lead: grow crops in raised beds with purchased soil, keep contaminated soil near the garden covered with a thick layer of mulch, and wash produce well when harvesting.

Adjusting Nutrient Levels

Below are some common nutritional deficiencies for edible crops, and organic sources for these nutrients.

Problem: Low Nitrogen

Signs: Plants are stunted, slow growing. Foliage may be yellow or pale green.

Quickly available organic sources: Blood meal, fish meal, liquid fish emulsion. Raw manure contains a lot of available nitrogen, but we advise against applying it directly to your soil. Compost it first to avoid potential pathogen risks.

Slow-release organic sources: Compost, seed meals (soybean, cottonseed), alfalfa meal, feather meal.

Problem: Low Phosphorus

Signs: Foliage shows a purplish color. Plants grow slowly. Fruiting plants have problems setting flowers and fruit.

Quickly available organic sources: Bonemeal, commercial high-phosphorus organic liquid fertilizer.

Slow-release organic sources: Rock phosphate, colloidal phosphate, composted manures.

Notes: Phosphorus is difficult for plants to take up when temperatures are cold. Using a high-phosphorus fertilizer when transplanting helps with new root growth.

Problem: Low Potassium

Signs: Yellowing/dieback of leaf tips (tip-burn); unhealthy, stunted fruit.

Quickly available organic sources: Sul-Po-Mag/sulfate of potash.

Slow-release organic sources: Greensand, kelp meal, composted manures, composted wood ash.

Notes: Potassium can be leached by excessive precipitation or irrigation. This is common in container gardens and in raised beds with limited depth.

Problem: Low Calcium

Signs: Blossom-end rot in fruits, leaf tip burn, plant grows poorly/is stunted.

Quickly available organic sources: Foliar feed with liquid kelp, chamomile tea, egg-shell tea, or a commercially available calcium spray (Calcium 25).

Slow-release organic sources: Lime (if you also need to raise soil pH), dolomitic lime (if you also need to raise pH and magnesium), gypsum (if you don't want to alter soil pH, also contains sulfur).

Notes: Calcium is very important for the structural health of your crops' fruit and foliage. Must be in proper ratio with magnesium (between 5:1 and 7:1 Ca:Mg).

Problem: Low Magnesium

Signs: Yellow tinge in leaves that first appears in between veins.

Quickly available organic sources: Epsom salts diluted in water and used as a foliar spray.

Slow-release organic sources: Dolomitic lime (if you also want to raise pH); Epsom salts (also a good source of sulfur).

Notes: Magnesium must be in proper ratio to calcium (between 5:1 and 7:1 Ca:Mg), so don't apply it unless you know you have a deficiency.

Problem: Low Boron

Signs: Variable symptoms. Hollow stems are characteristic of a boron deficiency in brassica crops.

Quickly available organic sources: Borax diluted in water and applied as a soil drench.

Slow-release organic sources: Borax, Solubor, Granubor.

Notes: Apply conservatively; boron can quickly become toxic if over-applied.

Problem: Low Micronutrients/Trace Elements

Signs: Variable symptoms.

Slow-release organic sources: Greensand (contains many micronutrients and potassium), kelp (liquid or meal, contains many micronutrients and potassium), Sul-Po-Mag/sulfate of potash (contains sulfur, potassium, and magnesium), elemental sulfur (contains sulfur, also lowers pH), compost (contains many micronutrients), gypsum (contains sulfur and calcium).

Notes: Using a blended fertilizer that contains kelp or greensand or using liquid kelp as a foliar spray will help to prevent imbalances.

Organic Soil Amendments

Sul-Po-Mag/Langbeinite/ Sulfate of Potash/K-mag
Application method: mix into soil, use as mixed fertilizer ingredient, or use as a soil drench (see page 126) at 4 tablespoons per gallon over 100 square feet
Nutrient percentage/use: 22% potassium, 22% sulfur, 11% magnesium

Borax (pure sodium tetraborate)
Application method: mix into soil or soil drench at ¼ teaspoon per gallon and spread over 30 square feet
Nutrient percentage/use: about 11% boron

Gypsum
Application method: mix into soil
Nutrient percentage/use: 22% calcium, 12% sulfur

Epsom Salts
Application method: mix into soil, foliar feed, or soil drench at 4 tablespoons per gallon of water
Nutrient percentage/use: 10% magnesium, 13% sulfur

Greensand
Application method: mix into soil
Nutrient percentage/use: 3% potassium, various trace minerals, improves structure

Kelp Meal
Application method: mix into soil or use as mixed fertilizer ingredient
Nutrient percentage/use: 1% nitrogen, 2% potassium (1-0-2) plus many trace minerals

Blood Meal
Application method: mix into soil or use as mixed fertilizer ingredient
Nutrient percentage/use: 12% nitrogen (12-0-0)

Rock Phosphate
Application method: mix into soil
Nutrient percentage/use: 3% soluble phosphorus (0-3-0), 20% calcium, 20% insoluble P

Bonemeal
Application method: mix into soil or use as mixed fertilizer ingredient
Nutrient percentage/use: 2% nitrogen, 14% phosphorus (2-14-0), up to 24% calcium

Calcitic Lime
Application method: mix into soil
Nutrient percentage/use: approximately 30% calcium, 5% or less magnesium

Dolomitic Lime
Application method: mix into soil
Nutrient percentage/use: less than 30% calcium, greater than 5% magnesium

Spreading Small Quantities

Spreading amendments at low rates over large spaces can be very difficult (boron is a great example; application rates are usually only a few pounds per acre). One way to apply small quantities of a given nutrient is to mix it with another amendment.

For example, if you're spreading lime on a 1,000-square-foot plot and need to spread a small amount of sulfate of potash over the same space, weigh out the amount of each amendment you need, mix them together thoroughly, then spread them. A push lawn spreader would be a good piece of equipment for this spreading job.

Alternatively, some amendments can be mixed with water and applied as a soil drench with a watering can or hose-end sprayer. This is realistic only for small and medium-size gardens, but it's a very easy and effective technique. See the Organic Soil Amendments chart (page 125) for soil drench application rates for a variety of amendments. Drench application is a highly effective technique for large acreages as well, provided you have access to a tractor with a boom sprayer.

Conversions for Amendment Application Rates

Small-scale production growers sometimes have it rough when it comes to determining how much of an amendment to apply. Many fertilizers and soil amendments have application rates listed in pounds or tons per acre, but most gardeners are dealing with square feet and are applying amendments with measuring cups and watering cans instead of tractor spreaders. Labels are improving as suppliers realize they need to meet the needs of small-scale growers. In the meantime, here are some conversion rates to help you figure things out:

1 acre = 43,560 square feet
½ acre = 21,780 square feet
¼ acre = 10,890 square feet
⅛ acre = 5,445 square feet

4' × 8' raised bed = 32 square feet
4' × 10' raised bed = 40 square feet
10' × 10' garden space = 100 square feet
Area (in square feet) = length (in feet) × width (in feet)

1 ton = 2,000 pounds
1 ton/acre = about 45 pounds per 1,000 square feet
1 ton/acre = about 4.5 pounds per 100 square feet

If you know how many pounds of an amendment you need per acre,

multiply it by 0.02 to determine how many pounds you need for 1,000 square feet.
multiply it by 0.002 to determine how many pounds you need for 100 square feet.

1 cubic yard of compost = around 1,000–1,600 pounds

1 cubic yard = 27 cubic feet

Setting Up Irrigation Systems

Water is one of the most important factors that determine the success or failure of a crop. Like most living organisms, plants comprise mostly water, and many fruit and vegetable crops contain an even higher percentage of water than other kinds of plants.

The watering requirements of your garden depend on a variety of factors, including the kinds of crops you choose, the structure of your soil, your region's climate, and the day-to-day variations in your weather. Rainwater is a great source of hydration for your plants, but it doesn't always arrive at the required time and in the required amount to sustain needy vegetables. In general, crops rarely yield reliable and robust harvests without supplemental watering at some point during their life.

THE CASE FOR IRRIGATION INFRASTRUCTURE

We strongly encourage high-yield vegetable gardeners to include a watering system with a timer in their initial garden plan. Building a watering system into your garden at the outset will save valuable hours as compared to creating an "aftermarket" solution that must be delicately placed around all of your established structures and plants. A watering system with automatic timers will save you countless hours managing hoses or otherwise attempting to keep soil moist by hand. Because a timed system can be set to deliver water regularly and at the best time of day for irrigation, your plants will be healthier and will produce a larger yield.

Even a perfectly built automatic irrigation system will need your ongoing attention. You still must make adjustments to the watering duration and frequency throughout the season; this practice will save water and ensure that your crops get exactly the amount of moisture they need. Additionally, normal wear and tear with some systems will inevitably cause small breaks and leaks that you'll need to repair. Even with these tasks, though, an automated watering system will reduce your total time spent dealing with water issues by about 90 percent versus hand watering.

Because we strongly believe that hand watering a large, diversified garden site is an inefficient use of time and resources, we won't even include it as a viable option for garden irrigation. In the peak of the season when irrigation is most commonly needed, spending valuable hours trailing a hose through the garden is, at best, a poor use of your time. With an established irrigation system in place, these hours can be used

identifying and managing pests, controlling disease problems, harvesting crops, and succession planting new crops.

The simple act of automating your watering program will completely change the health, yields, and appearance of your garden. Hoses and spray nozzles are still essential tools, however, for spot-watering the garden and watering new crops as you seed or plant them.

There are two principal methods of irrigating a garden: overhead irrigation and drip irrigation.

OVERHEAD IRRIGATION

Some growers prefer the evenness of watering with an overhead sprinkler. They feel that it better mimics the natural effect of rainwater. Overhead watering is especially beneficial for newly seeded crops while they germinate. The complete coverage and delivery to the top layer of soil can help ensure a good germination rate, which avoids having to reseed thin crop stands later. An overhead watering system also has the advantage of being much easier to set up as compared to a drip irrigation system.

Overhead watering systems do have drawbacks. They tend to use considerably more water than a drip system, and they tend to water areas (including pathways) that don't actually require irrigation. That, in turn, sometimes leads to additional weed growth (which then leads to extra time spent weeding). For certain crops, moreover, watering the entire plant rather than just the soil and root zone can encourage disease problems. Because it is much easier to over-water with a sprinkler system, its use may also lead to faster leaching of nutrients from the soil. Lastly, the large, heavy droplets can compact bare soil.

When using overhead irrigation, plan to water in the morning, as early as possible. This allows the water to soak thoroughly into the soil and gives plants a chance to dry off before the sun is at its most intense. Watering in the middle of the day is less efficient because water is lost to evaporation. Watering in the evening can increase the prevalence of fungal disease because the water sits on the leaves of your crops and the surface of the soil throughout the night.

Choosing the Right Overhead Sprinkler

When purchasing and setting up a sprinkler system, your most important consideration has to do with coverage. You need to have a system that is capable of adequately covering your garden space and able to *evenly* cover the space.

Oscillating. These are sprinklers that move a fan-shaped spray of water back and forth over an area. They're very inexpensive and easy to set up, and can be quickly moved around the garden if you feel that you need to water the space in more than one session. However, they usually put out much more water than the soil can absorb, and so are prone to wasting water. If not carefully used, they can also cause erosion and soil compaction.

Impact. Most small farmers who use overhead irrigation will choose impact sprinklers — those that shoot a narrow jet of water in a circle. This type of sprinkler is more efficient at using water than oscillating sprinklers, and when placed on a tall post, impact sprinklers can distribute water over your crops in a 360-degree radius. They also have the advantage of generally being easier to adjust to fit specific needs because they can be set to water in specific ranges, from a narrow spray all the way up to a complete circle.

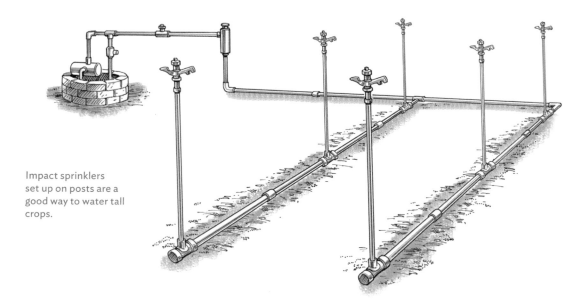

Impact sprinklers set up on posts are a good way to water tall crops.

Setting Up Multiple Sprinklers

Setting up a system with more than one sprinkler is not hard to do, but does take a little extra setup time and materials. To run multiple sprinklers in the garden, set them to run in succession so that the second starts shortly after the first has finished, the third starts shortly after the second has finished, and so on. In order to do this, you will need either a timer with multiple outputs (so that several hoses can be attached to the source at once) or for the system to branch out in the garden with timers attached at each junction. Some sprinklers have inlet and outlet hose threads and can be set up to run in series; however, this kind of setup is feasible only if your system has enough water pressure. Typical water pressure in a home water line is 40–70 psi (pounds per square inch). The pressure can vary greatly depending on whether or not other appliances (dishwasher, shower, and so forth) are in use. Water pressure might also depend on water use throughout your neighborhood. The simplest way to determine if you are able to run a system in series is simply to set up the sprinklers and test them.

If you have sufficient water pressure, a series of sprinklers is a simple and cost-effective way to irrigate a large garden.

Sprinkler Setup

Attach a hose thread timer to the water spigot that is nearest to your garden, attach a hose to the timer (make sure the hose can reach from the spigot to the farthest reaches of the garden space), and then attach the sprinkler to the business end of the hose.

Find the right location for the sprinkler in the garden. If your garden is an odd shape, you may have to move the sprinkler to a few different locations to determine where you will receive the best coverage. Depending on the strength of the sprinkler, you may have to water the garden in two or three sessions, moving the sprinkler each time to achieve even coverage. Alternatively, consider setting up a few separate sprinklers and setting them to slightly different times so they do not compete for water pressure. Doing so ensures that the whole garden receives its proper dose of water.

Watering Duration and Frequency

Set the time and date on the timer and run a watering session to establish an appropriate duration for your sprinkler to run. Try starting with a 15-minute irrigation session, then finger test the soil to determine if the time should be extended. To perform the finger test, poke your finger into the soil — if it feels moist about an inch down, you've watered sufficiently. If it's wet on the surface but dry below, you need to water for a longer duration. If water is pooling on top of the soil, wait until it has absorbed before watering again. You want the soil to feel moist but not overly saturated.

Plan to adjust the duration and frequency of irrigation sessions throughout the season. There is no way to preset a sprinkler to manage the irrigation timing based on rainfall and soil moisture levels. This means you will be responsible for checking the soil moisture every few days to determine if the system should be adjusted. Remember to turn it off during spells of rain. And don't forget to take the system apart and store it before freezing weather sets in.

Winterizing the Overhead Irrigation System

Assuming that all portions of your overhead irrigation system are aboveground, or shallowly buried, shutting the system down for the cold or wet season should be easy. Turn off the water source and remove hoses and timers (also remove the batteries from the timers). In cold climates, turn off the water main leading to the spigot or cover the spigot with a frost-protecting cover. Coil up all hoses and tubing, allowing the water to drain from the low end as you coil. Store all hoses, timers, and sprinklers out of the weather, ideally hanging them up off the ground in a garage or tool shed. Even small amounts of water left in a plastic sprinkler or timer can freeze and crack the tool.

DRIP IRRIGATION

Applying water directly to the soil surface is the most resource-efficient way to irrigate your plants. Drip irrigation reduces weed growth in bed edges and pathways because only the portions of the garden planted in crops receive water. Drip lines also make planting in straight rows easier (you can plant directly along the side of the line), which can make it easier for you to evenly space your plants. For example, a drip system with emitters spaced every 12 inches makes a perfect guide for planting kale or any other crop you might want to space at 12 inches; simply put a transplant right next to each emitter.

A well-functioning automated drip system (meaning there are no leaks) can deliver the appropriate amount of water with very little waste. Although drip irrigation systems typically take longer to set up than overhead systems, and require more tools and materials, they're much easier to install and manage than you might think. All you need is a free weekend (sometimes just a day), a working water spigot (hose bib), a few tools, and a handful of supplies.

Components of a Drip System

We like to visualize our irrigation systems from the top down, so let's look at the various parts you'll need, starting at the water spigot and working our way into the garden beds.

The Right Amount of Water

We encourage you to experiment with different watering schedules so that you may find what works best for your climate, soil type, and crop selection. Water crops deeply every few days. Doing so promotes the growth of large root systems; the plants are encouraged to chase the water deep into the subsoil. The most important thing, however, is that the plants appear to be healthy, continue to grow at an appropriate rate, and produce abundant harvests.

Gardeners often compare soil to a sponge. When it dries out completely, it will turn rock hard, and it takes some effort to convince it to absorb water again. If it stays completely saturated with water, then it becomes a funky mess. The goal is to keep soil moisture in the "golden range" for plant growth. This range is comparable to the feel of a damp sponge after you've wrung it out. The standard test is to squeeze a handful of soil in your palm: If it holds together in a ball, it has the right amount of moisture. If it falls apart, it is too dry. If you drop the ball of soil from waist height, it should shatter; if it doesn't, the soil is too wet.

To achieve that golden range, irrigate the soil until it is saturated, and then let it dry out enough so that the habitat for fungus and mold is reduced.

When the soil is ready, water it again. You never want to see your crops wilt due to lack of water. A wilting crop is water stressed, and this can lead to low yields and susceptibility to disease. We highly recommend that you develop a feel for your own soil to learn its tendencies: what it looks like when it's too dry, too wet, and just right. Feel your soil when it's really dry, after watering, and after a heavy rainstorm. Taking the time to understand your soil will allow you to easily and quickly identify its watering needs and keep the plants in your garden on track.

As you identify where a part goes in your system, you can label it on your working irrigation map for future reference (see Making an Irrigation Map, page 138). This will help tremendously when you are adding up parts to place an order or heading to the store.

Fittings for Constant Pressure

Some irrigation components are designed to be used under constant pressure (with water pressure against them at all times), and some are not. In most cases, the backflow preventer, the Y-valve or manifold, and the timer are the only components that are appropriate for constant pressure. All other components should be placed after the timer (meaning that they are only under pressure when the system is running). Failure to do this can cause the system to leak, which always seems to happen when you're out of town.

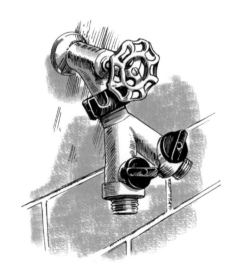

A Y-valve is a great way to run an irrigation system and a garden hose off a single outdoor hose bib.

Backflow preventer/anti-siphon valve. This piece ensures that water will not flow backward through your irrigation system into your home water pipes. To prevent reverse siphoning, this piece also empties out water from the system when the spigot is not in use. Make sure the piece has hose threads on both the inlet and outlet sides; these are labeled FHT or MHT (you do not want a piece with pipe threads, which are labeled FPT or MPT). These threads allow you to screw the piece right onto your spigot. Many newer water spigots have a built-in backflow preventer, meaning that a separate backflow preventer is not needed. A built-in backflow preventer might look like a small cylinder with holes in the side, and will be attached to the outlet of the spigot. It might also look like a plastic or metal "cap" on the top of the spigot. If in doubt, note the model name and number of the spigot and give your local plumber or plumbing supply store a call.

Y-valve or manifold. Using a Y-valve or multiple-line splitter (manifold) will give you the option to attach both a hose and an irrigation system to your water supply at the same time. Because each is independent, you can use the hose as necessary and leave the irrigation system connected all season. Because you won't have to disconnect the irrigation system to use a hose, you won't forget to reattach the timer after you finish using the hose.

Timer. For most home vegetable gardens, a battery-operated timer with hose threads is the best option. They are cost effective and easy to set up, and they don't require that the water source be located near an outlet. Larger, plug-in timers are great if you're creating a system with multiple irrigation zones (see page 135). Installing such a timer and the associated system can be a complicated procedure. (See Resources, page 307, for information on books that discuss complex irrigation system design.) If you want to set up multiple zones in your irrigation system, you can get hose thread battery timers with two outlets. You could also use a manifold on the spigot and attach multiple timers to create many zones.

Pressure Regulator/Pressure Reducer

This fitting reduces the water pressure from the water spigot to a level that is appropriate for your drip lines. If the water pressure in the system is too high, the drip lines and

Using a manifold and multiple timers allows you to water different sections of your garden for different amounts of time. By staggering start times, you can get irrigation coverage on large areas if you have low water pressure.

fittings can blow out or shoot water up in the air, rather than dripping it slowly into the soil. Be sure to choose a regulator with a psi (pounds per square inch) rating that matches the psi required by your drip lines.

Filter

A filter will catch tiny particles that may be present in your water system. This will help prevent the drip lines and emitters from clogging. Choose a filter that's rated for your drip lines. Filters are usually rated in "mesh" sizes; the higher the number, the finer the screen. Most drip lines need somewhere between 100 and 200 mesh filtration. Remember to clean out the filter screen once or twice a season.

Mainline Tubing/Header Tubing/Supply Line

The mainline is a solid tube that brings water from the spigot to the garden beds. Most systems use 1/2-inch polyethylene tubing for the mainline. In an irrigation system, header tubing is superior to a regular hose because it is inexpensive, lightweight, and easy to cut to fit your spaces.

It's important for the brand of your fittings to match that of the tubing. Even if two brands are labeled the same diameter, the true size of the pieces will vary by fractions of an inch, making them impossible to adapt. You'll need an assortment of fittings for your system, the type and number of which will be indicated in your irrigation map. Here are a few essential pieces:

- *Header start fitting.* This connects the mainline tubing to the threaded end of the filter or pressure regulator.

- *Header end fitting.* This fitting closes up the ends of each branch of your mainline tubing. These may be figure eight fittings, flush caps, or another variation on an end piece.

- *Tees, elbows, and crosses.* You'll want to pick up as many of these fittings as necessary so that you can turn your mainline around corners, and to branch it to all of the garden beds. Get several extra of each, just in case.

- *Couplers.* Make sure to pick up a handful of straight couplers. Use these to attach the ends of two rolls of mainline together, and to patch areas that you accidentally puncture or cut too short.

- *Valves.* These are great for isolating different parts of your irrigation system. Many growers put a valve on each bed. This way water can be shut off to the empty beds or the crops that don't need it. Some growers put a valve on each drip line for even more precise control. (See page 136 for more information on drip line fittings.)

Stakes

Stakes are incredibly helpful for holding any tubing in place. If needed, look for irrigation stakes or any type of landscaping pins that will fit with your system.

Setting Up Zones for an Existing System

If your garden is very large, you might not have enough flow coming out of your hose bib (faucet) to water the entire space at once. Splitting the garden into different zones — areas that are watered on individual schedules — will solve this problem. Having different zones can be useful for other reasons, as well. For example, one area of your garden might get more sun, and so will need more water than less sunny sections. You might also want to put annual and perennial crops on different watering schedules.

If you're a wiz at irrigation and you have an existing underground irrigation system for your property, you may be able to adapt one or more of those zones into an effective drip irrigation system for your garden. Using this existing resource will eliminate the need to run a system off the water spigot and can save time and energy. If you have a zone that can be completely redirected to the garden, you are in luck.

Keep in mind that drip irrigation and pop-up lawn sprinklers are not compatible (the pop-ups take too much water pressure for the drip to work properly, and drip irrigation and sprinklers usually require very different run times). If you decide to use part of an existing lawn system, try to isolate the garden from the rest of the system or change the entire zone you're using to drip lines.

Options for Drip Lines and Emitters

Drip irrigation comes in a few forms, the most common being drip tubing, tapes, and bubblers. Drip lines come with the water emitters already built in at regular intervals, and bubblers (which are also called emitters) are meant to be manually inserted into the system wherever you want them. The advantage of drip lines is the simplicity of setup and evenness of watering throughout the system. The advantage of using bubblers is the ability to highly customize the system to place water only where you want it. A watering system can be built using both of these materials. Generally speaking, drip lines with set emitter spacing are the best choice for annual vegetable gardens.

Each type of drip line or emitter system will have its own complement of fittings. This includes fittings to connect drip lines and emitters to the mainline, end fittings, tees, elbows, crosses, couplers, and valves. As you fill in your irrigation map, the locations for these pieces should become clear.

Emitter spacing. Drip lines are available with many different emitter spacings (6, 8, 12, and 24 inches are common). Six-inch spacing works well for germinating direct-seeded crops, but this spacing uses more water than necessary for established and widely spaced crops. Emitters spaced 24 inches apart are good for perennials, but this is not ideal for annual vegetable gardens. We find that 8-inch spacing works well for most gardeners. Emitters spaced 12 inches apart are also effective, provided that closely spaced and direct-seeded crops are given a little extra care with the hose.

Drip tapes. These are flat, straight drip lines that are very cost effective and quick to set up. They are not particularly flexible, so they'll work only for setting up straight rows. Drip tapes are relatively easy to damage while gardening, but also very easy to repair if minor leaks do occur. They may come in variations with different flow rates. Lower flow rates will allow you to set up a larger system without the need to break

Pressure Compensation for Even Watering

Not all drip lines and emitters are pressure compensating, but we recommend you use parts that are pressure compensating whenever possible. Pressure compensating means that the emitters maintain a constant rate of flow at varying pressures. This allows for longer runs of drip line (pressure in the line is lower the farther it is from the water source), and allows the system to water the entire garden evenly. All drip lines (whether or not they're pressure compensating) do have a limited length they can be run from the mainline. Be sure to follow the guidelines for your chosen drip lines to prevent dry spots at the far reaches of the system.

it into zones (this is not usually an issue except in very large gardens); higher flow rates will deliver the desired amount of water in a shorter period of time.

Quarter-inch emitter tubing. These small hoses are very useful for container irrigation and beds with non-linear shapes (circles, ovals, and so on). This tubing is relatively easy to set up, although the small fittings can be challenging to put together. It is more durable than drip tape, but is not typically pressure compensating. Even so, it works great as long as the specified run length from the mainline is not exceeded.

Half-inch emitter tubing. This is a very burly and long-lasting drip line. The heavier tubing is more expensive than other options and can be somewhat awkward to work with, but once in place it will last virtually forever. We really like it for perennial crops that will be in place for a few years.

Bubblers. It is possible to set up solid tubing and insert your own bubbler emitters at the spacing and locations that you prefer. This customized type of system requires more setup time and can be more expensive, but some gardeners find the effort and cost to be worth it. A bubbler system can be especially useful when setting up a perennial bed with crops at different spacings that will be in place for a few years.

Black porous soaker hose. If at all possible, avoid using black porous soaker hoses. They are notorious for watering unevenly. Their quality degrades quickly, and they are easy to break.

Drip tapes (far left) are great for long, straight rows of annual crops. Bubblers (near left) work well for perennials, which stay in the same place from year to year.

MAKING AN IRRIGATION MAP

We highly recommend that you draw your drip system from the outset of your garden project. This is a good opportunity to make a photocopy or traced copy of your site plan. You can use it to sketch out the path of the drip system. Drawing the whole system on paper gives you the opportunity to think through design choices and make sure you are taking the easiest and least obtrusive path from the water source to the garden. You will refer to this irrigation map when you make a shopping list for your watering system (see Assembling the System, page 145).

Start with the Mainline

Start by identifying the nearest usable water source to the garden. You may be lucky enough to have a spigot in the garden area itself or very close nearby, or you may need to connect to a spigot on the house and run the irrigation to the garden. Look for the path of least resistance. The supply line for the system will need to be run in an uninterrupted line from the water spigot all the way to your beds. We find that it is often possible to run the tubing right along the foundation of the house until an opportunity arises to turn the tubing toward the garden. We like to follow the edges of existing structures like patios and decks to keep the tubing out of the way and easy to locate in case repairs are needed.

In regions with mild winters, shallowly burying the mainline is the best way to eliminate the possibility that someone will trip over, mow over, or otherwise be annoyed by the tubing. Light freezes won't affect the tubing in the winter because most of the water drains out through the drip lines when the system isn't running. If you live in a region with very harsh winters, consider burying the mainline below frost depth or bringing it indoors in the winter so intense cold will not compromise the longevity of the plastic. Here in the Pacific Northwest (USDA Zone 8), we usually bury mainline about 4 inches deep and leave it in place year after year.

Map the Branches and Drip Lines

After you have identified a path to the garden, then map out how the system will branch out to reach all of the beds. You can use tees, elbows, and crosses as necessary to get the mainline where it needs to go for the branch line setup. Draw the path of the tubing as it reaches each bed. You'll make your installation job easier if you take the shortest path to each bed and keep the branching to a minimum. Consider including a valve on each line that enters a bed so that you can shut off the water as necessary on a bed-by-bed basis.

Now draw the arrangement of the drip lines within the beds. Drip lines should be set up to provide even coverage of the entire square footage of each bed. Since you'll be planting different crops at different spacings over the course of the year, and from year to year, you will want the drip lines to provide water for all crop and spacing placements (you can also add valves to individual drip lines). This way you don't have to retrofit the system mid-season or from year to year. If you already have crops in place, avoid the temptation to run lines directly to each plant; you'll only have to redo everything next year when you plant something different in that same space.

We usually space drip lines approximately 12 inches apart. The water dripping from each emitter will spread out to about an 8-to 12-inch circle below the surface of the soil (a larger circle in clay-rich soil, smaller in sandy soil). Emitter spacing on most drip lines is between 8 and 12 inches, so spacing the lines 12 inches apart will provide water to the entire bed. In addition, consider which direction is easiest to orient the lines and how this will influence your planting arrangements and access to the beds. Generally, running the mainline parallel to the short length of the bed and running the drip lines parallel to the longer length is the best way to go.

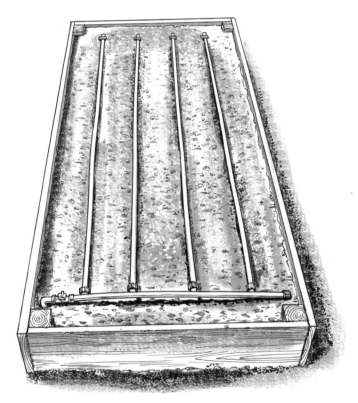

These drip tapes, spaced 12" apart, give even irrigation coverage over the entire square footage of the bed.

CONNECTING A SINGLE TIMER HOSE BIB LINE TO GARDEN BEDS

Ryan and Kiwi figured out an easy way to irrigate all of the backyard garden beds from one water source — the hose bib (faucet) located near the northeast corner of their house. The system is set up with a battery-operated timer attached to the hose bib. After installing all of the necessary fittings (such as a pressure regulator, filter, and backflow preventer), they ran a ½-inch mainline tubing to each garden area. The entire watering system can be run on a single timer. Ryan checks the soil moisture at least once a week and turns the irrigation up or down depending on need. It usually operates for about one hour each day, five days a week, during the summer. He always direct seeds his arugula plantings, so he is mindful to maintain a consistent level of moisture on the surface of the soil to ensure good germination.

The branch of the mainline that irrigates the bed on the south side of the house runs underneath the back deck. Once it reaches the south side of the house, it elbows around the corner. From there, a 15 mil drip tape runs north–south in each keyhole to provide even watering to the bed.

Mainline tubing runs along the north and south side of the deck to provide water to the potted herbs. A short piece of ¼-inch mainline runs to each pot and a spiral of ¼-inch emitter tubing is placed in the top of each container.

The longest section of mainline runs out to the wood-framed raised beds and the bed along the side of the garage. The irrigation to the garage bed mimics the setup for the bed on the south of the house. When the mainline reaches each raised bed, a short branch line tees off and runs underneath the edge of the bed. Once under the bed, that short mainline turns with a 90 degree elbow that brings it to the surface of the bed. The mainline elbows again to run across the short dimension of the bed. Four 15 mil drip tapes are spaced evenly across the bed running north–south. The first tape is 6 inches from the edge of the bed and each subsequent tape is spaced at 12-inch intervals.

The remainder of the landscape is planted with somewhat drought-tolerant perennials that include grapes, horseradish, and lavender. After a few seasons of hand watering, these plantings are pretty much on their own unless a massive heat wave threatens their health. There is always a hose attached to the Y-valve on the backyard spigot. An additional spigot is set on the front of the house for hand watering as necessary.

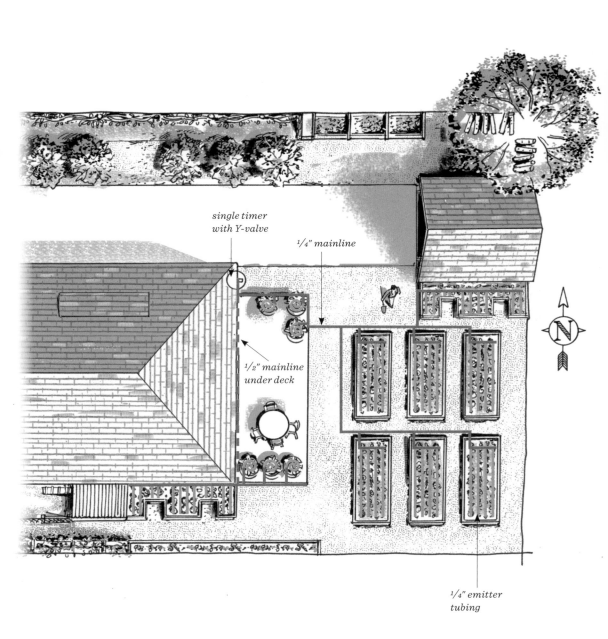

single timer
with Y-valve

$^{1}/_{4}$" mainline

$^{1}/_{2}$" mainline
under deck

N

$^{1}/_{4}$" emitter
tubing

SEPARATE SYSTEMS FOR FRONT YARD AND BACKYARD

Jason's house has a hose bib on the front and back. He's set up two independent drip irrigation systems to manage watering in the different parts of the yard. Each hose bib has a Y-valve, so he can always keep a hose hooked up for hand watering. There is an additional hose attached to the rainwater catchment tank on the back porch that he uses to irrigate the perennial herbs and flowers from time to time.

The hose bib on the concrete back patio is located close to the back door, so he ran the ½-inch mainline tubing along the back of the patio and off the south side of it. After reaching the south edge of the patio, the mainline tubing is buried about 4 inches and runs underground across the rest of the site except where it junctions into beds to connect to drip lines.

The mainline branches off to deliver water to perennial beds and to the greenhouse. For simplicity, he has used the same 15 mil drip tape for all backyard irrigation. The tapes are spaced farther apart in the perennial beds because he knows these plants require less water than the rest of the plants in the garden.

FRONT YARD

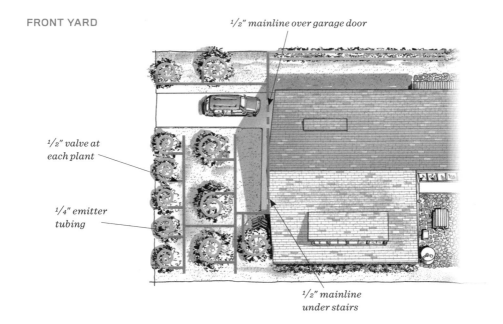

½" mainline over garage door

½" valve at each plant

¼" emitter tubing

½" mainline under stairs

He has included a manual ½-inch valve at this juncture and at every individual bed because he likes the flexibility to turn off any part of the garden that is fallow or between plantings (he also likes the option of water stressing his tomato plants).

The mainline tubing services each raised bed and continues to run past the end of the garden on the two principal sections. These mainlines end with flush caps that allow Jason to flush out sediment and easily drain the irrigation system each fall. He also likes the fact that it will be easy to add irrigation onto the system from there if he ever decides to add new beds to the garden.

In the front yard, the mainline tubing runs along the front walkway and tucks underneath the front stairs to access the main part of the yard. He had to run another branch up and over the garage door, connecting the tubing to the house with ½-inch pipe clamps, to reach the north side of the driveway. He also ran a coil of ¼-inch emitter tubing around each blueberry bush and fruit tree, and installed a valve at each plant because he plans to turn off the irrigation to the fruit trees and raspberries after two or three seasons, but will keep the water flowing to the blueberries year after year.

BACKYARD

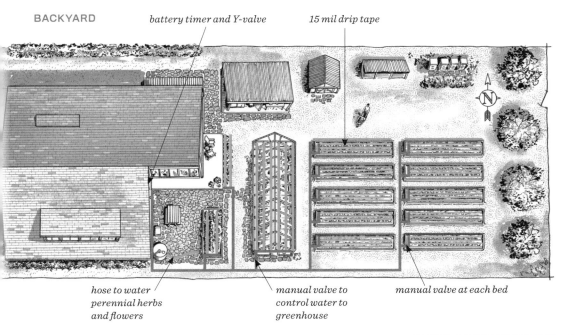

battery timer and Y-valve

15 mil drip tape

hose to water perennial herbs and flowers

manual valve to control water to greenhouse

manual valve at each bed

A TWO-TIMER SPRINKLER SYSTEM

Fortunately Dave and Erin had the foresight to install a hose bib just inside the garden fence when their garden was under construction. This hose bib has a four-way manifold that allows them to keep a garden hose attached, have an open spigot for filling buckets and watering cans, and operate two individual battery timers. Because they move the production area around from season to season, it was important for them to build a system with maximum flexibility. Each timer attaches to a standard garden hose, which then terminates into a powerful impact sprinkler.

At the beginning of each season, they set up one sprinkler in the center of the strawberry bed and one in the center of the vegetable garden. The two sprinklers are set to run at different times so that there is enough water pressure to cover each quadrant.

When a cover crop is first planted and germinating, Erin will occasionally move the strawberry sprinkler into this quadrant to make sure things get a healthy start. After the cover crop is established, they don't irrigate it for the rest of the season.

At the end of the season, the system is disassembled and stored in the tool shed. In the spring they bring the system out and set it back up in the appropriate production quadrants.

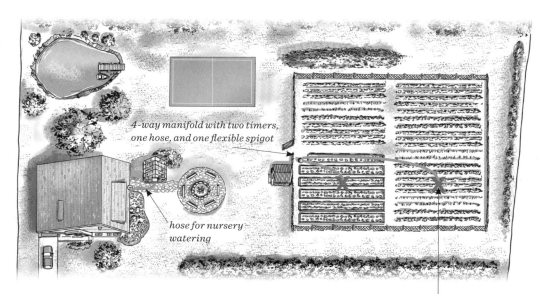

4-way manifold with two timers, one hose, and one flexible spigot

hose for nursery watering

impact sprinkler on a 4' stand, covers one quadrant

ASSEMBLING THE SYSTEM

Consult your irrigation map to create a parts list for your watering system. Drip and overhead watering supplies may be available at local garden centers and nurseries, and are readily available online. Before buying any irrigation supplies, make sure that you can find a full set of compatible materials. Remember: *Different brands of irrigation materials may not fit together, even if the diameter of the tubes and fittings are the same on the packages.* There is nothing more frustrating than trying to fit two sets of parts together that almost — but not quite — fit.

The Right Tools for the Job

The following tools will help you quickly and easily set up and maintain your drip irrigation system.

- *Hole punch.* This is a tool specifically designed to create the right diameter hole into tubing so that you can insert drip lines or emitters. Buy one that's designed for use with your particular system.

- *Cutting tool.* Use a pair of scissors, a knife, tin snips, or any other cutting tool to cut pieces of tubing and drip lines to length (don't use your gardening hand pruners or they'll get really dull).

- *Wrenches.* Keep two pairs of wrenches handy. Some drip fittings need to be tightened beyond "hand tight." Wrenches are also handy to have in case the water spigot itself has a leak. Channel locks, locking pliers, or crescent wrenches work well.

- *Teflon tape.* Also called plumber's tape, this white, stretchy tape can be wrapped around threaded fittings. It is not essential, but it can really help tighten up the system and keep it drip-free.

- *Rags.* A few small rags can be incredibly helpful to clean dirt off irrigation pieces that you might accidently drop in the soil or otherwise get dirty during the installation process. Remember, keeping soil out of the system prevents clogs.

- *Shovel and hand trowel.* Both of these tools might be necessary if you plan to bury any of the tubing, or if you need to move soil out of the way when adding tubing to an existing bed.

- *Drill.* Optional tool that you might use if you want to attach the tubing to the side of the house or side of a bed to help keep it in place. You can use $\frac{1}{2}$-inch pipe clamps to secure tubing to any workable surface.

When you have everything on hand, begin assembling the irrigation system at the water spigot. Take your time and fit the pieces together tightly. Take care when cutting lengths of mainline tubing to ensure they fit around the spaces you are working.

When the system is completely installed, remove the end fittings from your drip lines and run water through the system to flush them of dirt or bits of plastic that may have found their way in during setup. After running the system for a few minutes, turn off the water and seal up the ends of every line. Run the system once again, carefully examining every piece, fitting, and drip line for leaks. Take the time to tighten any dripping fittings.

MANAGING THE DRIP SYSTEM

It is a good idea to manually run the irrigation system every week or two while you're working in the garden. This allows you to check for new leaks, make sure the system is functioning properly, and provide appropriate water for the current weather conditions.

Your garden's need for irrigation will vary drastically over the course of the season. It may be that watering one day a week is sufficient at certain times of year and that five days a week may be necessary at other times. Once the system is in place, you can simply adjust the settings on the timer and carry on with your other essential garden tasks.

Keep in mind that with drip irrigation, your plants and seeds may need a little extra help when they are first planted or are germinating. The roots of seeds and newly transplanted crops are near the soil surface, and can't easily reach the subsurface moisture the drip system provides unless they're placed immediately adjacent to an emitter. This is the most sensitive time of their lives and it is essential that they do not dry out.

We suggest always hand watering new transplants and seeds. Depending on the weather and time of year, you may want to hand water a few more times, or at least check

Irrigation Repair Kit

Keeping a few repair pieces in your toolbox can make maintenance of an irrigation system a breeze. We keep a small bag of irrigation fittings with our gardening tools so that we can make minor repairs a cinch. After all, the easiest time to notice leaks is while you are working in the beds, and keeping materials on hand will make it easier for you to keep the system in working order.

If you have a drip irrigation system, you'll find the following items essential:

- *Teflon tape.* (See page 145.) Keeping a roll handy allows you to patch up small drips in real time.

- *A spare garden hose nozzle.* One of the most commonly broken garden tools. Having a spare on hand will ensure you are always able to hand water as needed.

- *Irrigation couplers.* For quickly patching up holes in the irrigation system.

- *Hole punch.* For moving around drip lines or making any other system repairs.

- *Goof plugs.* For plugging small holes in header tubing or for closing up an old hole when you move an irrigation line.

- *An extra battery.* In case your irrigation timer or any other battery-operated tool goes awry. Keep batteries in a plastic bag or other weatherproof container.

- *Sod staples.* We like to use short, U-shaped, sod staples to keep irrigation header and drip lines in place. Keep a few extras around to help pin down misbehaving irrigation parts.

soil moisture more frequently during the first week or two after planting to make sure crops get off to a healthy start. If germinating seeds during hot, dry periods, some growers will decrease watering duration and instead run their drip system every day for one to two weeks. This strategy is designed to prevent the seeds from drying out. These little bits of extra effort can pay huge dividends toward improving germination rates and encouraging early plant growth and development.

Duration of Irrigation

The length of an irrigation session will vary widely depending on the structure of your soil, flow rate of your drip lines, and the weather. Here is a starting guide for setting a watering system to run at the beginning of the irrigation season:

- *Drip tapes, low flow* (approximately 20 gallons per hour (GPH) per 100 feet of tape; 8-inch emitter spacing): 2 hours, 4 times per week

- *Drip tapes, high flow* (approximately 40 GPH per 100 feet of tape; 8-inch emitter spacing): 1 hour, 4 times per week

- *1/4-inch emitter tubing* (1/2 GPH per emitter): 30 minutes, 4 times per week

- *1/2-inch emitter tubing* (with 1/2 GPH emitters): 30 minutes, 4 times per week

- *Bubblers* (each emitter will have a designated GPH rating): 30 minutes, 4 times per week

After your first watering session, finger test the soil. If it seems dry, add 10 to 20 minutes to your watering cycle, and then test again after your next session. As the season progresses, and as necessary, add more time to the sessions, and add extra watering sessions. If your timer allows for it, set up a rain gauge, which will measure precipitation and cause the timer to self-adjust to match weather conditions.

Winterizing

Drip irrigation lines are not under pressure between watering cycles, so the tubing and drip lines tend to empty themselves of water after each session. This makes it possible to leave most types of drip lines in place through the winter. When cold weather is approaching, turn off the water spigot and remove the Y-valve, timer, pressure regulator, and filter, and put them inside for the winter. If possible, turn off the water supply to the spigot (unless it is a frost-free spigot) and/or cover the spigot with a thermal cover. Open up the ends of the mainline tubing to allow excess water to drip out. After leaving the system open for a few minutes, seal the ends back up to prevent dirt or insects from getting inside the system. If you live in a region with extremely cold winters, consider bringing tapes and mainlines into a garage or other protected structure to minimize fatigue of the plastic.

If your irrigation system does have components that don't drain easily (this is a problem with permanent sprinkler systems), use an air compressor to blow the water out of it at the onset of winter. Water left in small fittings and emitters can cause cracks due to freezing, so taking the time to properly drain your system will pay off in reduced repairs and maintenance in spring.

CHAPTER 7

Setting Up a Home Nursery

If your goal is to become a true high-yield gardener, we encourage you to produce as many of your own transplants as possible (growers use the terms "transplants," "plant starts," and "starts" interchangeably). Whether from seed or cuttings, establishing your own transplant production nursery — simply a protected space with adequate light and warmth to start plants indoors — enables you to care for thousands of small plants in a very limited space.

In addition to getting plants off to an early start in spring, a nursery also allows you to start successions of crops throughout the season, when space is not available in the garden beds. You will have good-size transplants that will be waiting and ready to plant as soon as space opens up. Even in the peak of summer, you may be growing out fall brassicas and late plantings of summer squash to replace the early-season crops in your beds. A home nursery can also create opportunities to sell/trade/give away extra transplants to other gardeners, and to experiment with new techniques like grafting or microgreen production in an easy-to-monitor situation.

INSIDE A HOME NURSERY

Creating and managing a nursery can be one of the most enjoyable aspects of food production. The controlled growing conditions ("controlled" being a relative term!) in a nursery setting allow you to monitor and tend to your crops more closely, making it possible to select the most robust and healthy plants for graduation to the garden beds.

In order for your nursery to be successful it will need light, heat, water, and ventilation. You can count on Mother Nature to take care of those elements in your garden beds (at least most of the time), but in your nursery, the environmental conditions are dependent on what *you* provide.

Adequate lighting. An ideal in-home or greenhouse propagation area should receive a full day of direct sun exposure. Areas like this might be hard to come by, but any space that receives a few hours of sunlight will make growing transplants that much easier. If the propagation area gets less than 12 hours of sunlight, your plants will be healthier if you provide supplemental lighting.

Heating. The primary reason for growing transplants in a nursery is that outside temperatures are too low for the plants to survive (or at least to grow properly). Therefore, it's essential that your propagation space be kept warm. Keep in mind that areas with supplemental heating may also require more frequent watering, as heaters reduce the humidity of the space.

Water. Make sure you have easy access to a water source, such as a hose spigot or sink, so that you can irrigate your transplants and wash out containers for reuse.

Humidity. If you live in a cold climate and your propagation area is inside a building or house with forced air heating, you might need to provide additional humidity to your propagation area. This can be done with a humidifier or a regular misting of plants or by placing a shallow tray filled with a layer of gravel or perlite in the propagation area. Keep the tray filled with water three-quarters of the way up the gravel. Such a gravel tray is necessary only in rare circumstances; regular watering of transplants is usually sufficient to maintain adequate humidity.

Ventilation. Every growing area requires adequate ventilation to minimize disease problems. Consider the location of windows, vents, and doors when locating your propagation area. Air movement is essential to help control pests and diseases, so placing the propagation space in a room with windows or doors will allow for a low-tech solution. Ideally, you'll be able to vent on opposite sides of the room for cross-ventilation. Depending on weather conditions, a window can be cracked open for part of each day (or the door can be propped open for a short time each day). Regardless, either method allows new air to move into the room. In an area with poor ventilation, a small fan can be used to keep air circulating.

Convenience. You want to make it as easy as possible to check up on your little plants. Placing the nursery in a location that is visible and frequently visited will make it a lot easier to check moisture levels, add fertilizer, and take note of germination rates. Regular check-ins will allow you to observe and deal with issues in the nursery before they become catastrophic.

The Home Nursery

1. **POTTING BENCH.** This might be inside your propagation space or in a separate area that can handle more debris and moisture. You'll use this space to mix and screen soil, and fill your flats and pots. A potting bench can even be a covered space outdoors where cleanup isn't that important, or an enclosed space that's easy to wipe down and sweep up.

2. **PROPAGATION AREA.** This is the space where flats and pots of newly seeded crops will live while they're germinating and growing for the first several days, weeks, or months of their lives.

    You may also want to set aside some space outside of the propagation area for hardening off flats of plants that are ready to be transplanted, or for holding them if you don't yet have a space open for planting. Consider a semi-shaded area where containers won't dry out as quickly and where plant growth can slow down to prevent the starts from outgrowing their pots before planting time.

3. **STORAGE.** You'll need some space — perhaps in the propagation room, under the potting bench, or in a tool shed — to store soil mixes, tools, and empty pots and flats.

4. **VENTILATION.** A fan improves air circulation and helps minimize disease issues.

LOCATING THE NURSERY

You may have a few options when considering where to place your nursery. Your choice depends on your space, budget, and the quantity of starts you plan to grow. In regard to location, most home gardeners choose to grow their starts either inside the home, in an attached sunroom, or in a separate greenhouse. Propagating your own starts takes a significant amount of time and attention, so take some time to think through what the best option is to meet the needs of your garden and lifestyle. Also, consider the quantity of plants you'd like to produce; trying to cram too many starts into an inadequately sized space will only lead to frustration, poor quality, and reduced yields.

In-Home Propagation

An in-home propagation area can be inexpensive, easy to set up, and highly productive. In fact, with the right kind of setup you can grow hundreds of transplants in a few square feet of space.

If you're planning to grow your transplants inside your home, chances are that natural light will be in limited supply. In-home propagation spaces typically require artificial lighting, even if they are set up near a south-facing window. Also keep in mind that a propagation area is a little messy. Consider placing a protective waterproof covering on top of any carpet, hardwood flooring, or other delicate material you may be working over. It also pays to clean the area regularly to avoid buildup of dirt and mold.

Also keep in mind that the invasion of insect pests is a real possibility when keeping transplants in the home. A well-tended, well-ventilated growing area can operate pest-free, but even the best managed space can succumb to the will of nature. See pages 234–235 for ideas on how to prevent and recover from insect invasions.

Sunrooms and Atriums

A sunroom or atrium attached to your home can provide an ideal location for transplant propagation. The best atrium growing areas are located on the east, south, or west side of a house and are not heavily shaded by trees or nearby buildings. A very sunny, warm sunroom may be able to support transplants with little or no supplemental lighting.

If your sunroom is attached to the exterior of the house and does not receive supplemental heat from the house, keep a thermometer in the room to monitor temperatures, and supply additional heating as necessary.

Stand-Alone Greenhouse

For most gardeners, the idea of setting up a stand-alone greenhouse is very tempting. Greenhouses can provide great winter work spaces where you can start transplants and produce crops all year long. The only real drawbacks of constructing and managing a greenhouse are the cost and relatively large amount of space they require.

Greenhouses can be expensive to purchase, expensive to build, and expensive to operate. That being said, they are one of the best investments you can make to increase the overall yield of your home garden space. You can use a small portion of your greenhouse for propagation, and the rest for the production of heat-loving crops in the summer and hardy crops in the winter. (Turn to page 261 for more information on greenhouse structures and their management.)

OUTFITTING YOUR NURSERY

You won't need many supplies on hand to establish a successful nursery, but the right materials are essential. Here's a look at what you'll need to create the right environment in your propagation area.

Lighting

In indoor and partially shaded spaces, there is rarely enough natural light to keep your propagation area in business. Supplemental lighting will help your seedlings grow quickly and stay healthy. Light-stressed plants develop thin, weak, "leggy" stems and are more susceptible to pest and disease attacks. Ultimately, such plants are poor producers. Setting up a grow light doesn't require an electrician's license and doesn't have to cost an arm and a leg, but high-tech options are available for those who love their lumens.

Time

Most vegetable transplants will grow at a healthy rate when provided with 12 hours of supplemental light per day. For ideal light exposure, lights can be manually turned on and off or set on a timer to mimic natural light cycles, 12 hours of continuous light, starting early in the morning and running until early evening.

Intensity and Spectrum

The intensity (or lumen output) of growing lights varies widely. The lower the intensity of the bulb, the closer it should be to the plants. Most grow lights come with large reflectors that are meant to efficiently use the available intensity of the blulbs and direct all of the light waves toward the plants.

Blue is good. It matters where your grow lights fall on the color spectrum. Generally speaking, light at the blue end of the spectrum supports vegetative growth, while the red end of the spectrum supports flowering and fruiting.

If you're interested in keeping plants under lights through maturity, you may need to invest in several types of lighting to provide light at various points in the spectrum. However, if you're like most growers and are producing young plants for outdoor production, you'll only need lights at the blue end of the spectrum. General full-spectrum lights (fluorescent, blue or white LEDs, or HID) work perfectly fine for growing young transplants.

Watch those Kelvins. The color of light from a bulb can also be expressed in Kelvins. It can be confusing because the term *Kelvin* is typically used to indicate temperatures, but with lightbulbs, Kelvin refers to the frequency of the light wave, which corresponds to the color of the light. To help vegetable plants produce healthy transplants, the bulbs should have a Kelvin rating of 5000K to 6500K (again, the blue end of the spectrum). If you plan to grow crops to maturity indoors, and need to support flowering and fruiting, the bulbs should have a rating of around 2700K (the red end of the spectrum).

Fluorescent vs. LED vs. HID

Your main options for supplemental lighting are fluorescent, LED, and HID (high-intensity discharge) bulbs. HIDs require large amounts of electricity, making them expensive to operate. Fluorescent bulbs and LEDs have much lower energy requirements, but also provide a lower quality of light.

Fluorescents. These are the least expensive type of fixture you can use for your lighting setup and they use a very small amount of energy to operate, making them very cost effective. If the lights show a Kelvin rating, make sure to pick out bulbs with a rating of 5000K to 6500K. Fluorescent lights contain very toxic chemicals (mercury), so take care not to break the bulbs, especially in the home.

Because of their low lumen output, fluorescents must hang 1 to 3 inches above the tops of your plants in order to provide sufficient lighting. Most growers install these lights on chains or ropes so that the lights can be adjusted as plants grow (another option is to place plants on shelves that can move up or down). This height requirement also necessitates having different light fixtures for plants that are at different stages of growth. It's not impossible, however, to provide proper lighting to one-day-old seedlings and three-week-old seedlings from a single fluorescent fixture.

Fluorescents are great for small production areas and for lighting stacked shelves of propagation flats. Consider using or building a series of shelves, each with its own light fixture.

LED (light-emitting diode). These bulbs are recent newcomers in the world of plant production. Because they generate low amounts of heat and consume tiny amounts

Grow lights and stacked shelves allow you to propagate a large number of plants in a very small indoor space.

of energy, there is an ongoing race to produce an ideal LED grow light. LED technology is constantly changing, but white and blue light LEDs are currently available for home-scale production growers. It is likely that purchasing an LED setup for your propagation area will require the largest up-front investment, but over time it should require the least amount of energy and replacement parts.

LED lights do not distribute light for great distances, so fixtures should be kept relatively close to the tops of your plants. The exact placement of LEDs can vary depending on the intensity of the light and the brand of the LED. Most are placed between 12 and 30 inches above the plants. LEDs do not emit heat, so if you notice any legginess in your transplants, simply lower the fixture closer to the tops of the plants. This limited light distribution means that several fixtures may be required to cover your propagation area. In fact, the biggest risk with LEDs is that you may accidentally invest in a set of fixtures that don't provide enough light for your plants. Be aware that the world of LED grow lights still operates with a Wild West mentality, meaning that most manufacturers overstate the "proven effectiveness" of their products.

HID (high-intensity discharge). These lights are considerably more expensive than fluorescents or LEDs, but can cover a larger area with a single bulb. The ballast (power source) and light fixture are typically separate units for HID lights. Many professional growers use this type of light to encourage robust growth and high yields when growing crops to maturity in an indoor setting. Because of the intensity of light provided by HID lights, the bulbs can stay in place and be fixed several feet above transplants (because they generate a lot of heat, HID bulbs can actually burn plants if they're placed too close to the foliage).

There are two principal types of HID lighting. *Metal halide* bulbs are best for vegetative growth. If you're growing transplants for planting in an outdoor growing location, this should be the only type of HID light you need. With a large-enough table space and reflector, a single metal halide light fixture would be sufficient for all of the transplant production needs of a home-scale grower. *High pressure sodium* bulbs are best for flowering and fruiting of crops. They're the bulbs to use if you plan on keeping plants in an indoor setting through their entire life and into fruit production. We encourage serious cost/benefit calculations before investing in the materials and energy to provide season-long supplemental lighting to your vegetables.

Heat Sources

If your propagation area is inside a house or building, you may not need an additional heat source to create an ambient temperature that is appropriate for seed germination (see the Planting Dates chart on page 56 for germination temperatures for different crops). If you're germinating seeds that don't need particularly high temperatures, you may be able to get away with using an unheated cold frame or low tunnel (depending on your climate and the time of year). For more information on cold frames and tunnels, or if you are using a stand-alone greenhouse for propagation, see page 255.

To supply heat, you have two options: heat the entire greenhouse or just the area where you'll be germinating seeds.

Heating a Greenhouse

Heating an entire greenhouse is usually done with a propane or LP (liquefied petroleum) gas heater hung from the framing of the greenhouse. Setting up the necessary infrastructure for heating an entire greenhouse is best done by a professional. If you purchased a greenhouse, you can consult with the company you purchased the greenhouse from for more information (see Resources, page 307, for suppliers). Some professional growers are also experimenting with alternative fuels, such as waste vegetable oil, waste motor oil, and biodiesel for heating their greenhouses.

For most home-scale production growers, heating an entire greenhouse for propagating a small number of starts is an unnecessary monetary and environmental expense. Instead, we suggest that you set up a heated area inside a production tunnel, or construct a small, separate kit greenhouse for propagation.

Heat Mats

If the nursery space is just a little too cold, consider purchasing a heating mat designed for propagation. These are available in various sizes, and are perfect for warming up a small space for propagation. They also work well in an outdoor greenhouse if you have access to electricity there. To provide additional warmth at night, you can cover the flats with a cold frame or row cover. This option works well for shallow seeding flats (a heating mat will only heat a limited volume of soil), and if the temperature in the greenhouse doesn't get too low.

Tips for Using Electricity Safely in the Greenhouse

We all know that electricity and water don't mix, so be very careful when using electric appliances in a greenhouse. Here are a few tips to help you stay safe:

- Do *not* use an electric blanket or other heating element that isn't designed for propagation.

- Keep plugs and extension cords away from the ground and from sources of water (we like to hang them from the ceiling).

- Shut off power and move equipment as necessary when watering.

- Hire a licensed electrician to run a separate circuit with GFCI outlets and moisture-proof covers. This is especially important if you'll be supplying electricity to a greenhouse on an ongoing basis.

- Only use an extension cord run from the house to the greenhouse for temporary, short-term use. Be sure it's plugged into an outlet in a dry location (or make sure it has a moisture-proof cover).

- Don't exceed the recommended load for extension cords (heaters and metal halide lights use a lot of electricity). A GFCI outlet is the safest option for this.

- Use extension cords that are rated for outdoor use.

Heat Cables

If you need more heated space than a heating mat can provide, you can set up your own heated propagation table using heat cables and a thermostat. Closely follow the setup instructions included with the product to avoid risk of shock and to ensure effective and even heating. The propagation table can also be covered at night with a cold frame or row cover to provide extra protection.

Space Heater

Another option is to set up a space heater underneath the table or rack that your transplants rest on. Make sure there's enough space between the heater and the table and any fabric so that the setup does not pose a fire danger. Also make sure you shut off the electricity and remove the heater when watering. Keep in mind that heat rises, so using a small fan will improve horizontal distribution of the heat. You can also cover the table with a row cover or greenhouse plastic at night.

Growing Media

Store-bought growing media are often referred to as "soilless" mixes. These mixes typically comprise ingredients such as peat moss, vermiculite, perlite, shredded coconut husks (coir), and compost. They generally don't contain garden soil, as it doesn't provide the aeration, drainage, and water-holding capacity necessary to maintain plant health in a container. Growing media are designed to hold water while still providing aeration and drainage in the somewhat artificial environment of a plant pot where insects and microbes are less present.

A heat mat with a row cover over it is an efficient way to heat a small germination area.

Heating without Electricity

If you'd like to avoid a spike in your utility bills, there are ways to heat a greenhouse without electricity or a major infrastructure investment. One effective (though admittedly labor-intensive) option is to build a compost bin in the greenhouse. Create a fresh compost pile early in the spring, and then place your seedling flats on a wire screen on top of the bin. The heat from the compost will warm the flats. Setting up low hoops and row cover over the plants will help maintain warmer temperatures at night. You'll need a significant amount of compost to generate enough heat to make this system work: a 3′ × 3′ ×3′ or larger bin should be adequate.

If you have livestock such as chickens or goats, you can bed them down at night in the greenhouse to generate additional warmth for germinating seeds. Use appropriate fencing to make sure the animals don't eat your tasty young seedlings. To avoid contamination of produce, we recommend that you don't house animals in production greenhouses while crops are growing.

A woodstove can work well to heat your greenhouse, provided you have a supply of wood and the time and skill to properly manage it. You'll also need to carefully monitor the humidity of the greenhouse.

Rocks, bricks, or jugs of water painted black and placed in the propagation area will absorb heat during the day and radiate it out at night. We've found that "heat sinks" like these are helpful, but are not sufficient on their own to supply enough heat for effective germination.

In this greenhouse, black drums of water absorb heat from the sun during the day and radiate it out at night.

You can find blends made specifically for germination, propagation, or just general use. Soilless mixes are often sterilized to eliminate disease spores and kill weed seeds. In a home nursery setting, sterilized soil mixes are not absolutely necessary and in fact, the lack of soil microbiology can lead to plant health issues during grow out. Growers will have different opinions about the cost/benefit analysis of sterile potting mix based on their personal experiences. We prefer to use a non-sterile mix with compost. We have found that, although sterile mixes work well in very controlled environments, the lack of beneficial microorganisms in the mix makes the plants more susceptible to diseases such as botrytis and damping-off in an organically managed propagation area. The beneficial microorganisms present in the compost help provide protection against these plant pathogens.

Germination Mix

We recommend that home gardeners grow transplants from seed in a special soil mixture known as germination mix. A germination mix is a finely screened, lightweight planting medium. The soil's small particles make it easy for young seedlings to push up through the mixture without being damaged or trapped under a large piece of bark or other material sometimes found in standard potting mix.

Make Your Mix

Creating your own soil mix can be a fun and cost-saving activity. Keep in mind that properly mixing soils requires time and patience, and bulk materials used to create mixes will take up a considerable amount of space.

Germination Mix

- 15 parts peat
- 4 parts compost
- 4 parts perlite
- ¼ part dolomitic lime
- ¼ part fine, granulated, balanced, organic fertilizer

Mix the ingredients thoroughly and keep them out of the elements. We like to use 5-gallon and 1-gallon buckets to measure out the ingredients. You can mix up a batch in a wheelbarrow by combining 2 cubic feet of peat (about three 5-gallon buckets), ½ cubic foot of compost (a little less than one 5-gallon bucket), ½ cubic foot of perlite (a little less than one 5-gallon bucket), 4 cups of dolomitic lime (¼ gallon), and 4 cups of fertilizer (¼ gallon). You can keep this mix in a clean plastic or metal garbage can with a lid for use all spring. It needs to stay dry to prevent the fertilizer from decomposing. Moisten only the amount of mix you'll be using, just before seeding.

Potting Soil Mix

- 1 part compost
- 1 part sand
- ½ part peat or perlite

Mix the ingredients thoroughly and use right away or store out of the elements for as long as necessary. You can add organic fertilizer to your potting mix at a rate of about 3 cups per 20 gallons of mix.

Depending on your scale of production, available time, and budget, you can buy ready-made germination mix or create your own. A standard germination mix consists of peat (or coconut coir), perlite, and lime. These mixes can be relatively expensive, but a large bag can last a long time for the home-scale nursery. If you'd like to create a germination mix at home, try our recipe (see Make Your Mix on page 158).

Potting Mix

As your plants mature, they'll require more nutrients than a germination mix can provide. If you pot up your young transplants to larger containers, it's important that you use a soil mixture with higher nutrient levels and more active microbiology. Potting up is a great time to mix in granular organic fertilizer. We also add a small amount of fertilizer to our germination mix. To learn more about using organic fertilizer, see page 203.

When potting up, you can use any store-bought, organic, all-purpose potting soil. Most potting soils contain perlite, bark, compost, and a variety of other materials (like worm castings and manure) and should provide a good starting point for almost any vegetable transplant. Because nursery plants require frequent watering (and thus leach nutrients), even the most nutrient-rich potting mix may require regular doses of liquid fertilizer as the plant grows. If you'd like to mix your own potting soil, try our recipe on page 158.

Containers for Large-Scale Seeding

Seeding flats or plug trays are great options for producing a large number of plants efficiently in a small space. Generally, flats are approximately 10 × 20 inches (but with the lip, they are actually about 11 × 22 inches). Flats are built to hold almost any number of plants: open flats can be seeded with hundreds of plants or plug trays are seeded in individual cells.

Open Flats

You can purchase open flats with no internal spacial divisions. These flats are designed to be filled with growing media and then seeded. They are inexpensive and easy to use, and they can be utilized for starting a variety of plant types. When using open flats, you must be very careful when removing young seedlings for potting up or transplanting. Roots will have grown together, and it is very easy to damage or kill plants when removing them from these trays. Some growers use these flats exclusively. We typically avoid seeding into these shallow open flats because of the difficulty of thinning and transplanting after germination.

Plug Trays

Most of our transplants are seeded into plug trays. Plug trays can be purchased in a wide array of cell sizes. Common cells per flat may be 36, 60, 72, 128, 144, and more. We primarily use 72-celled trays and 128-celled trays. Plug trays allow you to use your seed efficiently. We typically place 2 or 3 seeds per cell to reduce future thinning needs, ensure good germination rates, and make effective use of space. Seeds with very high germination rates or seeds that are very expensive may be seeded one per cell to stretch the seeds as far as possible and eliminate the need for thinning.

Seed 20 percent more. Keep in mind that, even under ideal conditions, seeds will rarely have 100 percent germination rates. Unless they're seeded with at least 2 or 3 seeds per cell, most plug trays will have some empty cells. For example, if you want to plant 72 peppers in the garden, make sure to either sow a few seeds per cell in a 72-celled flat or to sow more than one flat of the crop. As a general rule, always sow at least 20 percent more than you plan to use in the garden to account for unhealthy seedlings, mortality, and other unpredictables.

Transplanting. Most crops can be effectively grown out in a 72-cell tray and held for a few weeks until transplanting. Crops held too long in plug trays can become rootbound, or suffer from a lack of available nutrients, so keep an eye on growth and add consistent low doses of liquid fertilizer. Transplanting from plug trays is easy because the plant's roots will have filled out the soil in the cell by the time they're ready for planting out. Most crops will lift out of the tray easily if gently tugged by the leaves. To assist with transplanting, turn the tray on its side, squeeze the bottom sides of the cell, and gently pull each plant out by the leaves.

Soil Blocks

Many small-scale farmers use soil blocks for transplant production. A soil block is essentially a cube of soil that is used to germinate seeds without the structure of a plug tray. A soil blocker (also called soil-block maker) is a tool that will compress your growing media into multiple small cubes, which can then be seeded with the crop of your choice.

Soil blocks are great because plant roots will stop growing when they reach the edge of the exposed block (roots don't like to be exposed directly to air). This prevents seedlings from becoming rootbound and can ease their transition into the garden, because their root tips are poised to move beyond the edge of the block once they're placed into a garden bed. Soil blocks take a little more skill and care to use than plug flats, so be patient when learning the ropes of soil-block production. To ensure that your soil blocks hold together, use warm water when initially moistening the mix and make sure the mix is completely saturated. The consistency of the soil should be similar to a paste, much wetter than in other

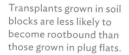
Transplants grown in soil blocks are less likely to become rootbound than those grown in plug flats.

applications. This initial work will help the ingredients form strong bonds and maintain their shape.

Other Containers

Many growers, when producing transplants on a small scale, find it easy to locate free containers for seeding. Egg cartons are a time-tested seeding tray, as are yogurt cups and pretty much any other small disposable container. Make sure to poke holes in the bottom of any container you use for propagation, as drainage is essential to prevent root rot and to maintain healthy plants. The only real disadvantages of using random containers are the inefficiency of space and the potential of poor drainage.

Larger Containers for Potting Up and Seeding

Potting up seedlings into larger containers can be useful for growing cold-sensitive crops, like tomatoes, in the protective space of the nursery for a long period. This is also a good strategy if weather conditions prevent you from planting outside on time. In general, though, because potting up requires additional time and materials, we encourage you to transplant directly from small containers to the garden whenever possible.

Four-Inch Pots

These are typically used to pot up seedlings from plug trays. It is also possible to seed directly into 4-inch pots. Starting in 4-inch pots will eliminate the need for potting up crops like tomatoes and peppers. The downside is that either more propagation space is needed or the selection of transplants will be limited. However, cucurbits like squash and cucumbers are commonly seeded directly into 4-inch pots because they can become stunted if potted up or transplanted roughly.

Direct seeding. If you're seeding directly into 4-inch pots, consider filling the pot almost entirely with potting mix and adding a thin layer of germination mix to the top of the container. This top layer creates a good seedbed, and the underlying potting mix provides the additional nutrients needed once the seedling's roots expand as the plant starts to grow.

Cleaning and Storing Your Trays

Trays and pots can be storehouses for pests and diseases that lie in wait for another crop to terrorize. If well cared for, your containers should last for a number of years. We recommend washing your pots with water and dish soap after each use, and then sanitizing with a mild bleach solution (1 part bleach to 10 parts water) or a peroxyacetic acid product. Pots should be allowed to air-dry and then stacked somewhere out of direct sunlight until their next use.

Gallon-Size Containers

Depending on the type of crops you're producing and how you've scheduled your seeding, you may want to use gallon-size or other large containers for your propagation nursery. If you like to start heat-loving crops like peppers and eggplants early in the season to get them as large as possible before planting out into the garden, you may end up potting up into a gallon or other large container. Larger containers reduce the chances that garden plants will become rootbound.

Direct seeding. Certain crops can be seeded directly into gallon containers. We often seed bulb onions and leeks into 1-gallon nursery pots. These large, deep containers allow these plants to grow out for several months before transplanting. Healthy onions can withstand a fair amount of handling during transplanting, so these can be seeded thickly into containers and pried apart at planting time. Use the same approach for filling gallon containers as you would for seeding into 4-inch pots.

Plant Tags

We can't stress enough the importance of proper and consistent plant labeling. Even if you're transcribing every activity into a notebook and even if you have a photographic memory, it's incredibly easy to mix up identical-looking young transplants. With some crops, it's virtually impossible to distinguish among different varieties when the plants are young.

When seeding an entire flat with a single variety, we recommend putting at least two tags in each flat (in case one falls out). If seeding multiple varieties together in a flat, plan to place a tag in each row. Your tags can then be placed in the garden when transplanting to help you identify and differentiate between varieties when you're out in the field. Wooden plant tags labeled with permanent marker make great tags because although they usually last for only one season, they can be left in the garden to decompose. Simple plastic plant tags labeled with grease pencils can be much less expensive if you are growing on a larger scale. These have the advantage of coming in bright colors, so they are easier to locate among large, healthy plants. However, they must be collected and disposed of after each crop is cleared. Plastic tags are usually UV damaged, worn out, and broken by the end of a season. Thicker plastic tags may be able to be cleaned and reused in subsequent seasons.

Watering Implements

You'll want something that can provide a gentle stream of water for your transplants. A standard watering can or hose with a nozzle both work just fine; some growers even hold a watering can up to the end of a hose as a makeshift nozzle while they water! If using a nozzle, try to find one with a gentle shower setting for everyday use and a mist setting for moistening very small seeds and misting grafted plants.

Tables and Racks

You'll need to place your nursery flats somewhere up off the ground (away from ground-dwelling insects and small animal pests) while the seeds germinate and the plants grow out. Any kind of table will suffice for this purpose — even just a pallet or a piece of plywood set up on blocks — as long as it can get wet and dirty. Common greenhouse and nursery tables have tops built from metal grating so that water drains easily away from the flats. Metal grating is a terrific long-term choice because, unlike a wooden tabletop, it will not warp or rot. You can make your own nursery tables with lumber and wire fencing. Consider using the space below your tables for storing supplies that can handle getting wet, such as empty flats, trays, buckets, and closed containers of potting mix.

Go vertical with racks. When setting up a nursery in a small space, you can stack flats on a rack with multiple levels to take advantage of vertical space. Any storage rack will work well for this purpose if the space between shelves is adequate to grow out your plants. A minimum distance of 12 inches is recommended for growing plants in one location for more than a few

weeks. If you plan to pot up the crops and keep them in a stacked situation for more than a few weeks, use a rack with 24 inches or more between shelves.

If you're stacking trays in this way, it's important to make sure all levels get adequate light exposure. Attaching a fluorescent or LED light to the bottom of each shelf will create a very condensed propagation nursery.

Some growers stack flats directly on top of each other or use unlit space while the seeds are germinating. This does work, but the plants will need access to high-quality light the day they begin poking out from the soil. Failure to provide light quickly enough will cause the plants to become leggy and unhealthy, so be very attentive if you decide to stack propagation trays.

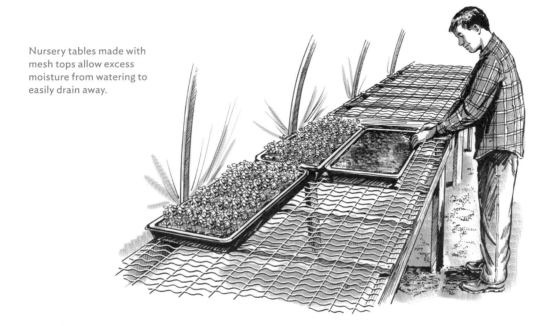

Nursery tables made with mesh tops allow excess moisture from watering to easily drain away.

CHAPTER 8

Starting Plants En Masse

Starting a nursery with a diverse array of crops and varieties requires significant planning, and the space must be well organized. The actual time investment to manage a home nursery is not incredibly significant; the key is to allow for short but frequent check-ups and tasking. Set aside a few minutes every day to check the watering needs of your starts. While there, you can scout for problems and, if you have a bit of extra time, seed new flats. Such diligence will pay huge dividends throughout the season. One key advantage of transplant production is that it gives you the ability to care for your plants in a controlled environment and get them off to a healthy start.

SCHEDULING YOUR SEED STARTING

Refer to your planting plan to determine how many transplants you need to produce for each crop, and seed your flats accordingly. (See chapter 2, starting on page 26.) Again, be sure to plant at *least* 20 percent more than you'll actually need. For example, if you need 30 tomato plants, plan to seed 50 cells of a plug tray. If you seed 50 cells, more than likely about 35 to 45 will germinate, which leaves you a little cushion in the event a few plants fail to grow. In order to fill the trays and avoid wasting valuable nursery space, we often place two or three seeds in each cell, and then thin them to one plant per cell a few days after they emerge. This technique is especially important if you have reason to suspect low germination rates (for example, if you're using old seed or are unable to keep your nursery at the ideal temperature for germinating that crop). Thin to one plant per cell and transplant only the 30 healthiest tomatoes to the garden. Ideally, you'll have a few extra plants to give away, sell, or trade at planting time.

While you're determining how many plants to start, plan your space carefully. You'll likely be starting seeds throughout the season, and possibly potting up transplants, so be sure to leave enough space open for flats later in the season.

Making a Schedule

After you've determined the quantities you'll need for each crop, prepare your seed-starting schedule. You can use a single schedule for the entire garden that includes a seeding schedule for the nursery, as well as outdoor seeding and planting dates. Or you can create a separate calendar just for the nursery area.

Your schedule should list the quantity of each crop to be seeded in a given week. At our nursery, we try to do each week's seeding on the same day each week (Monday), and this date is noted on a spreadsheet to help keep us on schedule. If we make changes to the schedule and seed on a Tuesday or Wednesday, we note the change in the schedule. Additionally, if we adjust quantities (for example, if we planned to seed two trays of lettuce but only seeded one), these changes are also noted. This gives us an accurate record of when and how much we plant, which helps us to project more accurately for future seasons.

We almost never follow our seeding schedule exactly as written. If a certain seeding of a crop fails, we need the flexibility to add to the next week's schedule to make up for it. Similarly, if early plantings of a crop are incredibly successful, we may choose to eliminate a seeding later in the season.

Depending on your location, your seeding schedule may last all year long, or it may stop for several months when the sunlight is not adequate for plant growth. Our schedule runs all year. Transplant production starts in January with onions and leeks, and continues in earnest through September. During the months of October through December, we don't start any seeds for outdoor transplanting, but we do seed flats of microgreens and sprouts for winter production.

To plan out your seed starting for the season, start by developing your planting plan and calendar as described on page 43.

Starting Seeds

Seed starting is a fairly simple process, but in order to ensure even, consistently high germination rates, it's important to do it properly.

1. Fill each flat with germination mix or screened potting soil. Use the bottom of a similar-size container to gently tamp down the soil, creating a level seeding surface ¼ to ½ inch below the rim of the container. If the soil mix is very dry, moisten it thoroughly before sowing.

2. Place the seeds directly on top of the prepared seed surface and sprinkle them with germination mix. (Seeds of different sizes require different sowing depths, so the amount of mix you'll need to cover the seeds will vary. Seed packets indicate how deeply the seed should be planted; as a general rule, seeds should be planted twice as deep as their diameter.)

3. Plant more than one seed per cell or pot. For most crops, two or three seeds per container should be adequate. In a small nursery setting, space is at a premium, and you don't want to dedicate heated propagation space to empty containers. After seeds emerge, thin to the single healthiest plant. (Crops that don't cope well with root disturbance should be snipped with scissors rather than uprooted; see the Tolerance of Root Disturbance chart on page 184.)

4. Water in the seeds after planting, to provide good seed-to-soil contact. Keep newly sown flats consistently moist during the entire germinating process, to ensure that seeds are able to absorb moisture during germination. If a seed dries out for even a few hours, the young sprout may desiccate and die.

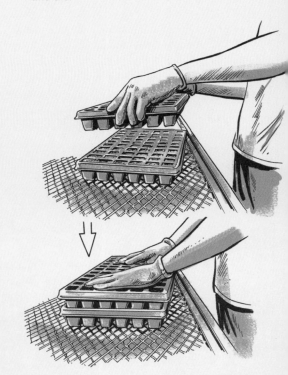

Once you've determined your crop amounts and transplanting dates, you can use the planting information chart on page 56 to figure out when to start your seeds. For example, let's say you want to have a broccoli start ready to transplant on the first of June. You consult the planting information chart and note that broccoli takes about four weeks to grow from seeding until it's ready for transplanting. This means you'll want to start the broccoli seeds in your propagation area on May 1 — about four weeks before June 1. (You can read another planning example in the profile about Jason's tomatoes, page 75.)

Some growers keep track of their seeding schedule right on their planting calendar (see the planting calendar template on page 72). Others make a separate seeding schedule to keep track of this information.

LARGE-SCALE SEEDING EQUIPMENT

As you scale up nursery production, hand seeding flats can start to take up a lot of time. Working quickly while still accurately seeding cells can present a challenge even to seasoned nursery workers. Fortunately, there is a range of tools that can help expedite and increase seeding accuracy.

Hand Seeder

This handy device is simply a small container with a single chute sticking out to the side. Fill the basin with your seed and gently tap the chute to help direct seeds into each cell of your flat or soil blocks. Using the tool effectively takes a little practice, but once you develop a feel for it you can double your seeding speed and accuracy. Some growers prefer to use a pen or pencil to tap the side of the chute rather than their finger because they believe it gives them more control. If you like high tech, you can also find electronic versions of this tool that will do the seed shaking for you.

Wand Seeder

Slightly more technical than the basic hand seeder, a wand seeder is a simple version of the vacuum seeder (described as follows). These contraptions typically use a hand or foot pump to suck up and deposit seeds. This tool is especially useful for managing tiny, hard to handle seeds like lettuce.

Vacuum Seeder

Probably the highest tech option out there, a vacuum seeder works by sucking a seed up to evenly spaced holes on a metal plate. Each plate is designed to fit a particular plug tray. For example, you can purchase a seeder plate for a 72-cell plug tray. Simply pour seed onto the tray and turn on the vacuum; the seeds will be sucked up into a place holder that aligns perfectly with each cell of your waiting flat. Place the plate over the flat, release the vaccum, and presto — the whole flat is seeded with a single seed per cell! This is a relatively advanced and expensive piece of equipment, but if you are considering high-volume nursery propagation, it might be worth checking into.

PROPAGATING FROM CUTTINGS

Growing transplants from seed is the most common form of propagation, but it's certainly not the only way to start new plants. If one of your goals is to grow quantities of perennial crops quickly and inexpensively, taking cuttings is your best bet. The various kinds of cuttings include:

Herbaceous cuttings are those taken from non-woody, herbaceous plants like basil and tomatoes.

Softwood cuttings are taken from soft, succulent, new growth of woody plants. New shoots and growth tips are cut when stems are springy and can be snapped off easily when bent. Softwood cuttings are common for perennial herbs like rosemary and sage.

Hardwood cuttings are taken from the mature branches of a woody perennial, such as bay laurel, when the plant is dormant.

The simplest type of cuttings to manage are herbaceous cuttings because they are the most likely to survive and require the least oversight (and they set new roots quickly). You can take cuttings and grow them out in your nursery from virtually any perennial herb, including anise hyssop, lavender, mint, oregano, rosemary, and thyme. Take cuttings in the spring, summer, or early fall when plants have new vigorous growth. Don't take them when the plant is flowering or water stressed, or right before frosty weather. This technique also works to propagate some annuals, including basil and tomatoes.

Similarly, if you hope to expand the productivity and health of fruiting crops like tomatoes and eggplant, it might be worth it to delve into the world of annual plant grafting, as outlined on page 170.

If one of your goals is to grow quantities of perennial crops quickly and inexpensively, taking cuttings is your best bet.

Making New Plants from Cuttings

1. Use a pair of sharp, clean pruners or scissors to cut off a 3- to 4-inch piece of stem from the plant. Make sure you are cutting new, soft growth from healthy branches. Cut the stem at a 30–45 degree angle; the extra surface area this angle creates will enable the cutting to send out more roots. Take 3 or 4 cuttings for each plant you hope to propagate. Often cuttings will fail for no clear reason, so hedge your bets by making a few extra.

2. Dip the cut end of the cutting into rooting hormone powder. Rooting hormone powder is a condensed, dried form of a compound found in all plants. It's usually harvested from willow plants, which have an unusually high amount of the compound. Rooting hormone can be found at any garden center or online. One package should allow you to make hundreds of cuttings.

3. Place the cuttings into a flat or small container filled with germination mix or straight perlite. To prevent the sensitive cutting from developing bacterial or fungal infections while it becomes established, do not include compost or garden soil. Keep the cuttings in indirect sunlight while they establish root systems. Some herbaceous and softwood cuttings can also successfully be grown directly in a container of water, with no other medium. (If employing this method, simply fill a cup or jar with water and make sure the leaves of the cutting sit comfortably above the water line. Change the water every few days to reduce the

potential of bacterial growth and skip to step 5.)

4. Keep the soil medium consistently moist. Cover the flat with a plastic cover (you can purchase one to fit over your flats, or you can make your own) and mist the cuttings with water as necessary to maintain a high level of humidity. Remove the cover periodically to allow excess water to evaporate (to avoid fungal problems). Remove any dying or diseased cuttings to prevent the spread of pathogens.

5. When the cuttings have rooted, pot them up into a larger container and monitor them in the nursery as they grow healthy root systems. Plant them into the garden in spring or whenever new herbs are needed. New plantings of herbs will take most easily when transplanted in spring or early summer. Once potted up in the nursery, allow them enough time to set out a root system that fills out the nursery pot, but not so long that they become rootbound. The easiest way to monitor their progress is to periodically lift one or two plants from the container (carefully) and examine the extent of root growth.

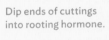
Dip ends of cuttings into rooting hormone.

"Stick" fresh cuttings into a flat of moistened perlite.

Pot up rooted cuttings into containers filled with potting mix.

GRAFTING FOR INCREASED PRODUCTIVITY

A centuries-old technique for all types of plants, grafting can be used to improve home vegetable crop production. Long practiced in Asia and Europe for annual crops, grafting has begun to catch on in the United States as a way to boost yields, increase vigor, and reduce susceptibility to pests and diseases. It is commonly practiced on solanaceous and cucurbit crops.

The idea is to select a variety for the rootstock (the part of the grafted plant that will provide the roots and lower stem of the plant) that is hardy, vigorous, and productive, and a variety for the scion (the upper part of the grafted plant that actually produces the fruit) that meets your needs for flavor, size, and shape. Grafting may be particularly helpful for heirloom varieties that taste great but have issues with disease or low productivity.

For solanaceous crops, it's important to order a specially selected rootstock variety seed from a reputable supplier. There are limited suppliers of these varieties as of this writing, but Johnny's Selected Seeds provides several tomato rootstock varieties. Challenging cucurbits such as cucumbers and melons are often grafted on to rootstocks of common, vigorous, hardy species, such as gourds and squash.

Because rootstock varieties are typically slower to germinate, plan to start the seeds for the rootstock about five to seven days before starting the seeds for the scion. Keep the temperature of the medium between 65 and 75°F to ensure consistent germination. Grafted plants need a few weeks to heal after the grafting process, so you might start them two to three weeks earlier than you would for non-grafted plants for the same crop (although their increased vigor often allows grafted plants to catch up to their non-grafted counterparts, even if they're planted at the same time).

When you're ready to start the grafting process, wash your hands and clean all materials before handling the plants. Use a new, clean, sharp razor blade or surgical scalpel to make the graft cuts.

MANAGING YOUR NURSERY

Managing a home nursery shouldn't take more than a few minutes a day. Changes happen quickly, though, so it's important to keep a watchful eye over the plants. Plan to check on the nursery a few times throughout each day to ensure that flats don't dry out and that the propagation area stays at the proper temperature.

Watering

Depending on your scale of production, you can use a watering can or hose to water your flats. Whichever one you choose, it's important that it have a rose or nozzle that can reliably deliver a *gentle* shower of water because most seeds are planted very shallowly in the flats and germination mix is very light. A heavy shower or stream of water can wreak havoc, washing seeds out of place or completely out of the flat.

Because of the limited soil volume and shallowness of the containers, flats of transplants can dry out very quickly. Plan to check moisture at least once a day, and potentially two or three times a day if the weather is hot and sunny.

Grafting New Plants

1. Plants are ready for grafting when they're about 4 inches tall and have two sets of true leaves and a strong stem.

2. Match the individual scion with the rootstock plant that has the most similar diameter.

3. Cut off the top of the rootstock plant at a 45-degree angle, just below the cotyledons (the first leaf). Discard the top of the rootstock plant so it does not get confused for the scion.

4. Cut the top of the scion plant at a 45-degree angle at a location above the cotyledon that matches the diameter of the rootstock.

5. Set the cut pieces together and firmly hold them in place while you attach a grafting clip or wrap the union in grafting tape.

6. As quickly as possible, place the flat under a humidity tent and keep it in a dark place for approximately 1 week while the healing takes place. Keep flats between 65 and 80°F.

7. Check on the flat twice daily to make sure moisture remains on the side of the humidity tent. Spray with water as needed to maintain a high level of humidity. It is essential that grafted plants remain humid and warm throughout the healing process.

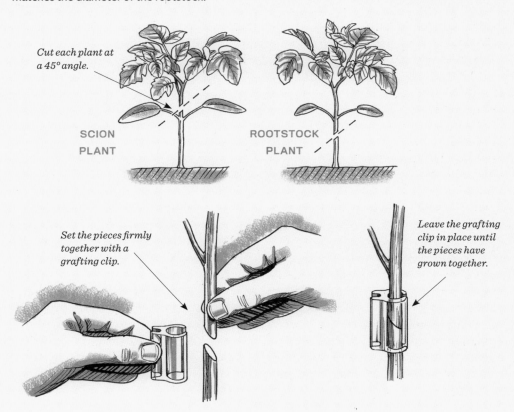

Cut each plant at a 45° angle.

SCION PLANT

ROOTSTOCK PLANT

Set the pieces firmly together with a grafting clip.

Leave the grafting clip in place until the pieces have grown together.

When seeds are germinating, it's essential that soil remain evenly moist until the plants have sprouted and begun developing a root system. Once plants have sprouted, allow the soil's surface to dry out a bit between waterings. Doing so will reduce pest and disease issues. Be wary of over- and under-watering! The goal is to keep the planting mix damp but not soaking wet — like a wrung-out sponge. Generally speaking, it's best to water flats before noon so the plants' foliage can dry off before dark.

Another technique is to bottom-water your flats once seeds have germinated. This allows you to keep water off of the new growth and deliver the water to the root zone more efficiently. Thanks to the wonders of capillary action, if your flat is set in a water-holding container, you can simply add water to this reservoir and let the water wick up into the soil from below. You can set each flat of plants in a solid-bottomed flat or plastic tub; on shallow plastic trays; or build a water-holding table.

Mature cuttings and grafted plants can be managed in much the same way as plants grown from seed. Once cuttings are potted up out of their initial root-out period, they can be watered from overhead or bottom watered.

Fertilizing

Proper nutrition for young plants is crucial, but it can be one of the more challenging aspects of nursery management. When plants germinate, they have a small store of nutrients that enable them to establish themselves as they begin searching for other nutrient supplies in the surrounding soil. Most germination mixes, including your own, should not contain high doses of granular fertilizers. High levels of fertilizer can reduce germination rates in sensitive seeds. Because fertilizers contain a variety of salts, excess amounts can affect the seed's ability to absorb water, potentially preventing germination entirely, so it's better to allow plants to germinate without fertilizers. Once the seedlings are up, then you can

Bottom watering is a good way to maintain consistent soil moisture in plug flats.

begin adding small amounts of fertilizer on a regular basis.

Because propagation containers are shallow and require frequent watering, nutrients leach much more quickly than they do in garden soil. Thus, frequent low doses of soluble fertilizer are much more effective than less-frequent doses at full concentration. Depending on the concentration of nutrients, plants can be fertilized every day (with very low doses), a few times a week, or just once a week.

If you pot up plants into larger containers, you can replace germination mix with a more nutrient-rich potting soil. This is a good time to mix in granular fertilizer. Be aware that it can be very easy to over-fertilize small pots with a granular fertilizer, so be judicious with your applications. Over-fertilization can lead to stress via salt buildup and can lead to fungal growth and damping-off. Consider applying a small amount of granular fertilizer

A hose-end sprayer works well for applying liquid fertilizer to young plants.

(or none at all) and continuing a routine of liquid fertilizer applications for the plants' entire nursery experience.

Cuttings and grafted plants should not be fertilized until they are out of the initial rooting phase and potted up. Plants are incredibly sensitive when undergoing the healing processes after cutting, and applications of any fertilizer is likely to cause much more harm than help.

To learn more about fertilizers and their applications, see page 203.

Potting Up Plants

The need to pot up plants depends on the specific crop, your climate, and the variables of the particular season. Many crops can be germinated in shallow flats (plug trays, soil blocks, open flats) and then moved directly into the garden. The most commonly potted-up plants are heat–loving and very cold-sensitive crops, such as tomatoes, peppers, and eggplant.

The standard nursery procedure is to germinate all crops in plug trays, choose the healthiest individuals from each variety for potting up, and graduate these to 4-inch pots or larger for continued indoor grow out. Almost any crop should be ready for outdoor planting directly from a 4-inch pot unless you start your crops incredibly early in the season, at which point potting up into gallon-size containers might be necessary or desired so that the plants can remain inside for a longer period without becoming root-bound and stressed. Depending on your climate, many crops can be planted directly from plug trays into the garden.

Hardening Off Transplants

Hardening off is the process of slowly acclimating your transplants to the stresses of the outdoor environment (cooler temperatures, direct sunlight, wind, and varying levels of soil moisture) so that they experience less shock when transplanted into the garden. Hardening off is most useful for transplants that have spent their entire lives in a temperature-controlled greenhouse. If transplants have been grown in an unheated cold frame, then they've already experienced low nighttime temperatures and will need less acclimating.

To harden off your plants, move them outdoors from the greenhouse or propagation area early in the morning or in the late afternoon/evening (avoid moving a plant from a greenhouse into direct sunlight at midday). If freezing temperatures are not a risk, you can leave the starts outside in their containers for about a week before transplanting into the garden. This will let them experience full sun and cooler nighttime temperatures (if nighttime temperatures do drop below freezing, you should bring the starts indoors overnight). Cut back a bit on watering to let the plants experience drier conditions (but don't let plants wilt or become water stressed).

There are many different theories about how gradually plants should be hardened off (or if it is even necessary at all). Some growers keep their plants in a shady area for

A cold frame can provide a protected space for growing out transplants.

the first few days and then move them into full sun; some bring the transplants indoors on the first few nights of the hardening-off process. In our experience in a variety of climates, simply getting the starts outside for about a week is plenty to harden them off for transplanting (additional coddling seems to be largely unnecessary).

Monitoring for Pests and Diseases

Greenhouses and indoor growing spaces can be prone to higher concentrations of pest and disease issues than outdoor spaces. Keeping your space clean and well ventilated will go a long way toward reducing or eliminating these problems. Whenever possible, open windows or vents for cross ventilation.

If fungal or disease issues arise, temporarily move the plants outside (weather permitting) and wipe down all surfaces with with a 10 percent solution of alcohol, bleach, or hydrogen peroxide. To make a 10 percent solution, mix one part of the sanitizing compound to nine parts water. Sticky traps and other low-tech pest catchers can also help keep persistent insect populations under control. Allowing the soil surface in your flats to dry out between waterings will reduce the possibility of insect breeding.

It is always good to know what issues might arise so you can quickly identify them if they do show up. Following is information about some of the most likely pests you may encounter in your greenhouse: whiteflies, aphids, thrips, and fungus gnats. Common greenhouse diseases include damping-off and botrytis. See page 231 for more information about using the following control techniques.

Insect Pests

Whiteflies. These are a common greenhouse pest. If you brush over a plant and a cloud of very tiny white insects poof up into the air, you have whiteflies. These insects slowly desiccate crops by sucking their sap. They're usually more annoying than harmful, but they can make plants more prone to disease problems. Sticky traps or soap spray is effective for killing them.

Aphids. These are tiny ($1/10$ of an inch long) pear-shaped bugs that hang out on the underside of leaves and suck the sap out of your crops. They can be a problem in the nursery and in the garden. If you see a leaf curling or looking anemic and yellow, check the underside for aphids. They are attracted to lush, green growth; if you have a serious infestation, it could be a sign that the plants are getting too much nitrogen, so cut back on your fertilizing. If aphids show up, you can carefully rinse them off your plants with a hose-end sprayer, or spray them with a soap spray. Moving nursery plants outside for several hours will sometimes dissipate early pest infestations.

Thrips. These are very difficult to see with the naked eye. Without the benefit of a magnifying glass, they look like tiny dots moving around on your crops. Silvery spots or streaks (sometimes with black spots of fecal matter) on plants are caused by thrips that scrape plant tissues and feed on their juices. Soap spray or neem works well for controlling them in the nursery.

Fungus gnats. These are black bugs similar in size and appearance to mosquitos. They're attracted to organic matter and moisture in your potting soil, and can often be seen hovering about the plants in a greenhouse. They don't cause much damage unless populations get out of control (they lay their eggs in the soil, and large numbers of larvae can damage plant roots). Keeping the greenhouse cleaned up and well ventilated helps limit the growth of these pests. Allowing the surface of the soil to dry out between each watering can significantly reduce their populations. Yellow sticky traps and pyrethrum-based organic insecticides kill them, and beneficial nematodes will kill their soil-dwelling larvae.

Diseases

Damping-off. This is a fungal disease that attacks the stem of young seedlings. The top part of the plant will tip over, and the stem will appear to be "chopped" through completely at the base, or may be black and rotted. Proper ongoing cleaning and sterilization of nursery equipment will help make sure this disease never becomes an issue. Adequate ventilation also goes a long way toward preventing this disease. Using a small amount of high-quality compost in your potting mix will also help control this disease because the compost provides a population of beneficial bacteria (these will compete with the damping-off fungus). If you see signs of damping-off, remove the affected plant or plants (burn diseased plants when possible or add to a hot compost pile), increase ventilation, and cut back on watering as much as possible. You can also try dusting cinnamon lightly on the soil around the rest of the plants, misting with a mild chamomile tea, or spraying neem oil. All of these have natural antifungal properties that can help combat the disease.

Botrytis. This is a fungal disease characterized by a gray fuzzy mold. It thrives in damp, cool conditions, and is often a problem for tomatoes and strawberries grown in high tunnels. It can also show up in minimally heated propagation areas. If you see signs of it, increase ventilation and consider using a fan to dry off foliage. If possible, raise the temperature in the propagation area above 75°F. Try spraying chamomile tea, a sulfur- or copper-based organic fungicide, or an organic spray that contains *Bacillus subtilis* (such as Serenade).

YEAR-ROUND NURSERY PRODUCTION

Now that you've set up a nursery or propagation area, why not use it as a year-round greens factory? Growing sprouts and microgreens is a great way to supplement what your garden produces and provides a steady flow of fresh greens during the winter months when your garden is less prolific. For the serious home food producer with an adaptable propagation space (or even just a kitchen counter), microgreens and sprouts can be worth their weight in greens.

Any crop that has a totally edible structure can be grown as a sprout. Obviously, you'll avoid nightshades and any other crop with potential toxins, but otherwise feel free to experiment with different salad greens and herbs. There is even a handful of unexpected crops like sunflowers and grains like wheat, buckwheat, and rye that can produce delicious winter greens.

Sprouting

There are dozens of commonly available seeds that are good candidates for sprouting. These include alfalfa, mustard, radish, and fenugreek. Motivated gardeners could collect enough seed from a few well-managed plantings of alfalfa and mustard to provide themselves with fresh sprouts through the winter months. Sprouts can be grown any time of year with minimal effort and space. If you are purchasing seed for sprouting, make sure the seed has not been treated with any fungicides or other chemicals. Many seed companies sell seeds that are labeled as "sprouting seeds." Sprouting seeds should not be treated and should be certified pathogen-free. Labeling requirements are somewhat vague on this, so check with your supplier to be sure.

What You'll Need

Glass containers. Depending on your scale of production, sprouts can be grown in quart-size mason jars or any larger glass container.

Sprouting lids. You can either purchase these or make them at home. The best lid will securely screw on to the top of a jar and provide a fine mesh screen that allows water to easily drain from the container but holds back small seeds.

Holding rack. You will need some sort of rack to support the upside-down jars so that they can drain effectively. Jars can be simply placed upside down in a bowl or set in a dish-drying rack near the kitchen sink.

How to Sprout

The technique for growing most sprout varieties is very similar: Simply measure a few teaspoons of seeds (or 1 cup for large seeds) per quart of container, fill the container with water, and let the seeds soak for 4 to 12 hours. The volume of seeds to use and how long they need to soak varies by crop. See the chart on page 180 for specific information on each crop.

Sprouting provides a source of fresh, nutrient-dense produce during winter months.

After soaking, drain the soaking water from the jar. Each day, fill the jar with water and quickly pour back out to rinse the sprouts (do this twice a day). Leave the jar upturned in a bowl or dishrack to drain. Sprouts can begin germinating in as little as 12 hours after soaking, but most take one to two days. Sprouts grow quickly, and after three to five days, most varieties of sprouts will fill their jar. The full jar should be placed in a refrigerator and be eaten within seven days.

When you're just starting out, we recommend sprouting two or three quart jars of sprouts per week (this volume presumes a household of one to three people). Make a schedule so that you can continue with your successions of sprouts each week to maintain a steady supply. Because of the quick turnaround time, it is easy to ramp production up or down based on your actual usage.

Microgreens

Growing microgreens is another great way to produce food year-round with a minimum of space and time. Microgreens are essentially sprouts that are propagated in a nursery flat on a bit of soil and allowed to grow until they put on tiny leaves (as the name suggests, microgreens are just very tiny salad greens). You can grow flats of edible greens, such as arugula, mesclun mix, mustards, or just about any other crop. Wheatgrass is typically grown as a microgreen and is used for making a healthful juice.

What You'll Need

Flats. Microgreens can be grown in virtually any tray or shallow container. We prefer to use standard nursery flats with a few small, bottom drainage holes. These containers retain some water, which helps keep the soil moist; however, it's important to avoid saturating the soil because that will drown the greens.

Soil mix. You can use potting soil, germination mix, or even straight garden soil as a medium for the greens. Plan to compost or dump the soil into the garden after use, as it will be full of miniature roots that need time and space to decompose. Fill each container with 1 to 2 inches of soil, which is about ½ of the depth of a standard flat.

Lighting. Microgreens can be grown with natural light or under any grow light. Supplemental light helps the plants grow more quickly and evenly, but amazing microgreens can be grown on a windowsill. Four to eight hours of supplemental light from your grow light system will make the greens grow faster and straighter.

How to Grow Microgreens

The quantity of seed needed for each flat of microgreens depends largely on the size of the seed itself. Generally, larger volumes of seed are needed for larger seeds, although the total number of seeds may be less. For example, a flat of the relatively large-seeded cilantro may use between 1 and 2 tablespoons per flat, whereas a smaller seed like mustard greens may use 1 teaspoon per flat. Use the chart on page 180 and your own personal trials to figure out the volume of seed that works best for you.

Microgreens are wonderfully easy to care for. They do not require any fertilization, although we do prefer to use a soil mix with compost so that the plants have access to some nutrients as they grow. We typically use overhead watering for flats of microgreens until they have germinated. Once they have emerged, we then switch to bottom watering. Bottom watering prevents the thin, tender sprouts from being knocked over and getting dirty.

After one to three weeks, depending on crop, temperature, and light levels, your microgreens should be ready to harvest. It's standard practice to cut them when they just begin to show their first true leaves (those that appear after the cotyledons), but you can cut them at any size you like.

When you're just starting out, we recommend sprouting between one and two flats of microgreens per week (presuming a household of one to three people). Make a schedule so you can seed flats once per week to maintain a steady supply. Because of the quick turnaround time, it is easy to ramp production up or down based on your actual useage.

An indoor nursery area can be used to produce delicious microgreens year round.

Crops for Sprouting and Microgreen Production

Many crops can be grown as sprouts and microgreens, but some are better suited to growing this way than others. For example, any brassica can be easily sprouted. However, broccoli and cauliflower seed are both more expensive and slower growing than mustard greens, so you may prefer to use mustard for sprouting and microgreens.

This chart contains our suggestions for the easiest and best crops for sprouts and microgreens. Some of these crops may be unfamiliar to you (like fenugreek) and others may be familiar (sesame, millet). Even though these are not typical vegetable crops for the home gardener, they are readily available at groceries and work well when creating delicious sprouting and microgreen mixes.

CROP	SPROUTING	MICROGREENS	QUANTITY OF SEED PER QUART JAR OF SPROUTS	QUANTITY OF SEED PER STANDARD FLAT OF MICROGREENS
ALFALFA	Y	Y	3 tablespoons	1.5 teaspoons
ALMONDS	Y		1 cup	
ARUGULA	Y	Y	3 tablespoons	1.5 teaspoons
BASIL		Y		1.5 teaspoons
BEANS, EDIBLE SOY (EDAMAME)	Y		1 cup	
BEANS, FAVA (BROAD)	Y		1 cup	
BEANS, LIMA	Y		1 cup	
BEANS, SHELL	Y		1 cup	
BEANS, SNAP	Y		1 cup	
BEETS		Y		1.5 tablespoons
BROCCOLI	Y	Y	3 tablespoons	1 teaspoon
BUCKWHEAT	Y		1 cup	
CABBAGE	Y	Y	3 tablespoons	1 teaspoon
CARROTS		Y		2 teaspoons
CELERY		Y		1.5 teaspoons
CHARD, SWISS		Y		1.5 teaspoons
CHICKPEAS	Y		1 cup	
CILANTRO		Y		1.5 tablespoons

CROP	SPROUTING	MICROGREENS	QUANTITY OF SEED PER QUART JAR OF SPROUTS	QUANTITY OF SEED PER STANDARD FLAT OF MICROGREENS
CLOVER	Y		3 tablespoons	
CORN, SWEET		Y		2 tablespoons
CRESS	Y	Y	3 tablespoons	1 teaspoon
DILL		Y		1.5 teaspoons
FENUGREEK	Y		½ cup	
KALE	Y	Y	3 tablespoons	1 teaspoon
LEEKS		Y		1 teaspoon
LENTILS	Y		1 cup	
LETTUCE, BABY MIX		Y		2 teaspoons
MILLET	Y		1 cup	
MUNG BEANS	Y		1 cup	
MUSTARD GREENS	Y	Y	3 tablespoons	1 teaspoon
OATS	Y		1 cup	
PARSLEY		Y		2 teaspoons
PEAS, SNAP	Y	Y	1 cup	¼ cup
PEPPERCRESS	Y	Y	3 tablespoons	1.5 teaspoons
PURSLANE		Y		2 teaspoons
RADISHES	Y	Y	1 tablespoon	1 tablespoon
RYE	Y		1 cup	
SCALLIONS		Y		1 teaspoon
SESAME	Y		1 cup	
SORREL		Y		1.5 teaspoons
SPREEN		Y		3 teaspoons
SQUASH, PUMPKIN	Y		1 cup	
SUNFLOWER	Y	Y	1 cup	2 tablespoons
TURNIPS	Y	Y	3 tablespoons	1 teaspoon
WATERCRESS	Y		3 tablespoons	
WHEAT	Y		1 cup	

CHAPTER 9

Transplanting and Direct Seeding in the Garden

All of your crops will be either transplanted or direct seeded into the garden. The particular method you use will depend on the growth habits of your crops, your climate, and your preferred management practices. Both methods require careful bed preparation, weather monitoring, and attention to detail.

Although transplanting requires much more work at the outset, compared to direct seeding, it can pay off because it reduces the amount of time you will spend thinning crops later on, and it avoids wasting valuable garden space on unhealthy specimens. Direct seeding, essential for many root crops, allows you to plant large areas of the garden quickly and can minimize the overall investment in easy-to-care-for crops like beans, peas, and salad greens.

CAREFUL TRANSPLANTING = PRODUCTIVE PLANTS

Transplants require a gentle transition from their containers into the garden bed. (You will especially appreciate their delicacy after having taken the time and effort to grow healthy seedlings.) If a plant is moved under stressful conditions, it may undergo serious "transplant shock." As a result, it may be unable to successfully send new roots into the soil. This can lead to wilting and stunted growth, and can even reduce the overall yield of the plant.

Prepare the Bed

Before bringing your plants to the garden, prepare the beds thoroughly, as described in chapter 5. Spread fertilizer (either broadcast it or add to individual planting holes), check the irrigation system for leaks, and set lines in the appropriate locations to help guide planting.

Many garden trowels are about 12" long, which makes them a great tool for spacing plants properly.

You can pre-dig holes for the transplants at the desired spacing, or you can remove the plants from their container and set them out on the bed at the desired spacing in preparation for transplanting. With some experience, you should be able to eyeball the spacing between plants pretty accurately. When starting out, or getting accustomed to new spacing, measure the distance between holes with a hand trowel or ruler.

Watch the Weather

Ideal transplanting conditions are overcast skies, relatively cool temperatures, and even a slight rain. Weather conditions like these will minimize transpiration (water loss from plant leaves), and soil moisture levels remain high enough to reduce damage to root systems and encourage quick new root growth. These conditions will reduce overall transplant shock and allow plants to more quickly transition back to healthy growth rates. If you have a lot of transplanting to do and the weather is hot and sunny, consider waiting a day or two if cool weather is in the forecast. If hot, dry weather is unavoidable, thoroughly water the garden soil and the starts before beginning transplanting. You can reduce heat stress to the plants by doing your transplanting early in the morning or in the evening.

Handle Transplants Gently

Crops tolerate a wide range of transplant conditions. The most tender plants tend to be cucurbits (squash, cucumbers, pumpkins) and legumes (beans, peas). When planting these sensitive crops, try to minimize disturbance to their roots as much as possible (pre-digging transplanting holes is ideal). Very carefully remove each plant

Tolerance of Root Disturbance

Some crops can tolerate (or even like) root disturbance at transplanting time. If you purchase a start in this category that has two or more plants in a single container, you can separate the plants by their roots and plant all of them. For crops that don't like root disturbance, snip all but one with scissors and transplant only the remaining plant.

Transplants That Can Tolerate Root Disturbance

- Basil
- Bok choy
- Broccoli
- Brussels sprouts
- Cabbage
- Cabbage, Chinese
- Cauliflower
- Celery
- Chard, Swiss
- Collards
- Eggplant
- Endive
- Fennel, Bulbing
- Kale
- Kohlrabi
- Leeks
- Lettuce (heads)
- Mâche
- Okra
- Onions, Bulb
- Parsley
- Peppers, Hot
- Peppers, Sweet
- Raab
- Radicchio
- Scallions
- Spinach
- Sweet potatoes
- Tomatillos
- Tomatoes

Transplants That Don't Tolerate Root Disturbance

- Beans, Edible soy (edamame)
- Beans, Fava (broad)
- Beans, Lima
- Beans, Shell
- Beans, Snap
- Corn, Sweet
- Cucumbers
- Dill
- Melon, Cantaloupe, Honeydew
- Peas, Shelling
- Peas, Snap
- Squash, Gourds
- Squash, Pumpkins
- Squash, Summer
- Squash, Winter
- Watermelon

Crops That Should Not Be Purchased as Transplants

- Arugula
- Beets
- Carrots
- Celeriac
- Cilantro
- Garlic
- Lettuce (baby mix)
- Mustard greens
- Parsnips
- Peanut
- Potatoes
- Radishes
- Rutabagas
- Turnips

Use scissors to thin starts that don't like root disturbance before transplanting them.

from its container, gently place it into the prepared hole, cover the roots with soil, gently compress the soil to help stabilize the plant, and immediately water it.

Brassicas, lettuce, and nightshades are much tougher. Some growers even intentionally disturb the roots of brassicas at transplanting time to encourage the development of new roots. To do this, tear the roots gently with your hands.

Water Well

It is important to water transplants as quickly as possible. This reduces the amount of time the roots are exposed to air. Watering the soil after the plant is in place settles the soil around the root tips and protects them. Consider watering in the plants with a low dose (typically ½ of a regular dose) of liquid high-phosphorus organic fertilizer (2-4-2 or something similar). See page 203 for more information on organic fertilization.

After watering in the transplants, go around the bed and finger test the soil for moisture near a few different plants. To finger test, simply put your pointer finger down into the soil up to the knuckle. The soil should be evenly moist all the way to this depth. If you feel dry space with your finger, continue watering the transplants until the soil is evenly moist on every finger test.

DIRECT SEEDING

Direct seeding — planting the seeds of a crop directly into your garden beds — is a very efficient way to get a crop started. It requires much less time up front, and an entire bed of crops can be planted in just a few minutes (though it can require more work later on to establish the crop and maintain it).

Making an appropriate choice between direct seeding and transplanting can greatly affect your yields. This choice is affected by many variables, including the space you have available in your garden (and nursery, if you have one), your general climate and microclimate, the conditions in your garden, and the crops you're growing. Many professional growers use both methods to plant the same crop at different times of the season. For example, in areas with cool spring weather, growers might transplant their first planting of summer squash to ensure a solid stand and good early growth when the soil is cold, and then direct seed the second and third plantings when the soil has warmed enough for good germination. Consider the benefits and drawbacks of direct seeding when making such choices.

Large-seeded crops such as peas are easy to direct seed by hand.

Planting at Different Depths

In most cases, the root mass of the transplant should be buried just below the surface of the soil in the bed. If the top of the root mass is not covered with soil, exposed root tips will be damaged and the entire root mass may dry out through evaporation. However, even though the roots should be completely covered, the stem of the transplant should be left exposed to minimize the chance of stem rot. There are several notable exceptions to this planting technique:

Brassicas. You can bury brassica stems without worrying about stem rot. In fact, young brassicas are notorious for their fragile stems, and burying the base of the plant up to the level of the first true leaves actually helps stabilize the plant in the soil.

Alliums. The stem and leaf portions of most alliums are planted deeply into the soil when transplanted. Bury leek stems 6 to 9 inches deep into the soil to help blanch them. The result should be a larger and more tender harvest. The same technique can be applied to bulbing onions and scallions. The majority of the young plant can be buried, though the top 3 to 4 inches of the plant should be above-ground so that it can continue photosynthesizing.

Tomatoes. A tomato plant will set roots from any portion of its stem that comes into contact with the soil. To take advantage of this vigorous rooting mechanism, remove the lowest sets of leaves from the transplant and bury the stem in the soil. You can bury the plant up to the top two sets of leaves. Some growers prefer to dig a shallow trench and bury the stem sideways in the soil, turning up the tip of

Burying brassica stems

Planting alliums

the plant above the soil. This technique keeps more of the root mass at a shallow depth where the soil is warmer, but it also carries the risk of breakage during planting because the stems are quite fragile.

Potatoes. Potatoes are planted from "seed potatoes." Seed potatoes are just healthy, disease-free individual potatoes from last year's harvest that are planted to grow a new crop. A single seed potato can produce up to 10 pounds of new tubers in a season. Plant small seed potatoes whole; cut larger ones into pieces to extend the planting stock. If you cut your seed potatoes, aim for a weight of 1 ounce per cut

piece. Each piece must have a healthy looking eye (this is where the new potato vine emerges).

Potatoes can be planted at virtually any depth, but deeper is typically better. To plant potatoes, do not initially cover the seed potato with any more than 4 inches of soil. As the vine grows, you can continue to add soil over the top of the plant as long as you leave the growing tip exposed to the sunlight. The more of the vine that is buried, the more tubers the plant will produce.

One way to plant potatoes is to dig a trench in the bed and leave the excavated soil in

mounds alongside the trench. Bury the seed potato in the trench under 4 inches of soil. Make sure the eye points upward when you place the piece in the planting hole or trench. Continue to add soil from the mound as the vine grows, until it reaches ground level and the soil is flat. Alternatively, you can plant the potato shallowly in a container and add soil as the plant grows. You can use any container that will hold soil, including stacks of straw bales, trash cans with drainage holes, or stacks of burlap bags.

Trenching a tomato

Trenching potatoes

Benefits of Direct Seeding

- Plant management in a propagation area is not needed, thus reducing the time, materials, cost, and attention needed to get the crop under way.

- Ability to rely on rain to keep seeds moist during germination.

- With sufficient rain or an irrigation system, crops need very little care during their early weeks of growing.

Drawbacks of Direct Seeding

- Increased weed pressure when the plants are young and most difficult to weed around.

- Attack from insects when the plants are young, and the likelihood that young plants will be severely affected or killed by such damage.

- The need to thin the plants to achieve desired spacing.

- The possibility of low germination rates due to the whims of nature (abnormally cold days, lack of rain, and so on).

- Slower germination rates in cool soil conditions.

Which Crops to Direct Seed

Certain crops grow best when they're direct seeded:

Root crops. Typically, it is a best practice to direct seed root crops — including beets, carrots, parsnips, radishes, and turnips. Root crops have been bred to grow substantial roots (your food source) at the expense of robust aboveground growth. Because these plants are root focused, transplanting can be stressful to them, and can lead to delayed or stunted growth, reduction in harvest, or death.

Baby greens. When growing *individual plants* for greens (head lettuce, frisée), it is helpful to grow them from transplants. However, when growing closely spaced, densely seeded crops like baby lettuce, baby arugula, braising mix, spring mix, and most other loose-leaf (cutting) greens, they'll produce best and be easiest to manage when they are direct seeded into the garden.

Cucurbits. Crops with very sensitive root systems, such as cucurbits (squash, cucumbers, pumpkins, melons) grow well when direct seeded. Assuming weather conditions are suitable, direct seeding these crops will eliminate the possibility of transplant shock and stunted growth. In many climates, unfortunately, the growing season is not long enough for direct-seeded cucurbits to reach maturity. In these locations, transplanting provides the solution. Take extra care when transplanting these crops into the garden. Consider growing them in soil blocks or peat pots to help reduce handling during the transplanting process. However, don't be afraid to grow these crops in your preferred transplanting containers; just be sure to handle them carefully.

Starting Indoors for Greater Success

For crops that can either be direct seeded or started indoors, we often prefer to start them indoors if nursery space is not a limiting factor. We find that plants are more successful when started in a controlled environment, pampered for several weeks, and then placed into the garden at the ideal spacing required for maximum production.

We are mindful that in regions with short growing seasons, many crops (like tomatoes) must be transplanted so that they have enough time to grow to maturity before cold weather halts their production. Typically, any crop that has a lifecycle longer than (or nearly as long as) your growing season should be started indoors or purchased as a transplant.

Tips for Successful Direct Seeding

Direct seeding crops proficiently is a fine art. By taking the time to properly prepare for and manage these plantings, you can dramatically increase germination rates, improve plant health, and save yourself tons of time and effort later in the season.

Create a fine seedbed. Create an environment that will make the seed's life easy from day one. As a seed germinates and begins to push roots down and send up a shoot toward the sky, large soil particles, chunks of wood, or small rocks can create physical barriers to root and stem development. So, before you sow, smooth and flatten the surface of your garden bed and remove large particles (or break them up into small pieces). If your soil is particularly clumpy or dense, you can sprinkle germination mix or a screened soil mix over the top of a newly sown crop.

Create a stale seedbed. Prepare your seedbed several weeks before you plan to direct seed your crop. Loosening the soil and irrigating the bed ahead of planting will encourage existing weed seeds to germinate. This will give you the opportunity to clear these weeds quickly and easily without worrying about disturbing your young crops. Prepare the bed, wait two weeks, cultivate the bed thoroughly, direct seed your crop, and enjoy lower weed pressure. This technique is especially useful with slow-germinating crops like carrots or parsnips.

Sow at the optimum soil temperature for each crop. All seeds have an ideal soil temperature range for good germination. Soil that is too cold may rot seeds before they have the chance to sprout. Soil that is too warm may kill seeds that are sensitive to higher temperatures. Your seed packet and seed catalog should indicate the ideal germination temperature for your crop (also see page 56). You can use your finger to test soil temperatures, though a soil thermometer will give you a more accurate reading.

Measure Soil Temperature

A soil thermometer is an inexpensive tool that can really help you keep track of real-time soil conditions. A soil thermometer provides information that can help you adjust planting schedules and monitor growth rates through the season. Different crops require different soil temperatures for germination, and using a soil thermometer will allow you to adapt your seeding schedule based on actual measurements, rather than a finger test or calendar dates.

Irrigate your garden bed on planting day. Unless the soil is already moist, plan to irrigate prior to direct seeding. Moistening the soil will settle it slightly. This helps the seeds to stay in place when you water them after planting. Water the bed, plant your seeds, cover with soil, and water the area again.

Monitor soil moisture as seeds germinate. Because most seeds are planted very shallowly in the soil, they are at risk of drying out during the germination process. As the sun hits your beds, the top ¼ inch of soil (where most seeds are located) can dry out very quickly. Even if the majority of the soil remains moist, a dry upper crust can wreak havoc on germination rates. Plan to overhead water newly seeded crops with sprinklers or by hand on a regular schedule until they have fully germinated (unless your garden is receiving regular and adequate rainfall).

Date your planting. Noting the planting date on the plant tag and in your records allows you to keep an eye on the rate of germination. If a crop is expected to pop up in five to seven days but no growth is seen in two weeks, you can reseed the crop right away without losing too many growing days. If you seed a crop and fail to monitor its days to germination, it will be difficult to know if the seeds are still viable or if the area should be replanted.

Plant an appropriate quantity of seeds. There's a fine balance between under-seeding and over-seeding. Too many seeds create crowding and makes thinning difficult. By contrast, under-seeding results in sparse plantings that need to be reseeded or that fail entirely. Even though a seed packet might indicate that a crop has a very high germination rate, keep in mind that this rate is applicable only to ideal conditions. In an outdoor real-time application, germination rates will be much lower. The seeding thickness and spacing will be different for every crop, but plan to seed at least two to three times as many plants as you want to harvest.

Seed in an orderly arrangement. Most crops are easiest to direct seed in rows or in other geometric arrangements. Keeping rows straight makes cultivating between and around crops much easier. Seeding directly along drip lines also increases

When to Broadcast Seed

An alternative seeding technique for closely spaced crops is called broadcasting. This is the practice of sprinkling seeds over a given square footage of a bed, and then raking or mixing them gently into the soil with the flat of your hand. This is a useful technique for planting baby salad greens such as lettuce mix or arugula because you can utilize the entire surface area of a bed for the crop. It's also useful for planting small-seeded cover crops. We don't recommend this technique for other vegetable crops because it's difficult to manage seeding depth and makes weeding very difficult.

germination rates and makes sure all parts of the planting receive adequate water throughout the season.

For closely spaced crops, try making a furrow (tiny trench) at the desired seeding depth of the crop you're planting, and sprinkle seeds at the desired rate into it. You can then firm soil over the furrow and water everything in. For example, carrots might be planted in ¼-inch deep furrows at two or three seeds per inch, with furrows spaced 6 inches apart.

For widely spaced crops like pumpkins or summer squash, place seeds directly into the ground at the desired spacing, and cover with soil to the desired depth. For example, you might place three cucumber seeds 1 inch deep in the ground every 2 feet in a bed.

Protect seeds as needed. Seeds and newly sprouted plants are particularly sensitive to pest damage. A single bite from an insect on a day-old plant may kill it. Similarly, birds have been known to swoop in and eat up a planting of direct-seeded crops before they have even had the chance to germinate. If you expect or are concerned about the intrusion of a certain pest, take preventive actions. Depending on local pests and the crop, this may include adding beneficial nematodes, covering seeds with floating row cover or bird netting, adding organic slug bait, applying diatomaceous earth, or putting out rodent traps.

Thin Your Direct-Seeded Plantings

We believe that in the home vegetable garden, where space is always at a premium, over-seeding crops and thinning — culling plants to allow adequate room for each maturing crop — is the most efficient way to use bed space and increases overall yield from the garden. Of course, this requires that you actually follow through on thinning the crops. Refer to the crop spacing chart on page 36 to determine the appropriate distance between any two plants of a particular crop.

Thinning is a relatively time-intensive activity, but it is very straightforward. Begin at one end of the row or planting, and work your way toward the other end by removing the extra plants. If you've accidentally overseeded, you may end up removing dozens or even hundreds of plants. (Keep in mind that, depending on the crop, you may be able to eat the thinning. So instead of lamenting the crops that could have been, be thankful for an especially early harvest.)

If the seeding is particularly thick, or if you want to make sure you have enough viable plants after thinning, consider thinning in two distinct passes. Once the crops have germinated and are tall enough to be easily distinguished and separated, thin the row to one-half of the eventual mature spacing. Two weeks later, make a second pass to thin to the final spacing. For example, if planting beets, the final spacing between plants should be 4 inches. On the first thinning, remove enough plants so each remaining beet is spaced 2 inches apart. On the second thinning, remove plants to achieve the final 4-inch spacing.

Direct Sow or Transplant?

ANNUAL VEGETABLES AND HERBS

ARUGULA	DS			LETTUCE, BABY MIX	DS		
BASIL	B			LETTUCE, HEADS	TP	E	B
BEANS, EDIBLE SOY (EDAMAME)	E			MÂCHE	TP	E	B
BEANS, FAVA (BROAD)	DS	E		MELON, CANTALOUPE, HONEYDEW	TP	E	B
BEANS, LIMA	E			MUSTARD GREENS	DS	E	B
BEANS, SHELL	E	B		OKRA	TP	E	B
BEANS, SNAP	E	B		ONIONS, BULB	TP		
BEETS	DS			PARSLEY	TP	E	B
BOK CHOY	TP	E	B	PARSNIPS	DS		
BROCCOLI	TP	E	B	PEANUT	TP	E	B
BRUSSELS SPROUTS	TP	E	B	PEAS, SHELLING	TP	E	B
CABBAGE	TP	E	B	PEAS, SNAP	TP	E	B
CABBAGE, CHINESE	TP	E	B	PEPPERS, HOT	TP		
CARROTS	DS			PEPPERS, SWEET	TP		
CAULIFLOWER	TP	E	B	POTATOES	DS		
CELERIAC	TP			RAAB	TP	E	B
CELERY	TP			RADICCHIO	TP	E	B
CHARD, SWISS	TP	E	B	RADISHES	DS		
CILANTRO	DS			RUTABAGAS	DS		
COLLARDS	TP	E	B	SCALLIONS	TP	E	B
CORN, SWEET	E			SPINACH	TP	E	B
CUCUMBERS	TP	E	B	SQUASH, GOURDS	TP	E	B
DILL	TP	E	B	SQUASH, PUMPKINS	TP	E	B
EGGPLANT	TP			SQUASH, SUMMER	TP	E	B
ENDIVE	TP	E	B	SQUASH, WINTER	TP	E	B
FENNEL, BULBING	TP	E	B	SWEET POTATOES	TP		
GARLIC	DS			TOMATILLOS	TP	E	B
KALE	TP	E	B	TOMATOES	TP		
KOHLRABI	TP	E	B	TURNIPS	DS		
LEEKS	TP	E	B	WATERMELON	TP	E	B

PERENNIAL VEGETABLES

ARTICHOKE	TP		
ASPARAGUS	TP		
CARDOON	TP	E	B
JERUSALEM ARTICHOKE, SUNCHOKE	DS		
RHUBARB	TP		

When transplanting a perennial, you may be using a whole plant, cutting, crown, root pieces, or bulb

PERENNIAL GARDEN FRUITS

BLACKBERRIES	TP
BLUEBERRIES	TP
CURRANT	TP
ELDERBERRY	TP
GOJI BERRY	TP
GOOSEBERRY	TP
HUCKLEBERRY	TP
JOSTABERRY	TP
LINGONBERRY	TP
RASPBERRIES	TP
STRAWBERRIES	TP
WINTERGREEN	TP

Most fruit and nut trees are best transplanted.

PERENNIAL HERBS

ANISE HYSSOP	TP	DS
BAY	TP	DS
CHIVES	TP	DS
CHIVES, GARLIC	TP	DS
FENNEL	TP	DS
HORSERADISH	TP	
LAVENDER	TP	
LEMON BALM	TP	
LEMONGRASS	TP	
LEMON VERBENA	TP	
MARJORAM	TP	
MINT	TP	
OREGANO	TP	
PURPLE CONEFLOWER	TP	
ROSEMARY	TP	
SAFFRON	TP	
SAGE	TP	
SAVORY, WINTER	TP	
SORREL	TP	DS
STEVIA	TP	
TARRAGON	TP	
TEA, CAMELLIA	TP	
THYME	TP	
VALERIAN	TP	DS

TP: *Transplant*

DS: *Direct seed*

E: *Either*

B: *Both; transplant early successions and direct seed later successions*

For plants listed specifically "TP, E, B," we suggest starting these indoors and transplanting to the garden, especially early in the season. This does not mean the crop cannot also be direct seeded, however. If you prefer, these crops can be direct seeded or you can plant each way.

MULCHING AT PLANTING TIME

Mulching is a great way to minimize weeding. Mulching also lessens moisture evaporation from the soil (in fact, with mulching you may be able to reduce irrigation needs by 50 to 80 percent, depending on your climate). Mulching also prevents erosion during periods of heavy rainfall and helps regulate soil temperatures. Mulching in the garden generally works best with transplanted or widely spaced crops.

For ease of application, consider spreading the mulch first, then making holes in it for setting transplants or direct seeding. If you use drip irrigation, lay the lines underneath the mulch. With transplants, you can water in the crop and then immediately pull the mulch back around the plant stem. With seeds, wait until the plant germinates and grows a bit before pulling the mulch back around the stem.

Here are a few cautionary notes on mulch:

- Mulch increases moisture levels and decreases airflow around the base of plants, so it could make any fungal problems worse. If your garden has had problems with damping-off in the past, wait to spread mulch until later in the season when the plants are well established.

- Avoid in-season mulching for closely spaced direct-seeded crops like lettuce mix and carrots.

- Mulch provides a great habitat for slugs and other dark- and damp-loving insects, so its use may not be appropriate if you have problems with these critters in your garden.

- Most mulching materials contain a lot of carbon, so it's best to not mix them into the soil unless they're very well broken down at the end of the growing season or winter. Consider raking them off before you plant and composting them instead. If you've used mulch during the growing season and it's still in good condition, you can leave it in place for winter protection.

- Avoid using bark mulch, sawdust, and wood chips on beds. Their high carbon content means that as they decompose they can tie up nitrogen when they're mixed into the soil the following year. They can also be difficult to rake off beds at planting time.

For ease of transplanting, spread mulch first and then make holes, through which you can plant your starts.

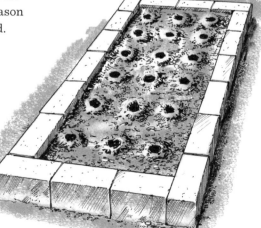

Mulches for the Growing Season

Compost
Mulching with compost mid-season supplies nutrients to your crops as precipitation passes through it.

Grass clippings
Don't let it contact plant stems directly as it can get hot during decomposition.

Shredded hardwood leaves
Can be left on the soil over the winter and turned into the soil in the spring to add organic matter and nutrients.

Plastic mulch
Helps warm soil and prevent weeds (though it can be a chore to remove in the fall).

Landscape fabric
Works well for weed prevention. Can be reused from year to year. Try laying it first, then cutting holes at appropriate spacing for transplants.

Rolled burlap or burlap sacks
An effective mulch, but can be difficult to lay in between plants. Don't turn these into the soil; instead, store and reuse them the following year.

Straw
Use a thick layer (4–6 inches). Avoid turning into the soil in the spring so as not to tie up nitrogen; instead, rake off remaining mulch and compost, or reapply when crops begin to mature. Whether or not your straw supplier is certified organic, it's important to verify that the straw you're buying was not sprayed with herbicides. Chemical herbicides can persist for some time, and unwittingly adding them to your garden via straw may lead to years of germination and crop health problems.

It is also essential that the straw not have seed heads. Adding straw with seeds can create a much more intense weed problem than the one you were trying to solve.

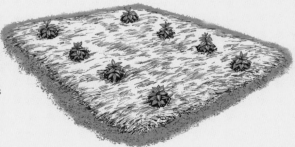

LEFT: Plastic mulch is an effective way to keep weeds down and warm up the soil for heat-loving crops.
RIGHT: Straw mulch suppresses weeds, moderates soil temperature, and conserves moisture.

SETTING UP SUPPORTS

Planting time is the best point to set up whatever trellises and other support systems you'll be using. Having the supports ready to use at this time will prevent disturbing the plants later on and will make it is easier to direct plants onto trellis. Plant stems can be floppy and fragile, so attempting to redirect them forcefully while they're growing is asking for trouble.

Often, though, plants will need some assistance locating and climbing a trellis. Keep an eye on your crops as they grow. Help them locate the structure and guide them upward as much as necessary. Don't hesitate to redirect an errant branch or tie them loosely to the structure with twine if needed.

Many of your crops won't need any additional support, but tall and vining crops may be much healthier and productive if properly supported. A little bit of extra help can likewise keep shorter crops from falling over if they have strange growth forms or heavy loads of fruit. Trellised and supported crops will benefit from a number of improvements in their living conditions. In general, trellises:

- Provide better air circulation, which helps to reduce the prevalence of pests and diseases

- Keep the fruit off the ground, reducing damage from ground-dwelling insects and animals such as mice and rats

- Allow for better sun exposure on more of the plant's leaves

- Give branches support, preventing them from breaking because of the weight of fruit or movement

- Help utilize space more efficiently; growing vertically allows you to grow more food in the same amount of space

- Improve the appearance of your garden — tall, well-managed crops add a unique structure and beauty to vegetable beds

Types of Supports

Some trellises can be easily built with common household materials (twine, wire, and so on). Others may require pre-fabricated structures (tomato cages, lattice, and the like). You may even want to purchase building materials and make your own. Creating a beautiful, functional trellis from materials found at a hardware store or plant nursery is entirely possible.

Twine for Large Numbers of Crops

You can create a simple trellis for tomatoes, pole beans, cucumbers, or any other vining crop when you attach a string of twine to an overhead structure. Tie the piece of twine to the sturdy overhead structure and loop the other end loosely around the base of your plant.

We find that this is a very cost-effective solution when trellising large numbers of vining crops. As a bonus, the twine can be cut down and composted along with the plants at the end of the season, reducing both the workload and the off-season trellis storage needs. The disadvantage is that crops will need ongoing assistance to make sure they stay on course and remain connected to or wrapped around the twine. Mid-season maintenance can be quite serious, but it has the benefit of forcing you to keep plants pruned and managed so that harvesting is a breeze.

UPPER LEFT: Twine trellises are a cost-effective way to train large numbers of vining crops.

UPPER RIGHT: Single stake trellises work well for tomatoes and encourage good pruning habits.

LOWER: A-frame trellises are a sturdy option for aggressive crops like winter squash.

Cages for Decreased Maintainence

Metal cages have long been used to support tomatoes, but you can also use them to trellis other crops like cucumbers, winter squash, and tomatillos. Cages come in different sizes, so be sure to check the mature height of your crop and select cages accordingly. Many gardeners prefer to build their own cages from hog wire or mesh fencing. Such custom structures are often sturdier than the store-bought kind.

The advantage of using cages is that there is virtually no ongoing training or manipulation of the vines once they are growing and attached to the structure. Mid-season plant maintenance is also quicker, as compared to a twine trellis. The downside is that these can take up a ton of storage space when not in use. In addition, finding and harvesting ripe fruits can be more of a challenge in a cage system.

Single Stakes for Simplicity

Consider using a short stake to support fruiting plants like peppers and eggplant. You can use wooden stakes, metal fence posts, rebar, or even branches from a tree. Size the stake according to the mature height of the crop and use twine to loosely tie the plant to the stake as it grows. Because these supports are minimally invasive, you can also use them to prop up any plant that starts flopping over in mid-season. This sort of ongoing trellising work will help keep plants off the ground, protect harvests, and simplify other maintenance tasks (like weeding). A few minutes of staking will save much more time down the road.

A-Frames for Aggressive Tendrils

An A-frame trellis will provide a sturdy structure for heavy, vining crops. Use this type of trellis for winter squash, cucumbers, peas, or beans. A simple ladder trellis can be built by creating a rectangular frame using 2 × 2-foot lumber and attaching wire mesh or garden netting to its face. We find these trellises particularly effective for crops with aggressive tendrils. Because of the sloped nature of the structure, once the plant has located the trellis they usually form tidy and attractive plantings. Harvesting from these structures is handy because fruits are easily visible above and below the mesh.

Doubling Up Crops with Tipi Trellises

Tipis have traditionally been used to grow pole beans, but they can be adapted to support any vining crop. A tipi can be built using bamboo poles, wooden poles, plastic poles, or whatever other tall, straight material you can locate. Tipi trellises are usually made with three or four poles, but you can use as many as you like. Push the base of each pole into the soil, and use twine or wire to tie the tops of the poles together. Consider planting a fast-growing crop such as lettuce mix or arugula in the center of the tipi to utilize this otherwise wasted space. Tipi trellises are inexpensive, easy to store in the off-season, and very sturdy.

Netting (and More) for Easy Setup

Any existing or newly built fence can serve as a structure for garden plants. You can use garden netting, twine, lattice, or hardware cloth to create a surface for plants to work up. If there isn't a fence in your garden, you can use a garden net (usually made from nylon rope or plastic) to create a fence-like trellis in the garden. Netting is inexpensive and easy to set up: simply place a support every three to four feet and tie the net to the support in as many spots as necessary to ensure that it stays up. Grow peas or beans between two sets of netting or use twine to help keep plants securely on the structure as they mature. This is a particularly useful technique when you're managing large plantings of vining crops. It is space efficient, easy to set up, and easy to manage.

Hilling

Some plants benefit simply from having soil hilled around their bases. Hilling can be especially effective for broccoli, kale, and other brassicas that have relatively shallow root systems and irregularly shaped stems. Hilling is also an effective way to keep bush beans from falling over and to bury the sprawling vines of your potatoes. To create a hill, simply mound soil around the base of a plant to support its stem.

Best Supports for Individual Crops

ANNUAL VEGETABLES	SUPPORT
BASIL	Hilling, single stake
BEANS, BUSH	Hilling, single stake
BEANS, FAVA	Hilling, single stake
BEANS, POLE	Cage, fence, frame, net, twine, tipi
BROCCOLI	Hilling, single stake
BRUSSELS SPROUTS	Hilling, single stake
COLLARDS	Hilling, single stake
CUCUMBERS	Cage, fence, frame, net, twine, tipi
EGGPLANT	Hilling, single stake
KALE	Hilling, single stake
MELON, CANTALOUPE, HONEYDEW	Cage, fence, frame, net, twine, tipi
OKRA	Hilling, single stake
PEAS, SHELLING	Cage, fence, frame, net, twine, tipi
PEAS, SNAP	Cage, fence, frame, net, twine, tipi
PEPPERS, HOT	Hilling, single stake
PEPPERS, SWEET	Hilling, single stake
SQUASH, GOURDS	Cage, fence, frame, net, twine, tipi
SQUASH, PUMPKINS	Cage, fence, frame, net, twine, tipi

ANNUAL VEGETABLES	SUPPORT
SQUASH, WINTER	Cage, fence, frame, net, twine, tipi
SUNFLOWER	Cage, single stake
TOMATILLOS	Cage, single stake
TOMATOES	Cage, fence, frame, net, twine, tipi
WATERMELON	Cage, fence, frame, net, twine, tipi

PERENNIAL VEGETABLES	SUPPORT
ARTICHOKE	Cage, single stake
ASPARAGUS	Cage, single stake
CARDOON	Cage, single stake
JERUSALEM ARTICHOKE, SUNCHOKE	Cage, single stake

PERENNIAL FRUITS	SUPPORT
BLACKBERRIES	Permanent trellis structure
RASPBERRIES	Permanent trellis structure

PART 3

Getting the Most from Any Garden Space

CHAPTER 10

Getting the Most from Every Plant

Once your crops are in the ground, you still have some work to do to maximize your yields. To get the highest production from each crop, you need to make sure its specific needs are being met until the point of harvest. Every crop has different fertility and cultural requirements, and taking the time to learn what they are and take action to meet them will help you get more out of your garden.

Some techniques are easy to learn and apply to a wide range of crops, and some are very specific to only a few crops. Of particular importance is the appropriate use of organic fertilizers. Almost every crop can benefit from increased fertility, and organic fertilizers can help you deal with nutrient and mineral imbalances immediately, while slowly building mineral reserves at the same time. And although pruning is usually associated with fruit trees, a wide range of annual crops are more productive when pruned selectively.

Effective garden management techniques will increase your harvests and make more efficient use of your time. Learning the skills in this chapter will help you get the most out of your high-yield garden.

STRATEGIES FOR FERTILIZING

Vegetable crops are needy plants. Even the lightest feeders need many more nutrients than the average ornamental plant in your landscape. Humus-rich soil and ideal conditions can sometimes supply all the nutrients vegetable crops need, but not always.

Crop-Specific Fertilizing

Since conditions usually aren't ideal, you'll need to use organic fertilizer to boost the nutrients in the soil. When temperatures are cold, for example, plants have difficulty taking up phosphorus. Using a high-phosphorus organic fertilizer during early spring planting will help to ensure the plants get all they need. Heavy feeders such as tomatoes, cucumbers, and winter squash often need more nitrogen than is available in the soil. A high-nitrogen organic fertilizer will help these crops remain vigorous through the season.

If you're growing multiple crops in one plot over the course of the season, or growing heavy-feeding crops, organic fertilizers are often required to keep nutrient levels high enough for good production. As you fine-tune your soil management over time, you may be able to minimize or even eliminate the need for additional organic fertilizers. In most cases, however, fertilizing will remain an important part of your soil fertility plan.

Using Slow-Release *and* Soluble Fertilizers

Generally speaking, the nutrients in organic fertilizers are not immediately available to your crops — these nutrients must be broken down by soil bacteria first and then become available slowly over a period of time. Because of this, organic fertilizers are often referred to as insoluble or "slow release." The slow breakdown rate is one of the great benefits of organic fertilizers (especially granular products) — there is less risk of losing soluble nutrients to leaching or off-gassing, and the plants can actually absorb and use the nutrients provided to them.

Unfortunately, you can't supply all of the nutrients your crops need in a soluble form at one time, but you can make soil management a top priority. Use compost and granular fertilizer before planting, then follow up with solubles. Note that blood meal can supply your plants with a shot of soluble nitrogen, along with a longer-lasting supply of insoluble nitrogen (blood meal can contain anywhere from 1 to 6 percent soluble nitrogen, depending on how it's processed).

Giving Plants a Quick Boost

Your plants might need a quick boost if they're experiencing nutrient deficiencies. Water-soluble nutrients found in liquid organic fertilizer are available to plants almost immediately upon application. Water-soluble nutrients can help reduce transplant shock at planting time and can help quickly turn around a crop that is showing visible signs of nutrient deficiency. If a long-season crop like a tomato or squash is stunted or showing discoloration, the addition of a liquid fertilizer can save the planting and get the plant back on track for an abundant harvest. Shorter-season crops may be less salvageable once showing visible signs of nutrient stress, but scheduled applications of liquid nutrients can help prevent nutrient stress in virtually any annual crop.

Foliar Feeding

Foliar feeding — providing nutrients to plants through their foliage — can give your crops a quick boost. Surprisingly, plants can take up nutrients very quickly and effectively through the stomata, or cell openings, on their leaves (even more than they can from their roots). However, it's not possible for plants to take up *large* amounts of nutrients this way.

Many growers apply foliar sprays at the onset of fruiting. Fruiting requires significant nutrient deployment, and a quickly absorbable feed can help plants stay healthy and improve overall yields. The timing of foliar feeding applications is crucial: applying foliar feeds in full sun can be damaging to the plant. We suggest waiting for a cloudy day, or applying sprays very early in the day (before eight o'clock in the morning).

Almost any organic liquid fertilizer can be used for foliar feeding, but it must be diluted as labeled to prevent burning the foliage. (See page 206 for our General Purpose Foliar Feed Recipe.) The fertilizer should be applied to the leaves in a fine mist. A hand pump sprayer such as those made by Solo work well for small applications; backpack sprayers are more efficient for spraying a larger space.

Apply the diluted fertilizer until you just start to see liquid dripping from the leaves. Adding a surfactant such as molasses or yucca extract will help the fertilizer adhere to the plant so that all of the nutrients can be absorbed. The most effective place to foliar feed is on the bottom of leaves. Most vegetable crops have the majority of their stomata (pores) on the undersides of the leaves, so spraying foliar feeds in this area will maximize absorption of the nutrients. This rule covers all dicotyledon plants (those with two cotyledons or seed leaves, such as brassicas). Monocots (plants with a single cotyledon, such as corn, rye, and other grasses) have equal numbers of stomatas on the top and bottom of the leaf.

When to Apply Fertilizer

We recommend applying organic fertilizer as follows:

Before planting. Add granular/dry organic fertilizer to the soil prior to planting any vegetable crop. For direct-seeded and closely spaced transplanted crops, broadcast fertilizer over the surface of the soil and mix it into the top 4 inches before planting. For widely spaced crops like tomatoes, potatoes, or winter squash, mix fertilizer into each hole before planting.

After planting. Side-dress heavy-feeding crops with granular fertilizer or liquid fertilizer, or apply a foliar feed, at two, four, and six weeks after planting. If using granular fertilizer, sprinkle the recommended amount around the base of the plant, and mix it into the top inch of the soil and water it in. If using liquid fertilizer, measure the desired amount into a watering can or hose-end sprayer and dilute it as recommended on the label. (Make sure to rinse out the can or sprayer after each use, as organic liquid fertilizer will stink and clog up screens and outlet holes.)

Here are a few suggestions for how to fine-tune your fertilizer applications:

- Apply low doses of liquid fertilizer to your nursery transplants two or three times per week. Applications can begin as soon as seedlings have emerged; continue until the starts are transplanted into the garden.

Reading the Label

The major nutrients that plants require for good growth are nitrogen, phosphorus, and potassium. Often called macronutrients, they are abbreviated as NPK. Calcium and magnesium are also highly important nutrients for plant growth, as are a host of important micronutrients and trace minerals, such as sulfur, boron, zinc, manganese, iron, and copper.

Every fertilizer is labeled with its ratio of NPK. For example, a fertilizer that contains 5 percent nitrogen, 5 percent phosphorus, and 5 percent potassium by weight will be labeled 5:5:5. Typically, several ingredients are mixed together to create the desired NPK ratio.

Sometimes calcium, magnesium, and other micronutrient amounts are labeled on the package, but the three numbers together always refer to NPK. If you want to keep things simple, you can use a "balanced" fertilizer for all your pre-planting and side-dressing needs. Balanced means that all three numbers are nearly the same — 5:5:5, or 3:2:3 — which in turn means the fertilizer supplies approximately equal amounts of NPK to your plants.

Nitrogen — responsible for early vegetative growth in plants

Phosphorus — crucial for photosynthesis, early root growth, and flowering

Potassium — helps with photosynthesis, fruit formation, and disease resistance

Calcium — vital for cell structural development, root growth, and nitrogen uptake

Magnesium — plays an important role in photosynthesis, and must be present in a 1:5 to 1:7 ratio with calcium in order for both nutrients to be available to crops

- When transplanting, use a high-phosphorus fertilizer (2:4:2 or something similar) to encourage quicker root development.

- Apply a foliar feed with lots of phosphorus, potassium, and calcium (0:5:5 or similar) to fruiting plants during early fruit set. Doing so should improve fruit quality.

- Side-dress leafy and brassica crops with a high-nitrogen fertilizer such as 5:1:1. This works especially well for leaf crops because they don't require large amounts of phosphorus and potassium. We use straight blood meal (12:0:0) for side-dressing garlic, onions, brassicas, arugula, and lettuce.

Side-dressing granular organic fertilizer is a good way to maintain consistent nutrient levels for heavy-feeding crops.

What's in Organic Fertilizer?

Organic fertilizers are made from a variety of ingredients that are derived from animal, plant, and mineral sources. Mineral fertilizer sources include greensand, rock phosphate, sulfate of potash, and glacial rock dust. Generally, animal byproduct ingredients come from livestock operations or fisheries. Common animal waste products include blood meal, cow or fish bonemeal, feather meal, crab meal, whole fish meal, bat guano, chicken manure, and worm castings. Animal byproduct–based ingredients are processed to kill pathogens and remove impurities. Common plant waste fertilizers include cottonseed meal, soybean meal, kelp meal, and alfalfa meal.

DIY Organic Fertilizers

You can make your own organic fertilizer by mixing different ingredients together to create your desired NPK (nitrogen, phosphorus, and potassium) ratio. (To learn about NPK ratios, refer to Reading the Label on page 205.) We've included a few of our favorite recipes here; you can find many others online or in other books. When mixing the fertilizer, be sure to do it outside and wear a dust mask. Use a 5-gallon bucket and a trowel for mixing smaller quantities, and a clean wheelbarrow and a shovel for larger quantities.

General Purpose Foliar Feed Recipe

For plants that are setting fruit, omit the fish emulsion.

- 1 gallon water
- 3 tablespoons fish emulsion
- 3 tablespoons liquid kelp
- 2 tablespoons molasses

General Purpose Mix (NPK approximately 4:4:3.5)

- 3¼ parts blood meal
- 1 part bonemeal
- 2¼ parts greensand
- 1 part kelp meal

High-Phosphorus Transplanting Mix (NPK approximately 4:6:2)

- 3¼ parts blood meal
- 1½ parts bonemeal
- 2¼ parts greensand
- 1 part kelp meal

Which Crops Need a Boost

We recommend supplemental fertilizing for heavy feeders or plants that need extra nutrition early on in life. Frequency of supplemental fertilizing will vary depending on whether you're applying granular, liquid, or foliar fertilizers. Soil and climate conditions also affect application frequency. Foliar feeding or liquid fertilizing is often carried out every week or every other week. If you're side-dressing with granular fertilizer, one to three applications are usually sufficient. Keep in mind that any crop may benefit from supplemental fertilization, especially those that show signs of nutritional deficiency. Whether or not they need additional fertilizer during the growing season, all the annual crops listed below should be fertilized at planting time. We also recommend fertilizing perennial vegetables and fruits before planting, and again in the spring of each growing season. Perennial herbs should be fertilized at planting time, but may or may not need a boost in successive seasons.

Annual Vegetables and Herbs That Need Supplemental Fertilizing

- Beets
- Broccoli
- Brussels Sprouts
- Cabbage
- Cabbage, Chinese
- Cauliflower
- Corn, Sweet
- Cucumbers
- Eggplant
- Garlic
  (in spring)
- Melon, Cantaloupe, Honeydew
- Okra
- Onions, Bulb
  (before bulbing initiates)
- Peppers, Hot
- Peppers, Sweet
- Potatoes
- Squash, Gourds
- Squash, Pumpkins
- Squash, Summer
- Squash, Winter
- Sweet Potatoes
- Tomatillos
- Tomatoes
- Watermelon

Annual Vegetables and Herbs That Don't Need Supplemental Fertilizing

- Arugula
- Basil
- Beans, Edible soy (Edamame)
- Beans, Fava (Broad)
- Beans, Lima
- Beans, Shell
- Beans, Snap
- Bok Choy
- Carrots
- Celeriac
- Celery
- Chard, Swiss
- Cilantro
- Collards
- Dill
- Endive
- Fennel, Bulbing
- Kale
- Kohlrabi
- Leeks
- Lettuce, Baby mix
- Lettuce, Heads
- Mâche
- Mustard Greens
- Parsley
- Parsnips
- Peanut
- Peas, Shelling
- Peas, Snap
- Raab
- Radicchio
- Radishes
- Rutabagas
- Scallions
- Spinach
- Turnips

PRUNING FOR PRODUCTION

Pruning — the practice of removing roots, stems, branches, leaves, flowers, or fruits from a plant — can serve many goals. It can increase a plant's productivity; speed up ripening; reduce the chance of pest and disease issues; prevent a plant from overwhelming and shading out neighboring crops; and simply keep the garden organized and tidy.

Prune for Air Circulation and Plant Health

Some crops simply grow too vigorously for their own good (or at least for *your* own good). Plants can put on tremendous amounts of foliage during the course of a season, and under certain circumstances, this extra vegetative growth may reduce overall yield. As an example, indeterminate tomato plants will continue to produce new growth shoots from their leaf axes. Removing these supplemental shoots during the fruiting period will help prevent the plant from wasting energy developing new branches that will not have time to ripen fruit before the season's end. By pruning, you can help the plant priortize where resources are allocated.

Dense foliage can also create conditions that invite pests and disease. Good air circulation around plants helps dry out wet leaves and stems, which reduces potential sites for fungal and bacterial infection.

Overgrown plants are harder to manage, and you are more likely to accidentally break off branches or otherwise damage an unwieldy plant. Accidental breaks also create sites for disease entry, so it's better to intentionally prune your plants to manage their size and shape, and to keep them healthy. Well-pruned plants will also make fertilization tasks and harvesting easier for you.

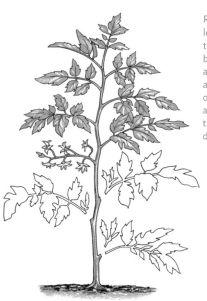

Remove lower leaves when they begin to die back, to promote air circulation around the base of the plant and prevent the spread of disease.

To keep the growth of indeterminate tomato plants focused on a single main stem, remove new shoots that develop in branch crotches.

Strategic Blossom Removal

Believe it or not, you can dramatically affect the productivity of crops by managing the timing of their blossoms. For every plant, there is a sweet spot during its life cycle when the development of flowers is most likely to result in the highest yield. If a fruiting crop flowers too early, its growth can be stunted, resulting in little to no viable harvest. If a fruiting crop continues to flower as the season draws to a close, it wastes energy that would be better diverted to existing underripe and developing fruit.

Pinching Early Blossoms

Ideally, plants shouldn't set blossoms until they're large and established enough to ripen good yields of quality produce. Fruiting plants that bloom and set fruit when they're very small will be inhibited from growing a large root system and strong branches for the fruits. Early fruiting also limits the overall size, yield, and quality of fruits.

If a transplant has become stressed during its nursery grow-out (the most common reason being that it has been in

Harvest Bolting Plants

Bolting is simply a term used to describe undesirable flowering — especially in root, stem, or leaf crops — and is usually a response to stress from unfavorable weather, lack of water, lack of nutrients, or other environmental stresses. Flowering takes a lot of energy, so once the plant begins to invest energy in flowers, the growth of its roots, stems, and leaves will decrease or stop entirely. Produce from a bolted plant commonly takes on a bitter taste because the plant has stopped supplying nutrients and sugars to its non-flowering parts.

As a general rule, once the flowering mechanism inside the plant has been tripped, it is very difficult to prevent that plant from flowering again. Pruning a bolted plant will only buy you some time; cutting back a bolting flower stalk will usually result in a new flower stalk emerging within a few days. In most cases, once a plant starts to bolt, the best thing you can do is to harvest the crop and prepare the space for a new planting (unless, of course, you've chosen to leave the bolting plant in place in order to collect seed or attract beneficial insects).

How to Prevent or Delay Bolting

To delay bolting, lower a plant's stress level by growing it during the season it prefers, keeping it evenly and adequately watered, and providing it with nutrient-rich soil. It is even possible to select varieties of a crop that have been bred specifically to bolt more slowly. Even in the best circumstances, some crops will bolt. Among a healthy row of carrots or leeks, you may come across a few rogue, bolting individuals. Remove erratically bolting crops from healthy plantings as soon as you notice them. Leaving them in place will take up space, water, and nutrients that would be better utilized by healthy plants.

its container for too long), it may begin to set blossoms even while it is in a small pot or shortly after transplanting. If you notice early blossoms, simply pinch them off. Pinching back early blossoms for a few weeks while the plant becomes established will enable it to grow to its full potential.

Removing Late Blossoms

Fruiting crops may continue to flower late into the season. Indeterminate crops (like indeterminate tomatoes and pole beans) won't necessarily recognize that the season is coming to an end, and so will keep producing flowers in the expectation of having time to mature into fruits with viable seeds.

If you know your average first frost date, you can anticipate how many weeks of useful production these crops might have left. Several weeks before the expected change in weather, remove any new flower blossoms. By removing blossoms that have no

hope of producing usable fruit, you encourage the plant to ripen its existing fruits more quickly. The result should be a better quality late-season harvest.

Discouraging Flowers Altogether

Fruiting and flowering crops such as tomatoes, peppers, squash, and sunflowers must bloom in order to produce a harvest. However, for crops that are harvested for their roots, leaves, or stems, flowering generally signals the *end* of the plant's usable harvest. You'll want to actively discourage these crops from flowering by regularly cutting or pinching off any emerging flowers.

Root Pruning

Root pruning is a technique that can help speed up the ripening process of crops. Often employed to help spur quicker ripening in tomatoes and other long-season fruiting crops, the technique is simple. Use a shovel

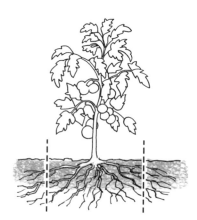

Root pruning can encourage a crop to ripen its fruit earlier.

or hand tool to sever the root system of the plant in a semicircle around its base. Cutting the roots will shock the plant into emergency mode. It will speed up the ripening process in an attempt to create viable seeds before its imminent demise.

Pinching for Higher Yield

Some plants will produce much higher yields if pinched back to encourage branching. Particularly effective on basil and related herbs, pinching can dramatically increase your season's harvest. Use your fingers, scissors, or pruners to snip off the top of each branch of the plant. If you snip back to the next set of leaves down the stem, the plant will send out two new branches from those leaf axes. When these new branches have grown to harvestable size, pinch them both back and double your harvest again.

Pinching to Contain Vining Crops

Trellised vining crops, such as peas, beans, or vining squash, can be maintained at a particular height by cutting back the primary growth tip (also called the apical meristem). This can be effective if you want to prevent the plant from growing past the top of a trellis. Simply use your scissors or hand pruners to snip off the top of the plant at the desired height. It may be necessary to cut back this top growth several times through the season to maintain this height.

Pruning for Propagation

The root systems of many perennial vegetables, herbs, and flowers will spread out as they become established and flourish. This can present a management issue over time. In situations where a plant is overly vigorous, root prune and cut it back each season

Pinching or cutting the top of a basil plant encourages its side shoots to grow, which greatly increases leaf production.

in an effort to prevent it from taking over a larger portion of the garden than you intend. However, hardy perennials also present opportunities to easily expand production. Many of these crops can be propagated in the garden by taking root cuttings, by dividing the plant, or by removing self-rooting branches and stems.

Stem Cuttings

Many herbs and other perennials can be reproduced by taking cuttings from their branches. Turn to page 167 to learn more about taking stem cuttings.

Layering

Layering is the process of encouraging a plant's branches to contact the soil in the expectation that it will set out a new root system. Mint and rosemary, for example, will layer themselves freely in the garden. But you can encourage other plants to reproduce in this way, too.

The layering process is simple. If the branches are near the ground, simply bend them toward the ground enough to cover a portion of the stem with soil. If the branch needs extra help staying put, use a pin or landscape stake to help hold it down. Once the branch has rooted, or if you notice that a plant's branches have rooted on their own, simply use your pruners to remove the branch from the host plant. You can find your cutting a new home in the garden, or you can pot it up in the nursery to hold it for future use.

For some perennials, including lemon balm, layering is a great way to produce your own rooted cuttings directly from an existing plant.

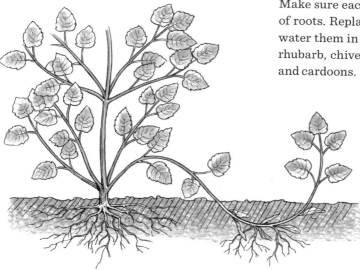

Root Cuttings

Root cuttings are exactly what you might imagine: portions of a plant's root system that are separated and replanted to grow another plant. Root cuttings are especially easy to take from perennial plants that are harvested for their roots. Examples are Jerusalem artichokes (sunchokes), horse-radish, and echinacea. When harvesting these crops, separate out as many healthy pieces of root as needed to supply your next crop. Replant them in the garden at the appropriate spacing as soon as possible after digging them up.

Division

Very similar to taking root cuttings, dividing plants is the practice of digging up the root mass of a plant and dividing it into multiple pieces. You can use a shovel or hand tool to separate the mass into a few distinct pieces (the number of divisions possible will depend on the size of the root mass). Make sure each piece has a healthy section of roots. Replant the divisions quickly and water them in well. This process works for rhubarb, chives, thyme, oregano, tarragon, and cardoons.

Types of Vegetative Propagation

PERENNIAL VEGETABLES	METHOD OF PROPAGATION
ARTICHOKE/CARDOON	Division
ASPARAGUS	Division
JERUSALEM ARTICHOKE, SUNCHOKE	Root cuttings
RHUBARB	Division

PERENNIAL GARDEN FRUITS	METHOD OF PROPAGATION
BLACKBERRIES/RASPBERRIES	Division, Layering, Root Cuttings
BLUEBERRIES	Cuttings
STRAWBERRIES	Produce Runners

PERENNIAL HERBS	METHOD OF PROPAGATION
ANISE HYSSOP	Stem cuttings
BAY	Stem cuttings
CHERVIL	Seeding
CHIVES/ GARLIC, CHIVES	Division, seeding
FENNEL	Division, root cuttings
HORSERADISH	Division, root cuttings
LAVENDER	Stem cuttings
LEMON BALM	Division, layering, root cuttings
LEMONGRASS	Division, root cuttings
LEMON VERBENA	Stem cuttings
MARJORAM/OREGANO	Division, root cuttings, stem cuttings
MINT	Division, root cuttings, stem cuttings
PURPLE CONEFLOWER	Division, root cuttings
ROSEMARY	Layering, stem cuttings
SAFFRON	Division
SAGE	Stem cuttings
SAVORY, WINTER	Stem cuttings

HAND POLLINATING FOR HIGHER YIELDS

You may find it desirable — or even downright necessary — to hand pollinate your plants. Pollinating by hand can boost yields of fruiting crops. It's especially helpful if you have a dearth of pollinating insects in your area, if you are growing fruiting crops under cover where insects may have a difficult time reaching them, or if you're selecting plants for seed saving. Cucurbit crops, in particular, benefit from hand pollinating because they're the most likely to suffer from low insect pollinator populations.

To hand pollinate, you must move pollen from the male part of the flower to the female part of another flower. It is a simple process, and most gardeners use a small paintbrush or cotton swab as their pollinating tool. You can also just use your finger (with or without a glove). Another option is to simply cut or pinch off a few flowers and use them as your handheld pollination tool.

In situations where there is a large crop and/or a crop with many flowers, it is possible to encourage pollination simply by shaking the plant to release pollen. Commonly done with greenhouse tomatoes and sweet corn, this technique can be useful on a range of fruiting crops. When flowers are open and fully developed, gently shake the plants to release pollen into the air and scatter it across the plants. Some of the airborne pollen will land on receptive flower stigmas, thus increasing the number and quality of fruits.

How to Hand Pollinate

To achieve successful pollination, it is crucial that you identify the parts of the flower to determine what kind of flowers you have. Some crops produce separate male and female flowers (these plants are called monoecious), others have both sexes on a single flower (hermaphroditic, or "perfect"), and others have separate male and female plants (dioecious). Follow these steps to hand pollinate:

1. Determine whether the crop is hermaphroditic, monoecious, or dioecious.

2. Locate the stamens and the stigma of the flowers.

3. Take your chosen tool and rub it against the stamens of the flower.

4. Transfer this pollen-laden tool to the stigma of the same flower or to another flower (depending on the type of flower) on the same plant or a nearby plant of the same variety (depending on the crop).

5. Repeat; and then wait for fruits to develop.

Anatomy of a Flower

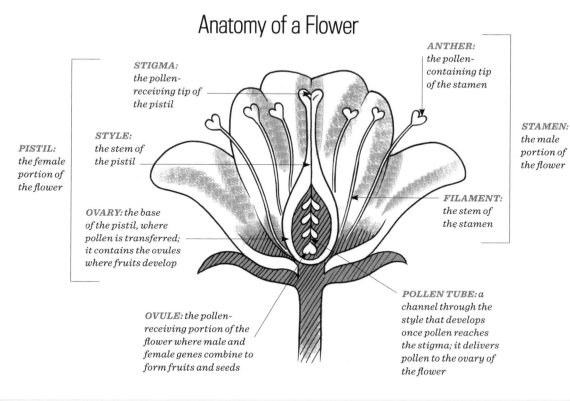

STIGMA: the pollen-receiving tip of the pistil

ANTHER: the pollen-containing tip of the stamen

STAMEN: the male portion of the flower

STYLE: the stem of the pistil

PISTIL: the female portion of the flower

FILAMENT: the stem of the stamen

OVARY: the base of the pistil, where pollen is transferred; it contains the ovules where fruits develop

OVULE: the pollen-receiving portion of the flower where male and female genes combine to form fruits and seeds

POLLEN TUBE: a channel through the style that develops once pollen reaches the stigma; it delivers pollen to the ovary of the flower

Glossary of Flower Terms

Complete flower: contains sepals, petals, stamens, and pistil

Incomplete flower: lacks sepals, petals, stamens, and/or pistils

Perfect: flowers containing male and female parts

Imperfect: flowers that lack either male or female parts

Pistillate: flowers containing only female parts

Staminate: flowers containing only male parts

Hermaphroditic: plants with perfect flowers

Monoecious: plants with separate male flowers and female flowers on the same plant

Dioecious: plants with male flowers and female flowers on separate plants

Gynoecious: plants with only female flowers

Andromonoecious: plants with only male flowers

Flower Types for Pollinating

When hand pollinating, use this chart to determine if the crop in question is hermaphroditic, monoecious, or dioecious.

ANNUAL VEGETABLES AND HERBS	FLOWER TYPE	SELF-POLLINATING?
ARUGULA	H	yes
BASIL	H	yes
BEANS, EDIBLE SOY (EDAMAME)	H	yes
BEANS, FAVA (BROAD)	H	yes
BEANS, LIMA	H	yes
BEANS, SHELL	H	yes
BEANS, SNAP	H	yes
BEETS	H	yes
BOK CHOY	H	yes
BROCCOLI	H	no
BRUSSELS SPROUTS	H	no
CABBAGE	H	no
CABBAGE, CHINESE	H	no
CARROTS	H	yes
CAULIFLOWER	H	no
CELERIAC	H	yes
CELERY	H	yes
CHARD, SWISS	H	yes
CILANTRO	H	yes
COLLARDS	H	yes
CORN, SWEET	M	yes
CUCUMBERS	M	variety dependent

	FLOWER TYPE	SELF-POLLINATING?
DILL	H	yes
EGGPLANT	H	yes
ENDIVE	H	yes
FENNEL, BULBING	H	yes
GARLIC	H	no
KALE	H	yes
KOHLRABI	H	yes
LEEKS	H	yes
LETTUCE, BABY MIX	H	yes
LETTUCE, HEADS	H	yes
MÂCHE	H	yes
MELON, CANTALOUPE, HONEYDEW	M	yes
MUSTARD GREENS	H	yes
OKRA	H	yes
ONIONS, BULB	H	yes
PARSLEY	H	yes
PARSNIPS	H	yes
PEANUT	H	not applicable
PEAS, SHELLING	H	yes
PEAS, SNAP	H	yes
PEPPERS, HOT	H	yes
PEPPERS, SWEET	H	yes
POTATOES	H	yes
RAAB	H	yes

H=hermaphroditic

M=monoecious

D=dioecious

ANNUAL VEGETABLES AND HERBS	FLOWER TYPE	SELF-POLLINATING?
RADICCHIO	H	yes
RADISHES	H	yes
RUTABAGAS	H	yes
SCALLIONS	H	yes
SPINACH	D	yes
SQUASH, GOURDS	M	yes
SQUASH, PUMPKINS	M	yes
SQUASH, SUMMER	M	yes
SQUASH, WINTER	M	yes
SWEET POTATOES	H	yes
TOMATILLOS	H	no
TOMATOES	H	yes
TURNIPS	H	yes
WATERMELON	M	yes

PERENNIAL GARDEN FRUITS	FLOWER TYPE	SELF-POLLINATING?
BLACKBERRIES	H	yes
BLUEBERRIES	H	no
CURRANT	H	yes
ELDERBERRY	H	yes
GOJI BERRY	H	yes
GOOSEBERRY	H	yes
HUCKLEBERRY	H	yes
JOSTABERRY	H	yes
LINGONBERRY	H	yes
RASPBERRIES	H	yes
STRAWBERRIES	H or D	yes
WINTERGREEN	H	yes

PERENNIAL VEGETABLES	FLOWER TYPE	SELF-POLLINATING?
ARTICHOKE	H	yes
ASPARAGUS	D	no
CARDOON	H	yes
JERUSALEM ARTICHOKE, SUNCHOKE	H	yes
RHUBARB	H	yes

PERENNIAL HERBS	FLOWER TYPE	SELF-POLLINATING?
ANISE HYSSOP	H	yes
BAY	D	no
CHERVIL	H	yes
CHIVES	H	yes
CHIVES, GARLIC	H	yes
FENNEL	H	yes
HORSERADISH	H	yes
LAVENDER	H	yes
LEMON BALM	H	yes
LEMONGRASS	H	yes
LEMON VERBENA	H	yes
MARJORAM	H	yes
MINT	H	yes
OREGANO	H	yes
PURPLE CONEFLOWER	H	yes
ROSEMARY	H	yes
SAGE	H	yes
SAVORY, WINTER	H	yes
SORREL	H	yes
STEVIA	H	yes
TARRAGON	n/a	no
TEA CAMELLIA	H	yes
THYME	H	yes
VALERIAN	H	yes

Flower Types for Pollinating <small>CONTINUED</small>

FRUIT AND NUT TREES	FLOWER TYPE	SELF-POLLINATING?
ALMOND	H	variety dependent
APPLE	H	variety dependent
ASIAN PEAR	H	variety dependent
CHERRY	H	variety dependent
CITRUS	H	variety dependent
EUROPEAN PEAR	H	variety dependent
FIG	H	variety dependent
HAZELNUT	H	no
MULBERRY	D or M	variety dependent
PEACH	H	yes
PLUM	H	variety dependent
WALNUT	M	yes

VINES	FLOWER TYPE	SELF-POLLINATING?
AKEBIA	M	no
GRAPES	H	yes
HOPS	D	no
KIWI	D	no

H=*hermaphroditic*

M=*monoecious*

D=*dioecious*

Suppress the Competition: Weeds, Pests, and Diseases

Weeding will always be a part of organic garden maintenance. One of the most important goals as a high-yield grower is simply to reduce the overall population of weeds in your garden. A good weeding strategy has two main benefits: reducing your crops' need to compete for nutrients, light, and moisture; and reducing the amount of time you spend weeding so that you can focus on more important tasks like planting, fertilizing, and harvesting. Weeded beds also have the side benefit of making your garden look more attractive!

DEVELOP A WEED-REDUCTION STRATEGY

A weed is any plant that is growing in the wrong place, whether it's a dandelion or a self-seeded tomato "volunteer." Some of these plants are edible and can create an additional harvesting opportunity (see page 279), but they can also crowd out more desirable crops and become a nuisance if allowed to spread without control.

Identify and Prioritize

Weed seeds can remain dormant in the soil for many years, waiting for the right conditions to germinate and grow. Freshly dug soil with regular summer watering might just be the opportunity they've been looking for, so if you've just created a new bed, don't be surprised if you start noticing weeds that you've never seen before. Learn to identify these unwelcome plants and prioritize their removal based on their aggressiveness.

Weed Early, Weed Often

Every garden has weeds, but if you diligently clear them from your garden throughout the season, you will keep their competition with crops to a minimum. The key to weed management is to start early and work often. Almost all weeds are easy to eliminate with minimal effort when they're small. Regular, weekly weeding sessions will prevent weeds from taking hold and, more important, will keep them from maturing and setting seeds. A flowering weed is a ticking time bomb and should be removed from the garden immediately (at a minimum the flower stalk should be cut down). If you stay on top of weeds and don't let them set seed, your weed issues will decrease from year to year.

Choose the Right Tools

Smaller gardens can be effectively weeded by hand with a trowel or hori-hori knife. We recommend keeping a weeding tool with you at all times in the garden, so that you can dig out weeds as you encounter them. Every little bit makes a difference! If your garden is larger, you may want to upgrade to using a stand-up weeding tool such as a hoe.

Weeding Efficiently with a Hoe

Clearly, using a stirrup hoe or collinear hoe can enable you to weed larger areas much more efficiently than using a trowel. If your garden is very large and has long straight rows, consider using a wheel hoe to speed things up. A wheel hoe is a long-handled tool with a wheel-mounted blade that disturbs the soil and slices through weeds.

Because it takes very little soil disturbance to kill small plants, cultivating small weeds with a hoe is best done on a hot, dry day. If you're digging up larger weeds with a trowel or shovel, they'll usually come out more easily if the soil is moist (wait until after a rain or an irrigation session).

In most garden situations, getting out and using tools like these once or twice a week should keep weed problems under control. Take the time to become comfortable with your weeding tool. Move through the garden intentionally so as to not damage your crops.

Hoes should be kept sharp and clean. The tool is intended to smoothly cut through plants, keeping your work as efficient and effective as possible, and disturbing your crops as little as necessary. Invest in a sharpening stone; a few minutes of tool care will save countless hours of work out in the garden.

Our Top Three Hoes

Humans have been designing cultivators for thousands of years, and you can find them in pretty much any shape imaginable. Gardeners and farmers tend to have particular preferences about the type of cultivating tool they use. Following are a few of our favorite contemporary hoes, but you should use whatever style of tool that works best for you and makes weeding most enjoyable.

Stirrup hoe. The business end of the hula hoe (also called the wiggle hoe or scuffle hoe) is shaped just like a stirrup. Both the front and the back of the stirrup are sharp, and the blade will move slightly forward and back as you weed so that it can cut weeds both coming and going.

Run the bottom part of the blade just under the surface of the soil and push and pull the handle back and forth to sever small and big weeds around your plants, in pathways, and anywhere else you have somewhat loose soil. In situations where weeds have grown out of control, you may want to weed with this hoe and then go back with a rake to gather up all of the accumulated debris.

Collinear hoe. A newer cultivating tool that is very popular with small-scale professional growers, the collinear hoe has a sharp, narrow blade that is great for weeding in small spaces (between rows and individual plants). It is specifically designed to use with small weeds, so it functions best when used regularly (which is also the best way to weed with any tool!).

A collinear hoe is highly effective for precision weeding between closely spaced crops.

A stirrup hoe (also called a wiggle hoe or scuffle hoe) is a great tool for efficiently cultivating larger gardens.

Wheel hoe. Only necessary if you're managing a fairly large space, the wheel hoe is a great friend to the small farmer. Operating almost like a tiny, manual tractor, the wheel hoe is simply pushed down the rows. The blade behind the wheel will cultivate the soil, pulling up weeds as it goes. A good wheel hoe actually allows you to change out blades, so you can use a hula hoe attachment, small tines, or any number of other shapes depending on the size and type of weed you are working with. Newer "low" wheel hoes are much easier to use than older "high" wheel hoes.

A wheel hoe works well for cultivating between long, straight rows. This tool is best used in very large gardens and small production farms; a stirrup or collinear hoe is more effective for smaller gardens.

Flame Weeding for Minimal Soil Disturbance

A flame weeder is simply a long steel torch attached to a propane tank. Once lit, the torch is waved over the surface of the soil to singe and kill weeds. Small flame weeders are relatively inexpensive and can be used effectively to suppress especially thick patches of small broadleaf weeds. Another benefit of flame weeding is that, since the process doesn't disturb the soil, new weed seeds are not brought to the surface. Flame weeders, however, are less effective against mature weeds or weeds with significant root structures, such as perennial grass.

It's not necessary to actually ignite and burn weeds with a flame weeder; a brief burst of heat just long enough to make the weed droop slightly is sufficient to kill broadleaf weeds. The best practice is to move at the pace of a slow walk while passing the torch across the bed, keeping the torch 4 to 6 inches above the soil surface. A successful pass wilts the weeds and/or turns them brown.

Pre-emergent Flame Weeding

Pre-emergent flame weeding is an effective method for controlling weeds early in the planting process. The goal is to direct seed a crop and then flame weed over the top of the garden bed just before the crop emerges. Any young weeds will be killed, and the crop will emerge in a clean bed. Pre-emergent flaming is most commonly done with beets and carrots, but it can work on almost any direct-seeded crop if it's timed properly. Here are a couple of tips:

- Cover the end of the direct-seeded row with row cover, plastic, or a glass panel or cold frame. The seeds under the cover should germinate a day or two earlier than the rest of the seeds in the bed. Remove the cover and flame weed the entire bed surface as soon as you see the seeds under cover emerge.

- Seed faster-germinating crops at the end of the row as indicators. For example, seed a row foot of beets at the end of a bed of carrots and flame weed once the beets have emerged but before the carrots pop up. Similarly, you could seed radishes at the end of a row of beets.

A Few Words of Caution

Flame weeding is a technique that might take a little practice to perfect, and for which safe practices must be followed. Flame weeding is best done on a hot, dry day with little or no wind. Always wear sturdy boots and nonflammable long pants when flame weeding, and stand upwind from the flame. Be aware of dry vegetation and other fire hazards near your garden, and don't flame weed when wildfire danger is high or if a burn ban is in effect. Keep a hose handy in case of an emergency. Always read and follow the manufacturer's directions when using a flame weeder.

Don't Forget to Mulch!

Covering pathways and garden beds around established crops with organic or inorganic mulch can drastically reduce the amount of labor and time spent controlling weeds. See pages 116 and 194 for more information on choosing and using mulches.

Flame weeding allows you to kill young weeds without disturbing the soil and bringing new weeds seeds to the surface.

MANAGE PESTS AND DISEASES

Regardless of the precision and care you put into crop planning and management, Mother Nature will inevitably come knocking at the garden gate, looking for a piece of the action. Unmonitored or unmanaged pest or disease issues can dramatically decrease your produce quality and overall garden productivity.

No matter how much thought you give to pest and disease control, and no matter how much you invest in it, the simple truth is that you can't eliminate all pests and diseases from your garden. Thus, your goal should be to *manage* the problem, not to *solve* it. Organic gardening, after all, is about communicating and engaging with the greater environment, not controlling it. Thus, pest and disease management techniques should disrupt the natural environment as little as possible, and should cooperate with and simulate natural processes as much as possible.

Growing food is always a humbling and profound meditation. The next time you're struggling with a difficult pest issue, try to appreciate the awesome power of nature and your small place within it. Nonetheless, some forethought and detailed planning go a long way toward managing pests and diseases in your garden.

Basic Concepts of Pest and Disease Prevention

We believe that managing pests and diseases in the garden starts with preventive and minimally invasive practices. These practices can be ramped up if specific problems get out of hand and more direct actions are desired. Maintaining a healthy

environment and keeping a watchful eye (in the right places) can help you avoid many problems before they start.

Start with Healthy Soil

Healthy, biodiverse soil produces healthy plants, and healthy plants have more resources with which to fight off pests and diseases. If you're following the right steps to build and maintain your soil (see pages 112 and 203), you're off to a good start in the effort to manage pests and diseases in your garden.

Be Vigilant

Pest and disease management (like all garden management) is much easier and more effective when monitoring happens frequently. Visit your garden every day, even for only a few minutes. Walk through the beds and inspect the crops. If you're constantly vigilant, you'll notice problems early on, and you'll have time to find solutions before things get out of hand.

After all, pests and diseases that attack vegetable crops spread very quickly. Just as your plants must grow and reproduce in a very short period of time (often just a few months), so do the pests and diseases that feed on them. Many of these insect pests produce several generations in a single season; some produce an entire new generation in the matter of a few days or weeks. If a pest population has weeks to establish itself before you recognize it, it will have already spread beyond its initial holdfast and will be much more difficult to eradicate.

Understand Your Crops

The longer you tend a garden, the faster and easier it will become to identify pest and disease problems. As you gain experience, you will likely come to understand the tendencies and peculiarities of the crops (and their varieties) you grow.

Imagine that you are in your garden on a hot day. You look at the leaves on your broccoli plants and discover that they are wilting. You wonder if the plants need water or if they are being attacked by a pest. Upon inspecting the soil, you find that it's adequately moist. You carefully dig around in search for root maggots, but find none. Still concerned about the drooping broccoli leaves, you do a bit of research and discuss the problem with a local gardening guru. As a result, you learn that brassica leaves tend to droop on very hot days (usually only if the temperature is above 90°F). You keep a close watch on the plants, and everything seems to return to normal when the temperature drops a bit. You're relieved because you are now certain that all is well.

It is this kind of vigilance, assessment, and follow-through that builds your knowledge base and helps you keep your garden thriving.

Finding Help with Pest and Disease Identification

Many different resources can help you proactively learn what garden pest and disease problems are most prevalent in your area. A quick Internet search is a good starting point. Start with a search for "most common vegetable pests and diseases in ___ (your area)." This will yield a great amount of information. The detail and accuracy of this information found on the Web is not always consistent or reliable, so it is a good idea to review numerous sites.

University Extension agencies are often the best and most knowledgeable on local pest and disease issues. They can even help identify particular pests and diseases for you. Depending on the school and the particular person you talk with, the suggested remedies may not always be appropriate for your garden (some Extension offices are proponents of chemical pesticides and fungicides). At the very least they can help you figure out the cause of a particular problem. Fortunately, many universities are beginning to research and develop support for organic agriculture. Your interaction with them might just help continue to push them in this direction, so don't be afraid to reach out.

Meanwhile, you should talk with local gardeners and experts about this subject. Local garden nurseries and garden clubs can be great sources of support. And books about garden pests and diseases make invaluable additions to your gardening library.

Whatever pest or disease problems your garden experiences, know that somebody out there has had the same issue — and probably solved it. Satisfactory solutions may come quickly to you, or you may have to do some serious sleuthing. If you enjoy the process, you'll learn a lot during each research experience.

Take Preventive Action

With proper knowledge and preparation, you can do a lot to minimize or even eliminate pests and diseases before they trouble your garden. Preparation strategies vary, as they depend on the issue at hand, but there a few highly effective and widely adaptable preventive techniques that you should consider.

Attract Beneficial Insects

The presence of insects in the garden can be a good or a bad thing, depending on the insect. Some insects might nibble on your crop plants, but others (referred to as "beneficial insects") will prey on pests and help pollinate your plants. Because the presence of insects is inevitable, you must come up with a way to live with them. Your best pest prevention strategy is to help build a diverse ecosystem in and around your property. Just like in a natural ecosystem, if you can achieve high levels of biodiversity, the population of any particular pest insect can be kept in check by the presence of benefical insects that prey on and parasitize them.

Add flowers. Planting a range of flowers in the yard is the easiest and best way to create habitat for a buzzing metropolis of insect life. You can add small and fast-growing flowers like alyssum to the edge of any garden bed; mix taller annuals like cosmos, bachelor buttons, and love-in-a-mist between edible crops; or create a dedicated space in the garden for perennial flowers like echinacea, cardoons (both of which also supply a crop), bee balm, and helinium.

Let a few crops bolt. Another strategy is to allow certain crops or a portion of a planting to flower instead of removing them promptly after their primary production has finished. Crops like cilantro, dill, fennel, basil, arugula, and mustard will produce flowers that beneficial insects love. Many of these flowers can also be eaten on salads or in recipes. Cilantro, if left to generate seeds, will supply you with coriander.

Flowers That Attract Beneficial Insects

Alyssum	Cosmos	Marigolds
Arugula	Dianthus	Mint
Bachelor buttons	Dill	Mustard
Basil	Echinacea	Parsley
Bee balm	Fennel	Sunflowers
Buckwheat	Helenium	Valerian
Cardoon	Hyssop	Verbena
Chamomile	Lavender	Zinnia
Cilantro	Love-in-a-mist	

Physical Exclusion

Putting up a physical barrier between the pest and the crop is often the most effective strategy for reducing pest pressure on your plants.

Floating row covers. When properly used, floating row covers will make it impossible for many pests to munch on or lay eggs near your crop. Since this option prevents insects from entering the bed, it is important to learn about the life cycle of the pest to determine when to apply the cover. This time is often immediately after seeding or transplanting. Depending on the pest and the crop, floating covers may be left on for a few weeks while the plant establishes itself, or all the way up to harvesting time. If you're growing a fruiting plant that needs insect pollination, the floating cover should be removed prior to flowering.

Know your pests before you install row covers. Some pests, such as tomato hornworm and squash vine borer, overwinter in the soil between seasons, and a row cover may trap the emerging insects right in the bed with your crops! If you know that the pests in your garden don't overwinter in the soil, then you can safely cover a cleared, prepared bed when you plant a new crop.

Row cover is especially helpful to control caterpillars, beetles, stink bugs, root maggots, and borers. Plants that benefit most from row-cover use vary depending on what pests are most problematic in your area (see the table on page 234).

Standard spun-bonded polyester covers used for season extension also work well for pest exclusion (lighter-weight fabrics are a good choice so that crops are less likely to overheat when temperatures are high). Some suppliers offer row covers made from fine mesh designed specifically for pest control (these allow more air circulation than polyester row covers). You can read more about setting up and managing floating row covers in chapter 13.

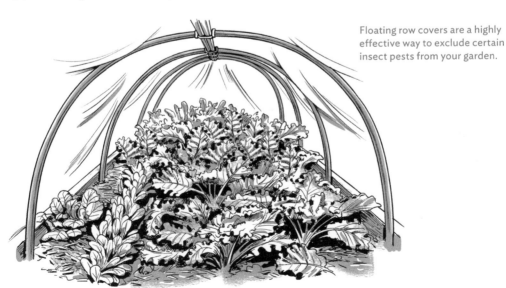

Floating row covers are a highly effective way to exclude certain insect pests from your garden.

Netting. Birds are especially attracted to sweet-tasting crops like corn and strawberries, but are also known to eat seeds right out of the soil and tear out young transplants, which then dry out and die in the sun. Black flexible polyethylene netting, called bird netting, can be used to protect crops from hungry birds. Bird netting can be attached to hoops, like floating row cover, or it can simply be draped over the crops. You don't need to leave bird netting on crops continuously; you can simply install it when the crop is at its most vulnerable point. Drape the netting over newly seeded crops until they've germinated and emerged from the soil. For sweet fruiting crops, use the netting right before fruits begin to ripen, and then remove the netting when harvesting is finished for the season. If transplants are being attacked, apply the netting at planting time and leave in place until the plants have become established, usually a week or two.

Fencing. Fences are an excellent solution to keep larger mammals out of the garden. The most common garden fencing is built to exclude deer and other large herbivores. A deer fence should be at least 8 feet tall to keep deer from jumping into the garden. Installing a deer fence also provides gardeners with an easy opportunity to exclude any other, smaller animals from the site. A fine wire mesh, like chicken wire, attached to the bottom 3 feet of the fence will effectively keep out rabbits and other small mammals. If tunneling pests are known to be a problem, the wire mesh should be extended 1 to 2 feet underground around the perimeter of the garden.

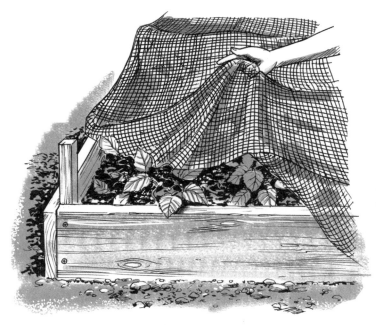

Polyethylene netting will prevent birds from eating ripening fruit crops. It will also discourage cats, dogs, and other small mammals from rooting around in the garden.

Preventive Applications

Some organic sprays and biological controls are most effective if applied before problems have begun. In order to use your time and money wisely, you'll want to use these methods only for pests that are known problems in your area or that you have had issues with in the past.

Nematodes. These microscopic creatures live in the soil and feed on insects, including fungus gnats, thrips, leaf miners, onion maggots, root maggots, caterpillars, cutworms, and armyworms. There are many different species of nematodes, but not all of them are beneficial to the garden. Each type will target specific insects, so a little research should reveal the appropriate nematode to apply for the particular pest you're dealing with. It is also possible to purchase packages of beneficial nematodes that include several different species. The idea is to apply a range of these helpful parasites and therefore have a better chance of keeping a variety of pest species at bay.

Nematodes will generally come in a plastic container that should be kept refrigerated until use. The dormant creatures will be hibernating in a medium that you add to water and soak into the soil. Because nematodes need a wet environment to survive, it is best to apply them when the soil is already moist (you can either irrigate or wait for rainy weather to soak the soil).

Applied nematodes are generally very short lived, which is a good thing ecologically speaking because it prevents these critters from becoming invasive. However, this also means you may need to apply them several times a season for maximum effect.

Diatomaceous earth. This is a very strange but effective organic pest deterrent. Diatomaceous earth is a white or off-white powder made from the fossils of very tiny, single celled organisms called diatoms. Although the powder feels relatively smooth to your hands, it has microscopic jagged edges that can slice open soft-bodied insects like slugs and snails. Be careful not

Creative Exclusion: Thwarting Root Maggots

There are many creative and surprising opportunities for pest-specific physical exclusion. Simply taking the time to learn about a pest's life cycle and habits might help you find a way to easily exclude it from your crops.

For example, root maggots can be a scourge on brassica crops. The maggots are hatched from eggs laid at the base of a broccoli or kale plant, where they burrow underground and feed on the roots of the crop. The adult form of the pest, a small fly that closely resembles the common housefly, prefers to lay eggs right next to the target plant. To prevent the fly from laying its eggs there, simply cover this area with an impervious material like plastic mulch, cardboard, or cut up pieces of landscape fabric.

Recipes for Preventive Sprays

There are many organically approved pesticides and fungicides that can be applied in spray form. The more potent of these organic sprays should be used only as a treatment for an existing pest problem so as to avoid the possibility of harming beneficial insects. There are some mild sprays, however, that can be used preventively to great effect to minimize the establishment of pests and diseases. We often use a baking soda spray preventively for fungal issues, and a hot pepper and garlic spray to prevent insect and animal pest damage.

Baking Soda Spray

Use this spray as prevention or as treatment at first sign of a fungal disease (powdery mildew, downy mildew, damping-off).

> 1 tablespoon baking soda
> 1 tablespoon vegetable oil
> 1 gallon water
> ½ teaspoon liquid dishwashing soap (or pure castile soap)

Mix the baking soda and vegetable oil with 1 gallon of water in a sprayer. Shake it up thoroughly and add the ½ teaspoon of liquid dishwashing soap (or castile soap). Be sure to agitate your sprayer while you work to keep the ingredients from separating.

Spray your plants weekly, preferably on overcast days to prevent the spray from burning the foliage. Cover upper and lower leaf surfaces and spray some on the soil. It won't get rid of the fungus on leaves that already have it, but it will prevent it from spreading to the rest of the plant.

Hot Pepper and Garlic Spray

The oils from hot peppers and garlic can deter birds, mice, rabbits, dogs, and a range of insect pests. Spray preventively or at the first signs of damage.

> 6 cloves garlic
> 1 small onion
> 1 teaspoon cayenne pepper (or 6 hot chile peppers)
> 1 quart water
> 1 tablespoon liquid dishwashing soap (or pure castile soap)
> 1 tablespoon vegetable oil or mineral oil (not olive oil)

Chop up or use a blender or food processor to mince the garlic, onion, and hot peppers (if using instead of cayenne pepper). Add these ingredients (and the cayenne pepper, if using instead of fresh peppers) to 1 quart of water. Steep the mixture for several hours or overnight in the refrigerator. Strain through cheesecloth and add 1 tablespoon of liquid dishwashing soap (or castile soap) and 1 tablespoon vegetable oil, and shake until well mixed.

Add mixture to a spray bottle. Spray to cover your plants, including the leaf undersides and on the soil under the plants. You can also apply it to the ground around your garden perimeter to discourage larger animal pests. Store in the refrigerator in a labeled spray bottle or jar for up to a week.

Note: Peppers (and this spray!) can cause skin and eye irritation. Be careful, wear gloves, and don't touch your eyes after handling the spray. When harvesting produce that has been sprayed with hot pepper and garlic spray, wash it extra carefully.

to breathe the dust, as it can be damaging to your lungs. Wear a dust mask and safety goggles when applying it. Diatomaceous earth can be mixed into the garden soil to deter soil-dwelling larvae like root maggots, or it can be applied to the surface of the soil to keep slugs and other surface-dwelling insects at bay.

Direct Actions

Sometimes preventive pest-control techniques just don't work out; you might need to take immediate direct action to get a situation under control. In many cases, you can address the problem simply by physically removing pests or diseased plants from your garden. This technique and the others that follow are effective in certain cases in small areas (especially in curtailing a problem early on), but are unsuccessful in larger gardens.

Hand Picking

Hand picking insect pests might seem gross, but becoming closely acquainted with your adversaries in this way will teach you a lot about their preferences (top of leaves versus bottoms of leaves, new leaves versus old leaves, broccoli versus cauliflower). Over time you'll be able to quickly locate pest problems. In the event you need to graduate to a more serious management strategy, your knowledge can guide you toward being more selective about the application of organic sprays.

It may take some time to recognize the pest you're picking. As an example, it may be very challenging to notice green caterpillars such as cabbage loopers or imported cabbage worms on your brassicas. But with a practiced eye, you will scan these plants for the particular color and shape of these pests and easily spot them.

When dealing with small pests such as aphids, simply squash them with your

If a plant is wilting and appears water stressed but there is adequate moisture in the soil, suspect root maggots or another root predator. This plant should be pulled up and the roots examined.

fingers rather than attempt to remove them from the plant. Running your fingers along a stem or leaf with slight pressure will allow you to kill hundreds of these tiny pests without sprays or any other supplies.

Hand picking can also be helpful in preventing the spread of disease. By removing the leaves or portions of the plant that are most affected, you may be able to slow down or even eliminate the spread of the disease without the use of sprays.

If a pest or disease is heavily attacking a small group of entire plants, consider sacrificing these plants for the greater good. Often, pests and diseases first appear on the weakest plants in the group. Quickly removing these plants also removes the pests and the potential subsequent generations of these pests.

Traps

Sticky traps can help reduce pest pressure with minimal management time. The most common garden traps are sticky yellow cards that are designed to be placed throughout a garden and/or nursery space. These cards can be purchased, or you can make your own by applying a horticultural pest glue such as Tanglefoot to bright yellow paper, plastic, or cardboard. A wide range of pests including aphids, thrips, whitefly, fungus gnats, leaf miners, and beetles can be attracted to these traps. Place traps on small stakes every 4 feet in the garden to help control flying pests. Sticky traps don't usually completely control a pest population, but they are helpful in reducing numbers and can help you notice the appearance of a pest problem early on.

What to Do with Diseased Plants

Although the composting process can be very effective at killing fungal and bacterial pathogens that cause disease, most growers agree that diseased garden plants (or weeds that spread aggressively by their roots or have set mature seed) should not be added to home compost piles or worm bins because the risk of reintroducing pathogens or weeds to the garden is too great.

If you're lucky enough to have a municipal composting system, you can put these plants in your yard waste bin or take them to the nearest collection facility and have them composted professionally. Commercial composting systems are more likely to reach high temperatures than home systems, so plant pathogens are more effectively killed.

Another option for home growers is to burn diseased plants. Alternatively, if you have woodland or unused space on your property, you can bury diseased plants away from the garden site. If none of these options are feasible, you can throw diseased plants in the trash. (We're loath to send organic matter to landfills, so we hope you'll use this option only if it's absolutely necessary.)

Sticky traps can help with early identification of a pest infestation.

Sprays

We intentionally left organic sprays for the end of this chapter because we think of them as the last resort in a pest management strategy. This is not to say that these sprays should never be used — only that it is important to utilize all of the aforementioned techniques first in an effort to reduce the need for these products.

Pests and diseases can develop a resistance to even the most benign organic pesticide. If a spray kills 99 percent of the existing population, the crop may be saved in the short term, but the remaining 1 percent of pests that are naturally resilient against the spray will survive to breed the next generation of pests that, in turn, will all have a better likelihood of also having this resistance.

The use of preventive strategies first, and the use of many different types of organic pesticides, will discourge pests from developing a resistance to a single pesticide. That is, by varying your control method, you prevent pests from selecting themselves for resistance to a specific method. Judiciously used in this manner, organic pesticides and fungicides can become an important tool for maintaining a productive garden.

It is equally important to keep in mind that many broad-range organic sprays can negatively affect the beneficial insects in a garden. Some pesticides affect only a narrow range of insects, but even these can kill innocent bystanders. For example, Bt, a spray intended to manage caterpillar pests like cabbage loopers and tomato hornworm, also kills butterfly larvae. Other sprays are broad spectrum and can kill a huge range of insects, pests and otherwise.

We list here only a select sampling of sprays. There are many organic pest and disease sprays available online and in garden stores, and new ones come onto the market routinely. Research any spray thoroughly before use so that you learn how to safely and responsibly apply it. Remember to read labels of all materials carefully before buying. Just like products at the grocery store, labels are often misleading — chemical pesticides may be labeled with very natural-looking imagery. The safest way to identify appropriate materials is to look for an organic certification logo.

Soap spray. Probably the most commonly used home gardening spray is a simple mixture of soap and water. This mixture can help control or eliminate hordes of insects. It's especially useful for aphids, but works on any soft-bodied insect including spider mites.

Management Strategies for Pests and Diseases

INSECTS

Aphids
Selective plant removal, sticky traps, attract beneficial insects, soap spray

Beetles
Floating row cover, selective plant removal

Cabbage loopers
Floating row cover, Bt, spinosad, attract beneficial insects

Carrot rust flies
Floating row cover, nematodes

Corn borers
Attract beneficial insects, selective plant removal

Corn earworms
Attract beneficial insects, hand picking, Bt

Cutworms
Hand picking, physical exclusion, nematodes

Hornworm
Floating row cover, Bt, spinosad, attract beneficial insects

Imported cabbage worms
Floating row cover, Bt, spinosad, attract beneficial insects

Leaf hoppers
Floating row cover, nematodes

Leaf miners
Floating row ccover, nematodes

Root maggots
Floating row cover, nematodes

Slug
Iron phosphate, diatomaceous earth

Snails
Iron phosphate, diatomaceous earth

Spider mites
Attract beneficial insects, selective plant removal, selective leaf and stem removal, neem

Squash borers
Floating row cover, selective plant removal, delayed plantings, traps

Stink bugs
Floating row cover, diatomaceous earth, soap spray, neem

Thrips
Attract beneficial insects, floating row cover, sticky traps, neem

Whiteflies
Attracting beneficial insects, floating row cover, sticky traps, neem

Wireworms
Cultivation, crop rotation

ANIMALS

Birds
Floating row cover, bird netting, hot pepper spray

Cats
Fencing, hot pepper spray

Deer
Fencing

Dogs
Fencing

Groundhogs
Fencing

Rabbits
Fencing

Raccoons
Fencing, bird netting, floating row cover

Rats
Traps

Voles
Traps

DISEASES

Anthracnose
Select resistant varieties, selective leaf removal, selective plant removal, copper spray

Bacterial wilt
Select resistant varieties

Blossom-end rot
Consistent watering regime, adjust soil nutrient balance

Clubroot
Increase soil pH, crop rotation

Damping-off
Provide air circulation, reduce watering schedule, reduce fertilization

Downy mildew
Selective plant removal, selective leaf and stem removal, baking soda spray, copper spray

Early blight
Selective plant removal, selective leaf and stem removal, copper spray

Fusarium wilt and rot (crown rot)
Select resistant varieties, selective plant removal, selective leaf and stem removal, copper spray

Gray mold
Selective plant removal, selective leaf and stem removal, baking soda spray, copper pray

Late blight
Selective plant removal

Leaf spot (*Cercospora*)
Selective plant removal, crop rotation, baking soda spray, copper spray

Leaf spot (*Septoria*)
Selective plant removal, crop rotation, baking soda spray, copper spray

Mosaic virus
Select resistant varieties

Powdery mildew
Selective plant removal, selective leaf and stem removal, baking soda spray, copper spray

Rust
Selective plant removal, crop rotation

Scab
Select resistant varieties, crop rotation

Verticilium wilt
Selective plant removal, crop rotation

The soap coats the insects and breaks down their cell membranes, drying them out and killing them relatively quickly. This spray is non-toxic and is safe to use around children and pets.

Soap spray should be used judiciously on crops because heavy and consistent applications can result in phytotoxicity (damage to the plant). Spraying early in the morning will help minimize this. To control aphids, spray the soap every two or three days for a week or two, and then stop applications. These repeated applications in rapid succession should disrupt the reproductive cycle of the insects.

To make your own soap spray, mix 1 tablespoon soap (liquid dish soap, castile soap, or a specialized insecticidal soap) with a quart of water in a spray bottle. Shake it vigorously and spray it on insect populations. This spray should keep indefinitely.

Bt (Bacillus thuringiensis). This is a strain of bacteria that, when ingested by caterpillars, paralyzes their digestive system. The bacteria prevents the affected insects from eating, killing them by starvation.

Different strains of Bt affect different species of caterpillars, and only some strains are approved for use in organic agriculture.

Bt is typically sold in liquid form that is then diluted and sprayed directly onto the leaves of affected crops. Bt remains active and alive only when wet, so there is only a short period of time when it can harm non-target insects. Apply Bt only after you have identified a serious infestation of a caterpillar pest, and spray as needed to keep populations under control. Consider alternating spray applications with spinosad (description follows) in an effort to reduce the chances that a pest develops resistance to Bt. In industrial agricultural crops, Bt genes have been inserted into genetically modified crops to create plants that produce their own insecticides. In some areas, the pest populations have quickly developed resistance to the pesticide, reminding us that these types of controls need to be used judiciously and appropriately.

Spinosad. Similar to Bt, spinosad is derived from a naturally occurring soil-borne bacteria — *Saccharopolyspora spinosa*. A compound found in the bacteria is isolated and manufactured into a liquid organic pesticide. The compound works by over-stimulating the nervous system of the target insect. The insects affected by this compound include caterpillars, thrips, mites, beetles, and borers. The spray is not persistent in the environment but can affect a wide range of insects, so it must be used carefully. Avoid spraying on flowering and fruiting plants to prevent damage to beneficial insects.

Neem. A potent broad-spectrum fungicide and pesticide, neem oil is derived from an Asian evergreen tree (*Azadirachta indica*), also called neem tree or Indian lilac. The seeds and fruits of the tree are pressed to release this strong oil, which deters an incredible range of pests including aphids, beetles, cabbage worms, caterpillars, fungus gnats, leaf miners, mites, scale, thrips, whiteflies; and diseases including anthracnose, black spot, powdery mildew, and rust.

Neem can be harmful to beneficial insects as well, so use only when necessary and avoid applications when pollinating insects are visiting your plants. Apply once and watch to see results; often one to three applications is adequate to control a problem.

Iron phosphate. An easy-to-apply slug and snail deterrent, iron phosphate is a naturally occurring soil component that has been isolated as an organic pesticide. It is known to be non-toxic to humans, pets, and wildlife. It replaces an older form of slug bait known as metaldehyde. (Metaldehyde is still available as a pesticide but is highly toxic and should be avoided. Read labels carefully!)

Iron phosphate typically comes in pellets, which are sprinkled on the surface of the soil across the bed or surrounding sensitive crops. Iron phosphate can be expensive and will mold in wet conditions, so we recommend using it judiciously. It is most effective when applied to protect germinating and newly transplanted crops when they are small enough to be fatally damaged by slugs or snails. Once crops are larger, reduce or eliminate use of this pesticide.

Maintaining Soil Quality

Because the quality of produce is dependent on the quality of the soil, we are big advocates of doing everything possible to make garden soil the best it can be right from the start, then working year after year to maintain and improve its quality. This process is necessary for any high-yield vegetable gardener expecting high production and multiple harvests from a single plot of soil.

Most existing soils, especially in a residential yard or urban plot, will not have enough available minerals or nutrients to grow high-yielding vegetable plants. Thus, it's vital that you take steps to add these amendments when building your garden, and continually maintain them over time. If you're doing a good job, the soil quality should improve with each gardening season.

There are four simple things you can do to maintain your soil quality from one year to the next:

- Add a 1- to 2-inch layer of compost over your garden once a year.
- Monitor and maintain proper soil pH.
- Use additional organic fertilizer every season to ensure proper nutrient levels.
- Protect your soil with mulch or cover crops, especially during the winter.

FIRST PRIORITY: BUILD UP HUMUS

Humus — the substance that is created when soil microorganisms break down raw organic matter — is an essential component for good garden soil. It acts as a "glue" to hold soil aggregates together and creates what growers call "tilth" (good soil structure). Humus gives garden soil a wonderful loose crumbly feeling, and yet such soil doesn't completely collapse into individual particles when it is worked.

Humus also acts like a sponge in your soil; it helps maintain proper moisture levels. In soil without humus, water will either leach away too quickly for plants to use (very sandy soil), or will make the soil waterlogged and difficult to work for long periods (very clay-rich soils). Humus-rich soil will take up water and hold it right where your crops can use it. As humus continues to break down, it releases nutrients that your crops can use to grow. Amazing stuff, that humus.

Just Add Organic Matter

Because humus breaks down, it must be maintained. This is done by adding organic matter to the garden on a regular basis. Compost is the best material to use because it is already partially decomposed and is much more easily converted into humus. Also, the nutrients in compost have already been stabilized, so they're less likely to leach from the soil as compared to raw organic matter. Good compost contains beneficial microorganisms, which help keep your soil biotic community in good health.

It's important to note, however, that not all compost is created equal. You might hear a recommendation such as "add X amount of compost to your garden each year, and you'll be able to grow wonderful vegetables without adding any other fertilizers." This might be true in some situations, but is often not the case. For example, compost made with animal manures may contain much higher nutrient levels than compost made strictly

Test Regularly

For most situations, testing the soil once every three years is sufficient. If you're really interested in learning how your amendments are affecting the soil each year, try testing once a year for three years. You can take these tests less frequently thereafter if your soil is changing in the way you want it to.

Over time, you might see that your soil test shows that your garden has high levels of soluble salts, which are usually brought about by excessive applications of organic fertilizer. To help avoid this situation, apply organic fertilizer only as recommended. If your soil does test high for soluble salts, you can leach them out

by running 2 to 4 inches of water through it. To do this, you can run your irrigation system with drip tape for 12 to 15 hours, or run your sprinkler until water pools on the surface of the soil. Then turn it off, let the water soak in, and repeat 4 to 6 times. Note that doing this can deplete other, desirable nutrients as well.

with plant material. Also, a well-managed pile will result in compost with higher nutrient levels than a poorly managed pile.

Regardless, finished compost will begin to supply nutrients quickly. But compost that's still breaking down may actually tie up nitrogen for a period of time because the soil bacteria are using it to process the organic matter.

PRODUCING LARGE QUANTITIES OF COMPOST

You can produce a surprising amount of compost by maintaining "catchall piles" — this is probably what you think of when someone mentions composting. It's the process of making a mound of your kitchen and garden scraps, yard waste, and other organic materials, and turning it frequently to allow oxygen in. If you maintain a proper carbon-to-nitrogen ratio (see page 242), keep the catchall pile evenly moist, and turn it regularly, you'll be able to produce quality compost.

Using Windrows Instead of Piles

If you're able to source large quantities of raw materials and want to make a lot of compost, make a windrow instead of a pile. A windrow is basically a long row of composting materials. It should be at least 3 feet tall at the peak and 6 to 7 feet wide, though it can be as long as you want to make it. The

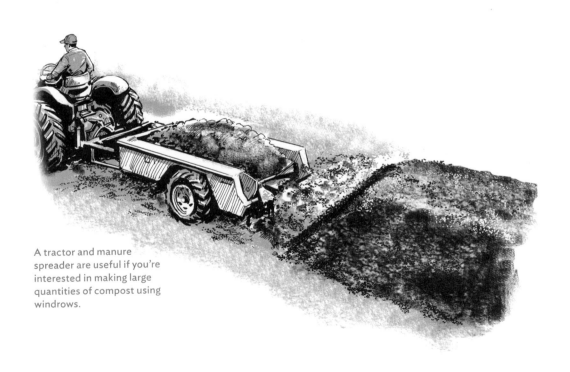

A tractor and manure spreader are useful if you're interested in making large quantities of compost using windrows.

advantage of the windrow shape is that it's easier to turn than a single massive pile. You can turn a windrow by hand if you're feeling strong, though most growers do this with a small tractor with a front-end loader or a specialized compost turner.

If you have a manure spreader for your tractor, you can use it to build a windrow. Fill the spreader with raw composting ingredients, set the spreader to unload as quickly as possible, and drive forward as slowly as possible. The spreader will unload the ingredients into a windrow shape (you'll need to fine-tune this method depending on your tractor and spreader). For suggestions on where to find more information on making large quantities of compost, see Resources, page 307.

Sourcing Bulk Materials to Compost

No matter the compost technique you choose, you may find yourself wishing you had more stuff to throw on the pile, especially after you've seen how beneficial compost can be for your crops. Here are some tips on acquiring more material:

- Many grocery stores will give you damaged or old produce for free. This makes a great high-nitrogen addition to compost piles. It's best if you bring your own containers (5-gallon buckets work well) to the store and show up at a set time that's convenient for the produce manager.

- Coffee shops and restaurants will often let you have their spent grounds (another nitrogen-rich compost feedstock). Ask if you can leave 5-gallon buckets for them to fill up.

- Check with neighbors who rake leaves in their yard. They'll probably be happy to hook you up with a few trash bags full. Hardwood leaves are a great carbon source and are loaded with minerals. Return the favor with a few bags of salad greens in the spring.

- Horse stables are often a great source for free manure. Manure mixed with straw bedding is easiest to compost. If the horses are bedded on sawdust or woodchips, add additional nitrogen to the pile and then compost for a full year before you add the finished product to your garden.

- Chicken, pig, and cow manure from a local farm are all great nitrogen sources for your compost pile.

- Keeping your own livestock is a great way to convert garden waste into manure for compost. Even urban dwellers with relatively small lots can successfully raise a happy flock of chickens (check out Resources, page 307 for more information).

Compost made with animal manures may contain much higher nutrient levels than compost made strictly with plant material.

Carbon-to-Nitrogen Ratios of Compost Ingredients

BROWNS

INGREDIENT	C:N RATIO	NOTES
BRANCHES	500:1	Use small-diameter branches and twigs or chip them before adding
DRIED GRASS CUTTINGS	50:1	
DRIED TREE DECIDUOUS LEAVES	70:1	
SAWDUST	400:1	
SHREDDED CARDBOARD	350:1	
SHREDDED NEWSPAPER	170:1	Make sure paper has natural-based inks such as soy
STRAW	75:1	
WOOD ASHES	25:1	
WOOD CHIPS	400:1	

GREENS

INGREDIENT	C:N RATIO	NOTES
COFFEE GROUNDS	20:1	
FRESHLY CUT GRASS	15:1	
GARDEN WASTE	30:1	
KITCHEN WASTE	30:1	
MANURE	20:1–40:1	Ratio will vary depending on animal source and freshness
PEAT	70:1	
WEEDS	30:1	Do not compost weeds with seed heads or very aggressive weeds

How to Make Compost

If you have the space, time, and access to ample feedstocks, making your own compost is a great way to feed your garden and process plant waste. Making compost is a skill that takes time and practice to learn. If you are planning to make your own compost, we suggest getting a book dedicated to the subject. We've provided a bare-bones review here of the basic techniques, and a few tips to make your compost more effective in your garden.

Getting the Right Ratio

When adding materials to the compost pile, it's important to get the right ratio of carbon ("brown" debris) to nitrogen ("green" waste). Your goal is to achieve a carbon-to-nitrogen (C:N) ratio of about 25:1. Bacteria will break down organic waste into usable compost most efficiently at this ratio.

Certain ingredients lend themselves incredibly well to this process. For example, the C:N ratio of horse manure is about 30–35:1, so horse manure on its own, or with a little bit of straw bedding mixed in, makes amazing compost. Chicken manure mixed with bedding makes great compost, as does young grass clippings or coffee grounds mixed with brown leaves or straw.

If you are like many home growers, however, you may be limited to the ingredients produced from your yard or that can be sourced nearby. Don't worry! If your compost is not top-notch, you can make up the difference in your garden soil with organic fertilizer and mineral amendments.

What *Not* to Include

Avoid composting vigorous weeds, and weeds that have set mature seed, in your home compost pile. The same is true with diseased or heavily insect-infested plant matter (see page 232 for how to deal with this situation). Also, avoid using sawdust, bark mulch, or wood chips, as their high carbon levels and low mineral and nutrient content create poor-quality compost.

Bigger Is Better

Composting works better when you go big — with a large pile it's easier to create the heat that helps drive the composting process. A pile should be at least 3.5' × 3.5' × 3.5' before you start turning it.

The compost pile should also be consistently moist (but not overly wet) — like a wrung-out sponge — to facilitate decomposition. Water the pile with a hose if it feels too dry. Cover the pile with a tarp during heavy rains to prevent nutrient leaching.

Turn, Turn, Turn

The more frequently you turn a pile, the more quickly it will break down. Frequent turning (every 1–2 weeks) will discourage rodents and limit odors from the pile. Less frequent turning (once a month to every 6 months) is fine if you don't have rodent issues and don't mind slow decomposition.

When turning a pile, you want outer layers to move to the middle of the pile, and the middle of the pile to end up on the outside. To do this, start by forking the top of the pile onto the ground next to the pile. Keep moving the pile over from the top down until you have a new pile (the top of the old pile is now at the bottom of the new pile, and vice versa).

Tracking the Temperature

Use a soil thermometer to help with monitoring the heat in the pile. After you've turned the pile, the temperature should rise, peak, and then start to fall. Turn the pile when the temperature drops back below 100°F. If it starts to fall before reaching 130–140°F, add more nitrogen-rich ingredients. If it gets over 150°F, it needs more carbon-rich ingredients. Turn the too-hot pile as soon as possible, as temperatures over 150°F can kill beneficial bacteria.

When ambient temperatures are low (especially below freezing), the composting process usually slows or stops. For this reason, home compost is most easily made during the late spring, summer, and early fall in most climates. During the winter, you can cover the pile with a tarp and let it sit until more favorable temperatures return in the spring.

Tips for Fine-Tuning Your Pile

- If your compost pile smells like ammonia, add more brown materials. If you accidentally get too many brown materials in your pile (or just have a lot of them and want to get them to compost), you can add blood meal or another high-nitrogen organic fertilizer to balance out the C:N ratio.

- Cover your pile with a thick layer (about a foot) of brown materials (straw or leaves work well) to minimize insect pests and odors and maintain heat levels.

- Add two to three 5-gallon buckets of garden soil to your pile. This inoculates it with bacteria that maintain the stability of the nitrogen in the pile.

- Add a little clay to your pile. This helps the organic matter convert more effectively into humus when you add the compost to your garden. One-half to one 5-gallon bucket is sufficient. You can dig clay from your own subsoil, or buy it in. Try mixing it with water to form a slurry, then sprinkling it onto the pile when you're turning it.

- Make compost in separate batches. When one pile has enough bulk to start turning, stop adding new materials. Start a second pile while you're turning the first one, and a third pile while you're turning the second. This allows all the ingredients in each pile to break down fully and uniformly.

- The compost is finished when it has a soil-like appearance and feels and smells earthy. A compost pile that is well balanced and turned frequently might be ready to apply to the garden in 3 months. A less frequently turned pile might take 6 months to a year.

Purchasing Compost

Many gardeners struggle with making their own compost (this is especially true for gardeners in urban environments). If you don't have access to quality feedstocks for your compost and a way to transport them (i.e., a truck) to your site, it can be difficult for you to build a large top-notch pile from scratch. If this is the case, don't worry. There's nothing wrong with buying compost. Even if it's only moderate-quality compost, you can still have a great garden if you use organic fertilizers and soil amendments appropriately. And if your compost ends up being sub-par, you can always try a different compost supplier the next season.

Ideally you will be able to locate a locally produced compost product that is made specifically for vegetable gardens. Avoid compost that is typically sold for use on ornamental beds, as it's likely to contain lots of high-carbon materials (undecomposed wood and bark), which can reduce the availability of nutrients for your plants.

Obviously, a certified organic product will help ensure quality ingredients, but well-made compost does not need such a certification to be a great product. Talk to the provider and learn how the product is made and what it is made from before purchasing it. Generally speaking, compost made with animal manure will provide more usable nitrogen, phosphorus, and potassium. Compost made strictly with plant waste is still a great source of organic matter, but will yield less of these nutrients. The following sections detail a few additional items that you should consider when purchasing compost.

Watch Out for Contaminants

Herbicides. Compost can become contaminated with certain persistent herbicides if they're present on the compost feedstock, which can in turn damage crops in your garden. This problem is rare, but it's worth checking to see if your supplier screens for it.

Arsenic. Some chicken confinement operations use arsenic in their feed, which can contaminate chicken manure compost. Again, ask your supplier if they screen for this.

Heavy metals. In the past, composted biosolids (human waste) often contained heavy metals that you wouldn't want in your soil. Today, sewage systems are more carefully managed and regulated and have become much cleaner. Composted biosolids can be a clean, viable option for food production. Such compost must be made to exacting standards to ensure that all pathogens have been killed, and should be tested for heavy metal content. If your supplier can't speak to these practices, avoid the composted biosolids they sell. Uncomposted sewage sludge should not be added to an edible garden under any circumstances.

Wood Isn't Good

Any compost made with large quantities of wood chips or sawdust is not suitable for vegetable production. In the short term, composts or other soil amendments that contain high levels of carbon — such as wood chips, bark, or sawdust — will actually decrease nutrient availability in the soil. (These materials, however, can be great for mulching around trees and perennials.) Many landscaping companies and nurseries carry compost made with woody materials; make sure you don't get the wrong product if you're buying from these sources. These materials may be labeled as compost, but are more accurately described as mulch.

Not Hot

Compost that is hot, steaming, or has a strong smell is probably not fully finished and could "burn" plants (either physically or with an overload of nutrients). Fully finished compost will have an earthy, "soil-like" smell and feel. If you happen to buy unfinished compost, you can pile it up and turn it a few times until it breaks down and cools off. It's also okay to add unfinished compost directly to the garden, but you'll want to wait at least a few weeks before planting into these areas. We like adding compost to the garden in the fall to make sure it's fully broken down before we begin planting in the spring.

PROTECT THE SOIL WITH COVER CROPS

Cover cropping is the practice of growing a crop specifically to generate organic matter, protect the soil, or capture nutrients. Cover crops are often planted in late summer or in the fall, which gives them time enough to mature so that they can offer good protection for the winter. Cover crops can also be a great midsummer soil management option between a spring and fall crop, or can be used to protect soil if you decide to take a bed out of vegetable production for the year (to let the soil rest or to break up pest and disease cycles). Most growers use a combination of a leguminous cover crop and a grass. The legume fixes nitrogen from the air and adds it to the soil, and the grass supplies carbon to balance the nitrogen from the legume.

The Impact of Climate on Compost in the Soil

Believe it or not, the climate you live in affects the ability of your compost to supply nutrients to your crops. Air temperature affects soil temperature, and soil temperature affects how quickly soil microorganisms break down organic matter and make nutrients available to plants. The warmer the temperature, the faster the organisms work. Thus, if you're growing in a warmer climate, you can expect to get more usable nitrogen, phosphorus, and potassium from your compost than you would in a cooler climate (so perhaps you'll need less organic fertilizer in a warmer climate).

This also means that in warmer climates your compost and humus break down more quickly and need to be replenished more frequently than in cooler climates. Phosphorus is notoriously unavailable in cooler temperatures, so using supplemental organic fertilizer is particularly important early in the season in the cooler regions.

Cover Crops as Living Mulch

You can seed a cover crop as a living mulch to grow alongside your primary crops. This living mulch will shade the soil from drying sunlight and suppress weeds. Living mulches can work especially well when used around tall, vigorous crops. If left unmowed, a living mulch will set seed and establish itself as a permanent fixture in your garden (a.k.a. a *weed*). Living mulches need to be mowed regularly to prevent this. Similar to other cover crop applications, we recommend starting small and experimenting to see if this technique works for you.

Use Cover Crops for Winter Protection

For winter protection, cover crops are the best thing you can do for the soil. As they grow, the crops take up excess nutrients left in the soil, which prevents them from leaching away. The roots provide a haven for beneficial mycorrhizal fungi throughout the winter (these fungi form a symbiotic relationship with plant roots and help them absorb nutrients from the soil). When cover crops are mowed and turned into the soil, they release usable nutrients and help build up organic matter.

For winter cover, you can choose between cover crops that winter kill (die at a certain temperature over the winter), or those that overwinter and grow through the spring. Winter-killed cover crops are relatively easy to turn under in the spring, and so are great for preceding early spring crops like broccoli or kale. Because overwintering cover crops continue to grow and generate biomass in the spring, they are best used with later-planted crops like tomatoes. It's important to know the particulars of your climate when choosing a cover crop because a given crop might overwinter in one area and winter kill in another.

It is also possible to leave the cover crop or its residue in place on top of your beds as a form of mulch. If you plant a cover crop that will winter kill, consider leaving the residue on the beds come spring and plant your crops into the decomposing matter. This method is best suited for beds where the crops will be transplanted (as opposed to direct seeded).

Start Small

Cover crops do have drawbacks for the small-scale production gardener. They take quite a bit of work to mow and turn in, especially for gardeners who rely on hand tools. Moreover, because cover crops take between three to five weeks to break down after they've been turned in, they can tie up valuable production space in the spring. So if the majority of your garden is planted in cover crops, you may not have enough room to plant early-season vegetables in a timely fashion.

Because of these drawbacks, we recommend starting small with cover crops. Don't plant more than 100 square feet in cover crops the first time you try them (especially if you're using hand tools to turn them in), and don't plant more than a quarter of your garden space with them. Once you get a feel for managing the cover crops, you can adjust your square footage to match your needs.

How and When to Seed Cover Crops

Start by clearing old crops and raking the soil smooth. You don't need to work the soil deeply unless it has become compacted. Once you have the seedbed established, sprinkle smaller-seeded cover crops (clover, rye, oats, vetch) over the surface of the soil. Use a rake to gently pull soil over the seeds, then water.

Cover crops can also be seeded beneath mature crops. By seeding while the previous crop is still in place (undersowing), you can establish the cover crop earlier in the season, allowing it to mature while weather is still good for quick growth. Undersowing can also lead to better germination rates because the seeds benefit from the shade and protection of the existing crops, and will be less likely to dry out or get snatched out of the soil by birds.

Keep the cover crops watered until they emerge. If you're planting larger-seeded cover crops such as field peas (see the chart on page 248), you'll need to create furrows so they can be buried a little deeper. If you are working on a small scale, use a rake or hoe to make 1-inch deep furrows that are

6 inches apart. Sprinkle the field peas into the furrows (aim for about 8 seeds per foot, but don't worry about being too precise), then rake soil over the furrows. If you're sowing rye or oats with field peas, start by making the furrows. Drop the peas into the furrows, and then sprinkle the rye or oats over the soil. Finally, rake it all in and water well.

Turning Them In

Plan to turn in your cover crop about a month before you want to plant vegetables. If the cover crop hasn't winter killed, you'll need to mow it first. On a very small scale, you can do this with a pair of long-bladed garden shears. For larger spaces, you'll want to use an electric or gas-powered weed whacker, string trimmer, or lawn mower. If

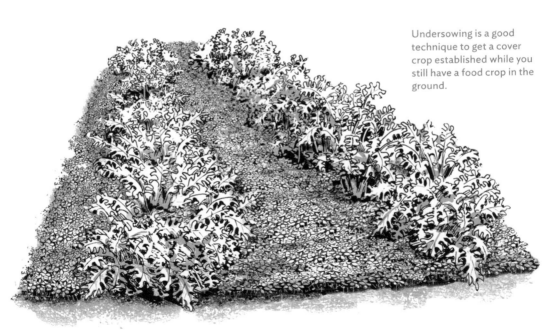

Undersowing is a good technique to get a cover crop established while you still have a food crop in the ground.

using a mower, use a mulching type so it drops the trimmings back onto the soil.

After mowing, work the cover crop into the soil. Use a spade shovel or spading fork to uproot the crops, turn them over, and chop clumps into pieces. Check the bed once a week, and further turn and chop any crops that are starting to resprout (this can be a problem in areas with rainy spring weather). A walk-behind rototiller makes this task much easier. We don't advocate habitual use of rototillers to prepare beds because overusing them can create a soil hardpan. Nonetheless, they do an excellent job of working in cover crops efficiently.

If your climate is very dry, you may need to water the bed to promote decomposition of the turned-in cover crop. After about four to five weeks, the beds should be relatively clear of debris and visible plant matter. If there are still lots of green/living bits of the cover crop, continue to work the soil until they've broken down.

If you're planning to add compost to the soil, you can use it to help kill your cover crop. After you mow and turn in the cover crop, spread the compost over top of it (this will help smother it). Mix this compost into the soil once the cover crop has decomposed and you're ready to prepare the planting bed.

Cover Crops for Every Garden

Many plant species can serve as cover crops. Your choice will vary based on your cover cropping goals, soil conditions, and the time of year. Some cover crops, such as clover and peas, are leguminous, which fix nitrogen from the air. Some, such as annual rye, create an allelopathic effect in the soil that helps prevent weeds from germinating. Some cover crops germinate in cold weather, which makes them a good choise for early and late-season plantings; others are very frost sensitive and grow best midsummer. It should be possible to identify a cover crop that meets your needs for virtually any situation.

BUCKWHEAT

Buckwheat grows very rapidly and has a short life span, so is useful as a mid-season cover crop between spring and fall plantings. It's quite tender, so will winter kill in most of the nation. It doesn't germinate well in cool soil, so it has limited applications for winter cover.

When to seed: spring–early summer
Management: mow at flowering and turn in
Winter kill temperature: 32°F
Seeding rate: pounds/square feet:
2–3 pounds/1,000 square feet

Alternate seeding rate: 8–12 cups/1,000 square feet

CLOVERS

Clover is a leguminous cover crop that is great for creating a long-term pasture (except crimson clover, see below). We don't use it very much in annual gardens because most types take too long to generate enough root and top growth to create organic matter and protect your soil. It also doesn't grow quickly enough if sown in the fall to effectively protect the soil for the winter. If you have space to grow it for a season, it's great for breaking up compaction and fixing nitrogen, and is an excellent forage for chickens. For all clovers, be sure to mow before seed set to prevent clover from becoming a weed problem; turn in when desired.

Red Clover

Most cold-tolerant clover.

When to seed: spring
Winter kill temperature: −20°F
Seeding rate: pounds/square feet:
0.5–1 pound/1,000 square feet, alone or with grass or grain
Alternate seeding rate: 2–3 cups/1,000 square feet

New Zealand White Clover

Longest lived clover; good for permanent pastures and areas with foot traffic.

When to seed: spring
Winter kill temperature: −20°F
Seeding rate: pounds/square feet:
0.25–0.5 pounds/1,000 square feet, alone or with grass/grain
Alternate seeding rate: 1–2 cups/1,000 square feet

Crimson Clover

Usually grown as a winter annual cover crop.

When to seed: late summer
Management: mow and turn in the following spring
Winter kill temperature: 0°F
Seeding rate: pounds/square feet:
0.5–1 pound/1,000 square feet, alone or with grass or grain
Alternate seeding rate: 2–3 cups/1,000 square feet

Sweet Clover

Especially good at renovating worn-out soil.

When to seed: spring–early summer
Winter kill temperature: −20°F
Seeding rate: pounds/square feet:
0.5–1 pound/1,000 square feet, alone or with grass or grain
Alternate seeding rate: 2–3 cups/1,000 square feet

FIELD PEAS

Field peas are a more manageable legume than vetch because they generate less top growth to turn in. Field peas winter kill in many parts of the United States, but overwinter well in the Pacific Northwest. An added benefit is that you can harvest and eat the growing tips when the plant starts to mature — delicious! Field peas are often sown together with oats.

When to seed: spring for mid-season cover, late summer for winter cover
Management: mow and turn in when desired; grown as a winter kill cover in cold climates
Winter kill temperature: 5–10°F
Seeding rate: pounds/square feet:
5 pounds/1,000 square feet alone,
3 pounds/1,000 square feet when sown with a grain or grass
Alternate seeding rate: 6–8 seeds per foot in furrows 6" apart

HAIRY VETCH

This vigorous legume grows well in the fall for winter cover and generates a huge amount of soil nitrogen for the following year's crop. Because of all the top growth, vetch can take a bit more work to turn into the soil in the spring. Rye and hairy vetch make a great combination for winter cover.

When to seed: spring for mid-season cover, late summer–fall for winter cover

Management: mow at or before flowering to prevent reseeding; turn in when desired
Winter kill temperature: −20°F
Seeding rate: pounds/square feet: 1 pound/1,000 square feet with rye or oats
Alternate seeding rate: 5 cups/1,000 square feet

MUSTARD

Research has shown that mustard greens can greatly reduce soil-borne diseases when grown as a cover crop, so you can use mustards as a "fall cleaning" cover crop in a greenhouse or field that has disease issues.

When to seed: early fall
Management: mow at flowering and turn in immediately for best disease suppression
Winter kill temperature: 5–10°F
Seeding rate: pounds/square feet: 0.25 pound/1,000 square feet
Alternate seeding rate: 1 cup/1,000 square feet

OATS

Oats are another commonly used grass. It's often grown in combination with field peas for a great winter kill cover crop in most of the United States.

When to seed: spring for mid-season cover, late summer for winter cover
Management: mow and turn in when desired, grown as a winter kill cover in cold climates
Winter kill temperature: 20°F
Seeding rate: pounds/square feet: 4 pounds/1,000 square feet
Alternate seeding rate: 9 cups/1,000 square feet

WINTER RYE (also called annual rye, not to be confused with annual and perennial ryegrass)

Rye is one of the most commonly used grasses for a cover crop. It's extremely hardy, and germinates well in cold soil. Rye requires vernalization to set seed, so it needs to be planted in late summer/fall if you want it to produce grain or straw.

When to seed: spring–early summer for mid-season cover, late summer to mid-fall for winter cover
Management: mow and turn in when desired; grown as a winter kill cover in cold climates
Winter kill temperature: −35°F
Seeding rate: pounds/square feet: 4–6 pounds/1,000 square feet
Alternate seeding rate: 9–13.5 cups/1,000 square feet

START A SOIL MANAGEMENT CALENDAR

There are a number of ways to manage your soil — and all kinds of ways to keep track of when you should carry out the tasks related to soil management. Use the following sample calendar of soil management practices as a general outline for your own plan.

Late Summer

- Test soil.
- Begin seeding cover crops, if they're part of your management plan.

Fall

- Turn in lime or sulfur to balance pH, based on soil test.
- Add compost to all beds.
- Mulch or continue seeding cover crops for winter soil protection.

Winter

- Review any fertility problems you had over the past season, actions you took to correct them, and what the results were. If the results were sub-par, winter is a great time to research new methods and amendments to try during the upcoming season.

Spring

- Turn in cover crops/prepare beds.
- Mix in organic fertilizer at planting time.

Summer

- Seed mid-season cover crops to precede fall plantings, if desired.
- Side-dress/foliar feed heavy feeding crops.
- Mulch crops as appropriate.

MULCHING FOR WINTER

During the winter, periods of high precipitation can leach nutrients and acidify the soil. Leaving the soil bare throughout the year can significantly decrease the population of beneficial mycorrhizal fungi. For these reasons, it is important to protect your soil in winter, either with cover crops or mulch.

Covering your soil with an organic mulch in the winter provides a physical barrier that protects against leaching. Mulching is much less management intensive than growing cover crops, though mulching does have a drawback as compared to cover cropping. Simply, mulch does not leave living roots in the soil, which is the best way to protect the beneficial mycorrhizal fungi. Following are a few options for winter mulches:

Compost: As with soil, nutrients can be leached from compost during the winter; however, it does provide soil protection and creates an easy to work with soil surface for the next season.

Grass clippings: When used as winter mulch, it can be turned into the soil in spring.

Hardwood leaves: Use a thick layer for winter protection (4 to 6 inches). Avoid turning into the soil so as not to tie up nitrogen; instead, rake off remaining mulch and compost.

Shredded hardwood leaves: Can be turned directly into the soil in the spring to add organic matter and nutrients.

Rolled burlap or burlap sacks: Don't turn these into the soil! Instead, store and reuse next year. Works for mid-season mulch, but can be difficult to lay in between plants.

Straw: Use a thick layer (4 to 6 inches). Avoid turning into the soil in the spring so as not to tie up nitrogen; instead, rake off remaining mulch and compost or reapply when crops begin to mature. Whether or not your straw supplier is certified organic, it's important to verify that the straw you're buying was not sprayed with herbicides. Chemical herbicides can persist for some time, and unwittingly adding them to your garden via straw may lead to years of problems.

CHAPTER 13

Extending the Growing Season

Season extension is the art and science of using protective covers like cold frames, low tunnels, and high tunnels to grow and harvest crops early in the spring, through hot summer spells, and late into the fall and winter. Along with storage crops and succession planting, season extension is one of the most important tools you can use to maintain a consistent supply of produce from your garden.

You can create very simple or complex systems for extending the growing season. What you build will depend on your needs. We recommend that you start small and scale up over time as you learn what works best in your climate and for your preferred crops.

GROWING IN EVERY SEASON

Although weather patterns and seasonality will dictate when the majority of your growing takes place, it is almost always possible to extend and expand your garden's productivity so that you can harvest throughout the entire year. Off-season productivity will be limited and plant growth slower, but surprisingly large jumps in yearly harvest totals can be accomplished with some simple technologies, planning, and practices.

Warming Up and Cooling Down in Spring and Summer

In the spring when it's cool outside, almost any crop will germinate and grow faster when it's protected by a low or high tunnel. You may be able to set out plantings of cold-tolerant crops such as peas, cooking greens, salad greens, radishes, turnips, and carrots as early as February, and use a row cover as additional protection to help them along through the cold weather. Using this technique, you can even sneak frost-sensitive crops such as tomatoes, cucumbers, and summer squash outside as much as a month before your average last frost date.

In summer, you can stretch the growing season of cool-weather crops and protect summer crops from abnormally hot weather. To help salad greens and brassicas keep cool — and produce tasty harvests even at the peak of summer — swap out your row cover with a shade fabric. Alternatively (or in addition to a shade fabric cover), you can use overhead irrigation on these heat-sensitive crops during hot summer months to help dissipate the heat from their leaves.

In areas with cool summers, tunnels provide the extra heat needed for heat lovers like tomatoes, peppers, basil, and eggplants. In this type of setting, a greenhouse can easily quadruple yields of these crops.

Strategies for Heat-Loving Crops

Greenhouses and high tunnels can help increase yields of heat-loving crops even in climates with relatively hot summers. Not only will the covered structure allow you to plant the crops earlier in the spring, it keeps precipitation off the leaves of the plant and the soil around it. This can reduce the risk of many diseases and give you more control of the post-harvest quality of produce.

For example, professional growers all over the country often choose to plant tomatoes in a greenhouse. This allows the plants to mature earlier in the season and produce later into the fall. Because many tomato varieties have indeterminate growth habits, they will continue to produce fruit as long as soil fertility and weather permit. Greenhouse growing can also reduce the incidence of early blight and increase marketable yields by reducing cracking and splitting during rain events.

Other examples of crops that are commonly grown in greenhouses to increase yield and quality are sweet and hot peppers, eggplant, trellised cucumbers, basil, and raspberries. Sprawling crops like melons and sweet potatoes also produce well in greenhouse culture, but are not as commonly grown because they require a large amount of space per plant.

It's important to remember that although greenhouse culture can reduce some diseases, it will create an environment that favors others. Problematic greenhouse diseases include *Botrytis cinerea* (gray mold), white and leaf molds, and powdery mildew. The best way to combat disease is to maintain adequate ventilation in your greenhouse and prune your crops to promote air circulation.

Extending the Harvest in Fall and Winter

The limiting factors to fall and winter cropping are cold temperatures, inclement weather, and lack of light. You can address the temperature and weather issues by selecting crops that grow well (and actually taste better) when grown in cold conditions, and by using protective structures. You can address the light issue by growing crops to maturity before day length begins to decrease.

Depending on your latitude, daylight hours may decrease to the point where plant growth slows down to a crawl. In northern regions, daylight will drop to less than 10 hours sometime in October or November, making it difficult for crops to grow without supplemental lighting. In these situations, then, you're not really *growing* crops in the winter; you're *storing* them.

You have two methods in this scenario. The first is to grow appropriate crops to a harvestable stage before light levels drop, meaning that you will be able to harvest them throughout the cold months. The other is to germinate seeds in fall, which will go dormant for the winter, and then wait until day length increases for an early-spring harvest. Skilled growers throughout North America, including frigidly cold northern areas in Maine and very low winter sun areas in the Pacific Northwest, use these techniques to harvest through the fall and winter months.

Choosing Cool-Weather Crops

Planting cool-loving crops is another great way to extend your growing season. Many crops can tolerate light frost, and some can take temperatures that are much lower. Cool-weather crops are great for growing in the early spring, and for growing in the fall to overwinter (depending on your climate and how much protection you give them).

The temperatures and planting dates we suggest in the following section are very general but should nonetheless give you a good idea of what is possible. We suggest that you read further (see Resources, page 307) about this subject, experiment with different crops, and make your own

Avoiding Nitrates in Winter-Harvested Greens

Some studies have shown that greens grown during periods of low temperatures and low light levels can take up nitrates from the soil into their tissues. Consumption of nitrates is believed to carry health risks, so for greens that are grown during late fall and midwinter, a best practice is to harvest them in the afternoon or early evening, and preferably on a moderately sunny day. This is because exposure to even a short period of sunlight drastically reduces the nitrate levels in the plants' leaves.

determinations about the best planting dates for your climate.

Salad Mixes

Our favorite way to take advantage of cool-weather crops is to grow a variety of baby leaf crops and combine them into unique salad mixes. For early-spring production, seed these crops in a high tunnel as early as you can work your soil, or seed them outdoors in a bed covered with a low tunnel or cold frame. For fall production, seed them in late August through September.

In most northern regions, you can maintain a harvest into the winter using a high tunnel or heavy polyester row cover. For overwintering and harvesting in the coldest months, you might need to use polyester row covers over top of crops that are inside of a high tunnel for maximum protection. For more details about tunnels, see Choosing a Structure, below.

Because establishing new plantings is difficult, if not impossible, to do in late fall and winter, using "cut and come again" culture works best for many of these greens. When the baby leaves are ready to harvest, cut them off cleanly about an inch above the soil level (if tiny new leaves are starting to emerge from the base of the plant, cut above them to maintain the quality of the next cutting). After harvesting, the tiny new leaves will slowly grow into a harvestable size (hence, cut and come again). Depending on the crop, soil, and weather conditions, you may get anywhere from two to four cuttings from a single planting.

Other Great Fall/Winter Crops

Carrots are sweetest when grown in cool temperatures and spend some time at close to freezing when mature. Carrot greens can tolerate below-freezing temperatures, but if the roots actually freeze they'll become fibrous and tough, or turn to mush. To prevent roots from freezing, cover overwintering plantings with 6 to 18 inches of straw or another easily removable protective mulch. To get a constant supply of carrots through the season, for example, we seed them as early as we can work the soil in the spring; and we seed our last outdoor plantings in late June to mid-July (sometimes into early August if we're using short-day varieties and a row cover or high tunnel).

Radishes tolerate frost well but lose quality if the bulb fully freezes. In the spring, seed as early as you can work the soil; then seed your fall plantings into early September (if using a row cover or high tunnel).

Scallions are extremely cold-tolerant, and in many climates can be grown outdoors without additional protection. Seed as you would radishes.

Baby turnips such as 'Tokyo Cross' and 'Hakurei' size up quickly in a short period (they're mature when at golf-ball size). The plants tolerate frost, but the roots should not be allowed to freeze. Seed as you would radishes.

CHOOSING A STRUCTURE

Using protective structures is the key to successfully extending a growing and increasing the high-yield potential of your garden. These structures fall into two general categories: short structures, such as low tunnels and cold frames; and taller structures, such as high tunnels and greenhouses. Short structures have the advantage of being less

Cold-Hardy Salad Crops

Baby beet leaves. Add color and flavor to salads; can also be sautéed. Can tolerate temperatures into the low 20s when leaves are young.

Baby chard leaves. Rainbow or 'Bright Lights' chard provides beautiful colors in salad mixes. Very cold-tolerant when leaves are young. Full-grown chard tolerates frost well, but not repeated freezing/thawing.

Baby kale. The baby leaf, especially the variety 'Red Russian', is excellent in salads. Cold-tolerant into the teens.

Bok choy/tatsoi/other Asian-type greens. These are all brassica family crops, and are excellent in salads as a baby leaf. They can be grown to maturity for cooking, too. Most are very cold-tolerant, but winter and early-spring plantings can bolt quickly when temperatures warm up.

Claytonia. Adds great weight and texture to salad mixes. Maintains its raw eating quality even when flowering. Thin plants to 4 inches apart for best growth. Extremely cold-tolerant (into the teens).

Curly cress/peppercress. Great flavor, good for multiple cuttings, and is easier to grow than watercress. Tolerant of light frosts and hard freezes.

Greens mixes. Many seed companies now sell mixes of different non-lettuce greens (mustard mixes, braising mixes, and so forth). These are great! We tend to avoid mixes that contain lettuce and other green types mixed together because they germinate and grow at different rates, which makes them difficult to harvest at a consistent size and quality.

Mâche. Some people love its unique flavor, and others find it off-putting. It is usually harvested as a whole plant; it doesn't regrow well for cut and come again. Tolerates temperatures into the teens, but can be a little finicky to grow.

Mizuna. This is a staple winter green for us. Its mild, bok choy–like flavor is excellent in salad mixes, and it can also be grown larger for braising or stir-frying. It recovers well from temperatures into the teens, and has strong regrowth for cut and come again culture.

Mustard greens. Adds a great kick to salad mixes as a baby leaf, and can also be grown full size for sautéing.

Minutina. Interesting flavor and texture. Can get tough and bolt quickly after the first cutting. Very cold tolerant.

Spinach. One of the most cold-tolerant crops (we've seen it recover from temperatures close to 10°F). You can use cut and come again culture when leaves are young (for raw eating), or you can pick individual larger leaves to extend the harvest over a longer period (for cooking).

Moderately Cold-Hardy Salad Crops

Arugula. This spicy green is mellow and delicious when grown in cooler temperatures. Handles light frosts well, but starts to deteriorate with repeated hard frosts. Can be cut several times, but quality is best at first cutting.

Baby lettuce mix. Lettuce tolerates light frosts well when leaves are at baby size, but it loses quality when temperatures dip into the 20s. Heads of lettuce grow well in cool spring and fall temperatures, but don't tolerate below-freezing temperatures well.

expensive to make and easier to install than tall structures. By contrast, tall structures allow for easier crop management and can accommodate a wider range of crops.

Low Tunnels

Low tunnels, also known as row covers, are structures that are not tall enough to walk into. They often comprise hoops or arches that support fabric or plastic covers that protect plants. The cover of a low tunnel must be removed to manage and harvest the protected plantings. Low tunnels are inexpensive and easy to set up, but because they're low, you can't grow tall crops to maturity under them.

For simplicity of construction and minimal cost, low tunnels are often built 2 to 4 feet tall. A 2-foot high cover will be perfect for salad greens and carrots, but will hamper the growth of maturing kale, peppers, or summer squash. A slightly taller tunnel (3 or 4 feet high) is appropriate for these and

other taller crops, such as tomatillos and broccoli. If you feel the structure needs to be any taller than 4 feet, consider upgrading to a high tunnel (see page 261).

How to Construct a Low Tunnel

It's pretty easy to improvise a structure for a low tunnel. Alternatively, you can purchase materials from a nursery or seed company (see Resources, page 307). Common materials for hoops are #9- or #10-gauge wire; or PVC pipe bent over rebar pins that are pounded into the ground. (We like to use 2-foot lengths of ½-inch rebar for pins, and 10-foot lengths of electrical conduit that are cut to size to fit over the bed.) Another easy option is to bend a section of wire fencing into a C-shape and attach the covering material to the wire with zip ties, twist ties, twine, or bungee cords. Low tunnel structures, especially taller ones, are more stable if they feature a top purlin (a lengthwise roof support between the hoops).

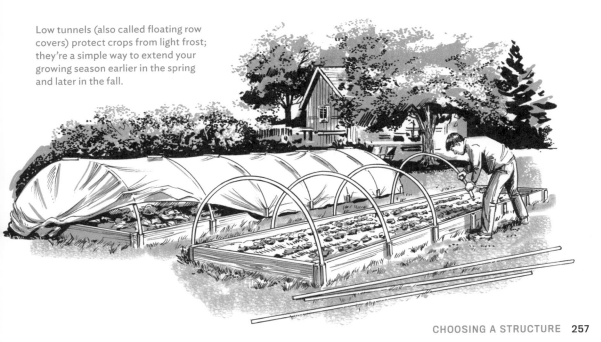

Low tunnels (also called floating row covers) protect crops from light frost; they're a simple way to extend your growing season earlier in the spring and later in the fall.

Low tunnels can be covered with a variety of materials, such as these listed here:

Spun-bonded polyester fabric. This material provides some heat retention and wind resistance but is also breathable and lets precipitation pass through (Reemay and Agribon are common brand names). It doesn't create the greenhouse effect like clear plastic, so you will not have to remove it when the sun comes out. You can purchase row cover in different weights — heavier weights provide the most protection from the elements; lighter weights are more breathable and are best for pest exclusion (see chapter 11 for more information). Row cover will let anywhere from 30 to 90 percent of the sun's rays pass through, depending on the weight of the fabric.

Greenhouse or UV-resistant plastic film. Using clear plastic to cover your hoops creates the greenhouse effect, and your garden beds will get maximum temperature gain. However, this material can cause your crops to fry on a sunny day (even in the middle of winter); you need to be prepared to open it partially or remove it for ventilation during sunny periods. It doesn't breathe and doesn't allow precipitation to pass through, so you will also need a way to water the crops underneath. Greenhouse plastic lets 80 to 90 percent of sunlight pass through. Avoid using clear plastic tarps or painter's plastic purchased from a hardware store; light transmission may be poor, and the plastic will break down very quickly because it's not UV stabilized.

Slitted plastic row cover. This is also a UV-resistant plastic cover but contains slits or holes that are desgined to promote ventilation and reduce temperature spikes in sunny weather. The slits remain closed when the plastic is cool, but when it heats up and expands the slits open and allow air to pass through. You still need to water underneath this type of cover, and open it up to ventilate during long sunny periods, but it's much more versatile and requires less management than a solid plastic row cover. Because it's less insulating than solid plastic, slitted plastic is more commonly used to warm up spring crops than to protect overwintering crops.

Cold Frames

Cold frames serve the same purpose as row covers, but have a sturdier structure that is built from wood or metal. Because of the sturdy frame, you can use heavier covering materials such as double-wall

Cold frames are more complicated to assemble than row covers, but are sturdier and provide a bit more protection.

Keeping It Together

You can use a variety of techniques to hold row covers in place:

Attach the covering to the structure. Purchase clamps or specially made clips to attach sheeting material to your hoops or other row cover structures.

Hold down the bottom edges. Most home growers use sandbags, rocks, or bricks to weigh down the edges of the fabric. This works well, but moving them around involves some labor. If you don't mind doing some extra digging, you can also use soil to bury the edge of the row cover. This method works particularly well if excluding pests is a priority, because you can effectively seal the entire edge of the cover with soil. Some growers use stakes or landscape staples to hold the covers in place, but this can destroy the fabric very quickly.

Close the ends. Seal the ends of the row covers by bunching the fabric or plastic together, and then holding it in place with weights or soil.

When purchasing materials for a low tunnel, make sure you get hoops and a covering that are wide enough to cover your beds adequately (don't forget to leave extra fabric to place weights on or secure with soil). An 83-inch wide row cover is just about the right size to span a low hoop over a 4-foot bed.

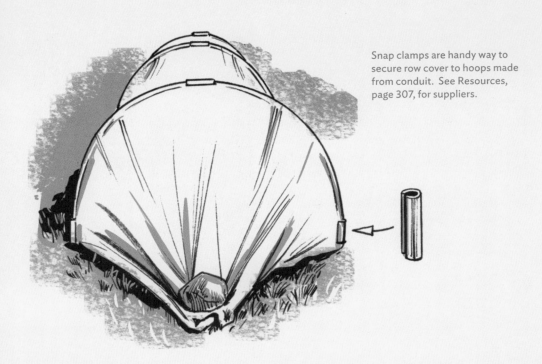

Snap clamps are handy way to secure row cover to hoops made from conduit. See Resources, page 307, for suppliers.

polycarbonate sheeting or salvaged windows (greenhouse plastic or spun-bonded polyester also work). Try to find plastic or tempered glass windows; old glass panes can break and leave shards in the soil.

The advantage of cold frames is that they are less likely to blow away than low tunnels and have a higher insulation value. Also, you don't have to assemble or disassemble them — you can just lift up the whole structure and set it over top of a garden bed. The drawback is that they don't cover a lot of square footage in the garden relative to the time and expense of building them. Also, they can be difficult to move around (most take two people), and you have to find somewhere to store them when they're not in use. We find that they're most useful for protecting small amounts of space-efficient salad greens, or for protecting a few flats of transplants while they're growing.

Almost any crop can be covered with a low tunnel or cold frame in the spring to enable earlier planting and harvest. For frost-tolerant crops, seed or transplant as soon as you're able to work the soil. Water in the crop, and then cover with plastic, slitted plastic, or spun-bonded polyester row covers. For frost-sensitive crops, transplant from two weeks to one and a half months earlier than suggested by the chart on page 56. The additional thermal and wind protection provided by the cover should accelerate harvest by one to five weeks.

The exact timing of your planting will depend on your local climate/microclimate and your tolerance for risk. We know a skilled professional grower in Pennsylvania who sets out his first planting of tomatoes under row cover on March 15 (two full months earlier than is recommended for his climate). If the spring works in his favor, he's the first in his market to show up with tomatoes. If it's unusually cold, he might lose the whole planting and have to set out another one. He feels it's worth the risk because early tomatoes are prized by his customers.

Closely monitor the temperature under the plastic and slitted plastic covers and be prepared to remove them when necessary. You also need to remove these covers for watering if you don't have drip irrigation installed underneath. You don't need to remove spun-bonded polyester covers unless the plants are flowering and need insect pollination, it's time to harvest, or if the plants need more room to grow (for tall crops like trellised tomatoes).

Extending Your Harvest in the Fall

Transplant or direct seed your fall crops, wait until temperatures and/or light levels start to drop, and then cover each of your crops with a floating row cover of your choice. For example, you might seed spinach on September 1 for fall harvest. If your early September temperatures are still 70°F or above, wait until late September or October to install row cover.

We like to use heavy row cover for this application because our primary concern is protection from wind and cold. We don't worry about blocking light because once it's October, there's not enough daylight for plants to do much growing anyway.

You can also use multiple coverings on your low tunnels. In the early fall, start with a spun-bonded polyester row cover fabric over your low tunnel. In the late fall or early winter, when temperatures and light levels drop, add a greenhouse plastic cover on top of the fabric row cover.

High Tunnels, Hoophouses, and Greenhouses

High tunnel, hoophouse, and *greenhouse* are essentially interchangeable terms — they all describe an arched or gabled structure that is tall enough to walk into. Some growers use the term *greenhouse* if the structure has a heat source in it and the term *high tunnel* if it's unheated (but this distinction isn't universally adopted).

High tunnels are more complicated and costly to set up than simple row covers, but they're much easier to work in. They also allow you to grow tall crops, such as tomatoes, to maturity. An added benefit to using a high tunnel is that you can keep precipitation off the leaves of disease-prone crops, which can help extend their season dramatically.

Usually, high tunnels have doors or windows on the ends for access and ventilation, and are outfitted with some way to open or roll up the sidewalls to provide for maximum ventilation during hot days. If you have access to electricity, greenhouses can be fitted with automatic ventilation

A high tunnel involves some initial expense and labor to set up, but provides an easy-to-work-in structure that can improve your yields year-round.

shutters, fans, and heaters for further season extensions.

Heating a greenhouse does have a high environmental cost in terms of fuel use and carbon emission, so we recommend doing so only when absolutely necessary (growing transplants is a good example). You can still dramatically extend the seasons and have amazing yield improvements by using an unheated or minimally heated high tunnel.

The Structure

The hoops and arches that support a greenhouse are usually made from bent steel pipe. You can purchase these pipes pre-made, or you can bend them yourself. Johnny's Selected Seeds sells a great bender for small-scale growers. These pipes are often used for the construction of so-called caterpillar tunnels (so called because their segmented structure makes them look like enormous insects). The materials to build these structures are easy to source. In fact, most component pieces are designed for chain-link fencing. (Check with your supplier for more information on appropriate components for your structure.)

Small high tunnels may only have hoops or arches (a "Gothic" arch shape is usually more expensive but is stronger and handles snow loads better). As these structures get larger, purlins, ridgepoles, corner braces, and trusses may become necessary. You can construct greenhouse (tunnel) end walls from steel pipe with customized fittings, or you can make them using standard framing lumber. Smaller greenhouse kits often feature a wooden or metal frame, and some even feature a gabled roof. You can indeed build an elaborate (hence expensive) greenhouse like this, but metal hoops/arches are the more cost-effective method for building larger greenhouses.

Finding the Right High Tunnel

You can choose from an astonishing array of brands and materials (and a wide array of specific hardware pieces) to construct

Challenges of Greenhouse Production

One issue with permanent high tunnels is that the soil under them is never exposed to precipitation and extreme temperatures. This can lead to nutrient imbalances (high salt levels in particular) and a buildup of pest and disease problems. Careful ventilation, fertilization, and irrigation will help deal with these issues. Some growers are pioneering techniques for using movable greenhouses to expose the soil to weather and allow for longer crop rotations. These movable greenhouses usually move back and forth on skids or tracks with rollers, but some are moved by hand and others with a small tractor. Alternatively, it's relatively easy to disassemble and move a high tunnel if crop disease problems arise.

your greenhouse. Identify a local or regional supplier and ask them to help you design the structure, if you need guidance (see Resources, page 307). If all you need is a 6 × 6 foot or 8 × 8 foot structure, consider buying a kit. Doing so saves you the trouble of figuring out all the fittings and parts needed to assemble a greenhouse using metal hoops. You can even create a greenhouse that moves from place to place in the garden. If you're interested in movable greenhouses, turn to the resources section on page 307 for more information.

Greenhouse Coverings

High tunnels are almost always covered with UV-resistant plastic film or acrylic panels. Greenhouses can be built with glass, but we suggest avoiding glass because it breaks easily and is difficult to repair. Double-wall polycarbonate panels are often used to construct end walls. These panels

have more insulating value than plastic sheeting, but are quite expensive.

If you have a high tunnel covered with plastic film, you can increase the insulation value by putting two layers of plastic on it, and inflating the air space in between the layers with a specially designed electric blower.

To provide maximum protection in cold northern climates, you can use low tunnels inside an unheated high tunnel to grow cold-hardy greens year-round (even when outdoor temperatures fall to 10°F and below!).

Site Selection and Orientation

When choosing a site for a high tunnel, consider its orientation. For summer production of heat-loving crops, some growers prefer a north–south orientation of the long axis because it theoretically allows for more even light distribution on the plants. In our experience in the northeastern and northwestern United States, we haven't

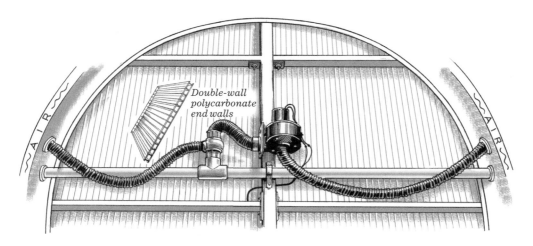

Double-wall polycarbonate end walls

Fitting the ends of high tunnels with double-wall polycarbonate panels will provide a bit more insulation than if you used a single sheet of plastic film. In addition, covering the high tunnel with two layers of plastic film inflated with a small blower will increase its thermal efficiency and minimize condensation on the interior.

experienced a big difference between east-west and north–south orientation for summer crops.

For fall and winter production of greens, many growers prefer an east–west orientation for maximum light intensity in the winter. Our experience has found this to be very effective.

For North America, we recommend the following guidelines for greenhouse orientation:

- If you're north of 40 degrees north latitude, orient your greenhouse east–west for maximum light intensity.

- If you're south of 40 degrees north latitude, light intensity is much less of an issue. Orient your greenhouse north–south for best light distribution.

Interior Layout

You have many options to consider when laying out beds in a high tunnel. The simplest option is to set up beds that run the length of the greenhouse, and adjust their width based on the total width of the greenhouse. If you grow trellised crops, such as cucumbers or tomatoes, this layout allows you to hang trellis strings from the purlins — an added benefit.

If your greenhouse features vertical sidewalls, then awkward spaces along the walls may not be an issue. But if you're using a tunnel with sloping sidewalls, you'll probably want narrow beds on the outside edges of the greenhouse. This design then places your path down the tall center of the tunnel. If your tunnel is tall enough, you may be able to walk through it without stooping. The perimeter of a high tunnel is usually the coldest space, so there are arguments for putting a path along the outside edge. Our experience with garden design and production growing, however, has taught us that good access is a primary consideration — if it's hard to access beds because you hit your head on the greenhouse frame, you won't want to work in that location.

Comb-shaped or keyhole beds maximize plantable square footage in a greenhouse. These are a little more complicated to lay out, and are a little harder to manage if using low tunnels within a high tunnel, but they allow you to plant more of the protected square footage inside the greenhouse.

Lighting and Heating

For most season-extension purposes, the expense and complication of adding a light and heat source to a greenhouse are prohibitive. However, there are circumstances for

Greenhouse Thermometer

Installing a thermometer so that you can gauge the temperature in your greenhouse is always a good idea, if only to see how much warmer the space is than the outside air. If you don't have automatic venting in the greenhouse, the thermometer will help you determine when to vent the space whenever inside temperatures get too high.

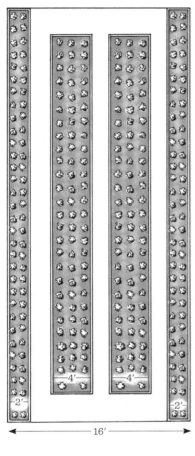

This 16'-wide high tunnel is laid out into rectangular beds for easy planting in straight rows. Note the narrower beds on the outer edges for ease of access.

This 12'-wide high tunnel is laid out into keyhole or comb-shaped beds to maximize usable square footage in the space.

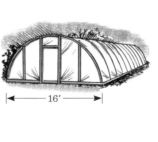

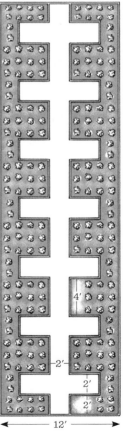

which these extra costs and work might be worthwhile, especially for growers who produce young transplants. Please see page 152 to learn about adding supplemental lighting and heating to your greenhouse.

Using High Tunnels/Hoophouses/ Greenhouses

For spring and fall planting, high tunnels are managed just like low tunnels. The major difference is that the high tunnel is still standing during the main part of the growing season, so you can use it to grow heat-loving crops such as basil, tomatoes, cucumbers, or peppers.

You can also use your high tunnel to grow crops throughout the year. A typical strategy for doing so is to establish fall crops in late August and September. These crops would be harvested into the late fall–early winter, or perhaps even over the winter (depending on crop choice, climate, and if you use an additional row cover over the crop). In the spring, any overwintered crops would be harvested and cleared as they finish producing or as they bolt. If necessary, warm-season crops could be relay-planted into the tunnel before the overwintered crops are removed.

When the warm-season crops have finished producing in the fall, fall greens could be planted again. Many warm-season crops are typically still producing in early September when fall planting should begin, so part of the greenhouse could be left fallow during the summer to allow for this.

Ventilation and Daily Management

Ventilation is crucial for moderating the temperature in a high tunnel and minimizing any diseases that might arise there. If you don't have automatic vents and fans in your tunnel, you'll need to be available on a daily basis to open the tunnel during sunny periods to prevent the temperature from getting high enough to damage your crops.

Cover Cropping or Fallow Periods in a High Tunnel?

Some growers who are focused on fall and winter crops may not use their high tunnel for vegetable production in the summer. Instead they might plant a short-season cover crop like buckwheat or mustard greens (see page 245 for more information on cover cropping). They do so because it is a good way to address soil quality and disease issues. Some growers who are primarily focused on growing warm-season crops in their greenhouse might leave it fallow in winter, or even remove the covering to expose the soil to cold temperatures and precipitation. Because a greenhouse provides such a valuable production space, most growers use high tunnels for growing crops year-round and address issues that arise by way of other organic methods.

Regardless, hang a thermometer in your high tunnel so you can easily monitor the interior temperature. Consult the Planting Dates chart on page 56 for guidance on what temperature is best for each crop. If you're growing peppers and tomatoes in the spring, you might wait until the temperature is above 75°F before venting the tunnel. If you're growing spinach or salad greens, you might vent it at 65°F.

To minimize disease, consider opening the greenhouse on cloudy days for a short period at midday, even if interior temperatures are still low. If you have electricity in your tunnel, use fans to circulate the air in the spring and summer (wind can damage crops when it's cold/below freezing, so we don't set up fans until temperatures are above 50°F). When temperatures are higher, fully open the ends and sides of the tunnel for maximum air flow (roll-up sides are helpful for this). In the fall and winter, close up the tunnel an hour or so before you lose sunlight to warm the air and soil before outdoor temperatures start to drop.

Use Inner Covers for Extra Protection

If you're located in a colder climate and are going for winter-long production of greens, plan to use low tunnels (inner covers) inside your high tunnels. Start by establishing the greens in your high tunnel, as previously directed. When outdoor temperatures start dropping below freezing, set up a low tunnel over the greens using a heavy-weight fabric or greenhouse plastic. If it's sunny, remove the inner cover after the temperature in the high tunnel is above freezing. Replace the inner cover in the late afternoon before the tunnel temperature drops below freezing. If it's cloudy and the temperature stays below freezing all day in the high tunnel, leave the inner cover on.

Roll-up sides are a great way to ventilate your high tunnel in hot weather.

For growing greens during the really cold months, use floating row covers inside of your high tunnel to extend the season even further.

COOLING IN SUMMER CAN INCREASE YIELDS

In hot climates, and even in temperate climates that are prone to heat waves, protection from very high temperatures may be necessary to keep crops thriving and productive. Most of the cool-season crops mentioned on page 256 can be grown longer into the hot season when given a bit of shade. Even heat-loving crops can suffer when temperatures jump above 90°F for extended periods of time. High temperatures can result in blossom-end rot and dropped blossoms in many fruiting crops. In extreme heat, tomatoes, peppers, and beans can stop setting fruit altogether. A heat wave that brings temperatures into the triple digits can stress out even the hardiest vegetable crops. If you adapt your irrigation regime to help cool crops, and utilize the semi-shady areas of your site or tunnel, you can stretch your garden seasons to their maximum limits.

Using Shade Cover/Cloth

Shade cover can reduce sunlight penetration and keep plants and soil cool. With a layer of shade cloth, almost any low tunnel, cold frame, or high tunnel structure can be adapted to help extend the summer growing time for cool-loving crops. Just remove the row cover or plastic from your structure, or build an entirely new structure to support a layer of shade fabric over heat-sensitive crops. If you're covering a greenhouse or other more permanent structure, you can drape a layer of shade cloth over the top of the structure to provide relief from direct sunlight. In these situations, be extra conscientious about ventilation.

In hot climates, or on abnormally scorching summer days, shade cloth can be worth its weight in lettuce. This cloth is breathable and lets precipitation pass through. Furthermore, you can select different fabric grades to control the amount of shade your plants receive. Very generally,

Shade cover can help you grow crops that like it cooler during midsummer heat. You can set up shade cover using the same techniques for setting up floating row cover.

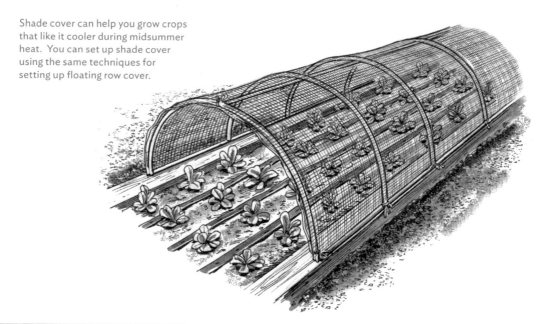

30 percent shade works well for protecting fruiting crops from sunburn in hot areas and for growing lettuce and salad greens in midsummer in the cooler regions. Fifty percent shade cloth works well in hotter climates for shade-loving plants, such as lettuce and salad greens.

If you live in a particularly hot climate, consider setting up a shade cloth over the entire garden in peak season. Using tall stakes, you can set up a temporary lean-to over the garden to cast shade with minimal investment and time.

Planting in Partial Shade

Try to use the portions of your garden that receive a little less sunlight for summer plantings of heat-sensitive crops. You may even consider building a special bed in a semi-shady location and dedicate it to summer greens, thus taking advantage of a space where sunlight is ample enough to allow the plants to grow but not so excessive that they become heat stressed. A good location for such a bed is the east side of a house, which allows the plants to receive morning light but provides reprieve by mid-afternoon when the sun is at its peak intensity.

Overhead Irrigation

Even if you've decided to use drip irrigation for your garden watering needs (which we strongly encourage you to consider), a quick and easy overhead irrigation setup can work wonders for cooling crops in summer. Sprinkling crops from overhead will cool down the leaves, stems, and fruit of the plant, as well as the soil around them. You won't want to turn on sprinklers in the middle of the day, but in very hot weather you can overhead irrigate in the morning and again in the late afternoon. The afternoon watering will help cool down the plants before night but will be early enough in the day so as to allow some of the moisture to dissipate from their leaves. We have seen growers harvest perfect heads of lettuce in the middle of July by employing a regular schedule of watering in this way.

CHAPTER 14

Timely Harvesting and Storage

Harvesting your crops is a singularly rewarding experience. After all of your planning, preparation, and hard work, you finally reap what you have sown. There is much to be appreciated about the growing process itself, but harvesting is what probably inspires you to keep going.

The goal of the high-yield vegetable gardener might be to produce as much food as possible from the space available, but this goal only makes sense if those crops are put to good use. Proper harvesting technique, timing, and storage will ensure that the fruits of your labor do not go to waste.

Experimental Harvesting

Don't be afraid to experiment with harvesting a crop before or after its normal harvest stage. Sometimes you'll discover a whole new taste or texture that you enjoy. For example, arugula is generally considered best when harvested young and tender, but we've come to enjoy cutting it large and tough and sautéing it like kale, or letting it flower and using the petals to spice up a salad.

BECOMING A SKILLED HARVESTER

Harvesting is an important skill unto itself. When and how you harvest can contribute greatly to the eating quality and storage life of your produce. Crops are ready to harvest at different stages depending on what part of the plant you're harvesting, and at different times of year based on the crop's planting date and life span.

Through proper planning and management, you can spread the harvest out over as much of the year as possible, but in every garden calendar there is always a peak harvest season. In temperate climates, peak harvest season happens in the late summer and fall. In hot climates it may be later in the year, or in the spring. No matter when your climate sets the stage for optimal plant growth, you should be ready for action.

Harvest Crops at Their Peak

Every crop has a characteristic size or appearance that indicates when it is ready to harvest. Anticipating the approach of harvest and recognizing these signs will ensure that you pick your crops at the peak of their flavor and freshness. Harvesting is a skill; it pays to keep a regular eye on your crops to watch how they change in form as they grow.

It also pays to do some experimental trial-and-error harvesting. If you're growing a new crop for the first time, start tasting it before you think it's ready to harvest, when the crop appears to be at its peak, and when it's a little past its prime. In this way, you can train your eyes to know when a crop is right at its ideal flavor and texture. The chart on page 272 will help guide you, but keep in mind that the peak harvest point for a crop can vary depending on who you're growing it for. For example, some chefs prefer arugula to be harvested very small when the leaves are extremely tender and the flavor is mild. Other chefs like the leaves a little bigger, tougher, and with stronger flavor, so that they stand up to a robust dressing.

Harvest "Hidden" Crops

In addition to the obvious harvests that you have been looking forward to all year, you may be able to find a few hidden surprises in your garden, yard, and neighborhood. To work toward your highest-yield garden, look for extra harvests wherever you can.

Eating the Whole Crop

Many garden crops contain extra sustenance, and creative gardening and cooking preparations can reveal surprising results. For example, carrot tops are delicious in soups, and beet leaves can be prepared just like kale or chard. Bolted cilantro can be kept in the garden until seed heads form for a harvest of coriander. Broccoli leaves can serve as a replacement for kale or cabbage when you need cooking greens; squash blossoms are a summertime delicacy; and even grape leaves are edible.

Keep in mind that not all parts of all crops are edible. For example, don't eat tomato leaves or rhubarb leaves. Get to know all of the plants in your garden. You will be amazed at how many hidden foods are already available to you.

When to Harvest

ANNUAL VEGETABLES AND HERBS

Arugula

Cut with a knife or scissors about 1 inch above soil level when leaves are desired size (usually 3–5 inches).

Basil

Pinch set of 4 leaves at the top of the plant early on to encourage growth of side shoots, then pinch 4 leaf sets heavily from the whole plant about once a week. Conversely, cut the top third of the plant off and strip the leaves.

Beans, Edible Soy (Edamame)

Pick pods after they've plumped out, but before they turn brown and leathery.

Beans, Fava (Broad)

Pick pods after they've plumped out, but before they turn brown and leathery.

Beans, Lima

See Shell Beans.

Beans, Shell

For fresh shell beans, pick pods after they've plumped out but before they turn brown and leathery. For dry beans, pick after most of the plant's leaves have fallen and pods feel dry and crunchy. Continue drying in a covered, well-ventilated space if weather is not conducive for field drying.

Beans, Snap

Pick when pods are about the thickness of a pencil (before inner seeds start to swell).

Beets

Harvest when roots reach desired size (you can harvest them small for "baby" beets).

Bok Choy

Cut plant at base with a knife when it reaches desired size, but before stem elongates and flower stalks appear (4–8 inches for baby, 8–16 inches full size). Different varieties are mature at different sizes.

Broccoli

Cut main head when "beads" are swollen, but before they separate or open. Continue harvesting side shoots for 1 to 4 weeks after main head is cut.

Brussels Sprouts

For earlier and more uniform harvest, cut the loose head at the top of the plant when sprouts are about ½ inch in diameter (late August–early September in many climates). Pluck individual sprouts when fully sized up, or cut entire plant at base if desired. Flavor improves when sprouts experience a few frosts.

Cabbage

Cut head at base when it feels dense, firm, and well filled out (before the top of the head starts to separate).

Cabbage, Chinese

Cut heads at base when they reach desired size (Chinese cabbage doesn't feel as dense as standard cabbage).

Carrots

Dig when roots reach desired size (dig one or two up to check; you can't tell from aboveground). Carrots can be harvested young for "baby" crops, but make sure they have full coloration (very young carrots are pale and don't have fully developed flavor).

Cauliflower
Cut head when it reaches desired size, but before the curd starts to separate. White color can be maintained by tying outer leaves around head when it's small.

Celeriac
Harvest when roots reach desired size (3–5 inches across).

Celery
Harvest when stalks reach desired size. Celery can be blanched for milder flavor by wrapping/covering the stems during the growing process (keep the top leaves exposed). Try a half-gallon milk jug with the top cut off for individual plants, or two boards placed on either side of a row of plants.

Chard, Swiss
Harvest outer, larger leaves (with stem attached) about once a week when they reach desired size. Don't remove more than 30 percent of the leaves at one time for best future harvests.

Cilantro
Cut with a knife or scissors about 1 inch above soil level when leaves are desired size.

Collards
See Chard.

Corn, Sweet
Harvest when ears feel well filled when squeezed, and when kernels are plump and "milky" (you can peel back the wrapper leaves and puncture a kernel with your thumbnail to check). This usually happens about 18 to 24 days after ear silks first show.

Cucumbers
Pick fruit by hand or with shears when they reach the desired size (well before cracking or yellowing appears). Once bearing begins, pick every other day to maintain best quality.

Dill
For dill weed (foliage), cut with a knife or scissors when leaves reach a desired size. When plants are small, cut and come again culture is possible (see Arugula), or individual branches can be harvested on a weekly basis (see Chard). For seed heads for pickling, harvest seed cluster (called an "umbel") when seeds have

filled out (you can also use flower clusters before seeds have formed for this purpose. For dill seed, wait until seeds have turned dry and brown on the plant.

Eggplant
Harvest fruit with shears at desired size. Pick regularly for best production.

Endive
Cut head at base when it reaches the desired size. For milder flavor, blanch the head by tying the outer leaves together over the plant, or covering it entirely with a reused nursery pot or other container 1 week before harvest.

Fennel, Bulbing
Cut bulb at base after it has swollen and reached desired size.

Garlic
Harvest by lifting entire plant with a spade or trowel when half of the leaves have browned out (half should still be green). See text on curing on page 287 for more information.

Kale
Harvest outer, larger leaves (with stem attached) about once a week when they reach

desired size. Don't remove more than 30 percent of the leaves at one time for best future harvests.

Kohlrabi

Cut bulb at base after it has swollen and reached desired size (3–8 inches in diameter, depending on the variety).

Leeks

Harvest by lifting plant with a spade or trowel when it has reached the desired size (approximately 1- to 2-inch-wide stem, depending on the variety). Trim roots and leaves with shears for washing and storage.

Lettuce, Baby Mix

Cut with a knife or scissors about 1 inch above soil level when leaves are desired size (usually 3–5 inches).

Lettuce, Heads

Harvest by cutting head at base well before stem elongates or flower stalks appear.

Mâche

Cut entire plant with a knife or scissors about 1 inch above soil level when it's reached desired size (usually 2–4 inches).

Melon, Cantaloupe, Honeydew

Assessing melon ripeness varies by variety and takes some experience. Most melons are ripe when the fruit shows some yellow coloration and detaches easily from the vine by hand (known as "full slip"). Honeydew and charentais melons are overripe at full slip and should be cut from the vine using shears. Read as much as possible about the variety you're growing before harvest.

Mustard Greens

Cut with a knife or scissors about 1 inch above soil level when leaves are desired size (2–4 inches for salad eating, larger for braising and sautéing). The greens become spicier as size increases.

Okra

Harvest pods with shears before they get tough (about 3–4 inches long). Harvest every 2 or 3 days for best production and quality.

Onions, Bulb

For baby bulbs and usable greens, harvest at any size when leaves are still green. For best size and storage, wait to harvest until tops have browned and died back.

See page 287 for curing information.

Parsley

Harvest outer leaves (with stem attached) about once a week when they reach desired size. Don't remove more than 30 percent of the leaves at one time for best future harvests. A well-harvested parsley plant will produce for an entire season.

Parsnips

For best flavor, dig when roots are fully sized up in mid–late fall, or early in the following spring before tops begin to regrow.

Peanut

Dig peanuts 120 to 160 days after planting, depending on the variety (peanut plants flower at around 40 days, and start producing the actual peanut underground after flowering). Loosen a 24-inch diameter circle around each plant with a spade, then pull the entire plant (including the roots) from the ground, and strip peanuts off the roots. This is best done when the soil is relatively moist.

Peas, Shelling

Harvest when pods are plump and well filled.

Peas, Snap

Harvest when pods are plump and taste sweet (you might need to experiment a bit with different varieties to determine best harvest stage; if you're too early, the peas aren't as sweet; too late and they get tough and stringy).

Peppers, Hot

Harvest when fruit is desired color (green through fully colored — red, yellow, orange, and so on). Picking the first full-size peppers at the green stage will improve overall yield of the plant.

Peppers, Sweet

Harvest when fruit is desired color (green through fully colored — red, yellow, orange, and so on). Picking the first full-size peppers at the green stage will improve overall yield of the plant.

Potatoes

For new potatoes, dig at about 8 weeks after planting. For full-size potatoes, dig when foliage is brown and has died back.

Raab

Cut whole plant at base when buds appear, or pick only buds for extended harvest.

Radicchio

Harvest as you would head lettuce.

Radishes

Pull plants from the ground as soon as the stem reaches the desired size (varies with each variety). Many radishes have a short harvest window and split or become tough or pithy if harvested when overmature.

Rutabagas

Harvest when roots reach desired size. For best flavor, wait until plant has experienced a few light frosts.

Scallions

Lift plants from the ground with a trowel or spade when they reach the desired size (about twice the thickness of a pencil). Overmature scallions can still be harvested, but are tougher so benefit from cooking like a bulb onion.

Spinach

For baby spinach, harvest like baby mix lettuce. Avoid cutting into the new leaves emerging from the base of the plant to maintain quality of the next cutting. For extended harvest and larger leaves, pluck larger outer leaves from plant and leave inner young leaves to size up (this method produces the best regrowth for winter crops).

Squash, Gourds

Harvest by cutting stem with shears. Point of harvest varies by variety.

Squash, Pumpkins

Harvest by cutting stem with shears when fruit is fully colored.

Squash, Summer

Harvest fruit by twisting off or cutting the stem with shears when it reaches the desired size. Smaller squash are most tender, larger squash have more flavor. Harvest before outer skin becomes tough.

Squash, Winter

Harvest by cutting stem with shears. Point of harvest varies by variety, but many winter squash are fully ripe when they have a distinct "ground spot" where they've been resting on the ground.

Sweet Potatoes

Dig roots in the fall before soil temperature drops below 50°F.

Tomatillos

Pluck fruits when they've filled out and their husk starts to split.

Tomatoes

For fully vine-ripened fruit (and maximum flavor), harvest when the tomato is fully colored and is somewhat soft to the touch. Tomatoes ripen well off the vine; for longer shelf life or shipping, harvest when fruit is partially green and harder to the touch.

Turnips

Pull plant from the ground at the desired size (varies depending on the variety; golf ball size for baby, 3–4 inches or larger for full-size varieties).

Watermelon

Cut fruit from vine with shears when tiny leaves on tendril close to fruit have turned brown (a ground spot is also a good indicator of ripeness).

PERENNIAL VEGETABLES

Artichoke

Cut flower buds from plant while tight and firm (artichokes become tough once buds start to open).

Asparagus

Break spears at soil level when they're 7–9 inches tall and the tips are still tight (spears toughen when the tips open and begin to fern out). Harvest every other day for best quality. Harvest for 3 weeks after initial emergence during the second season the plant is in the ground; and for 6 to 8 weeks the third season after planting and all following years. Once the harvest window is over, allow plants to fern out and grow to maturity to feed the roots and preserve the longevity of the planting.

Cardoon

Blanch stems for 3 to 4 weeks prior to harvest by wrapping them in burlap, landscape fabric, or other materials. Cut stems with a knife or shears, remove leaves and thorns with a knife or scissor, then use a vegetable peeler to remove the majority of the tough fibers on the exterior of the stem.

Jerusalem Artichoke, Sunchoke

Dig tubers in late fall, mid-winter, or early the following spring. Flavor is best if tubers have experienced cold temperatures.

Rhubarb

Break larger outer stalks from plant and remove most of leaf from stalk with a knife or shears (a tiny bit of leaf left on the stem will keep it crisp during storage). Rhubarb leaves are toxic; make sure to remove them completely before cooking. Pluck about two-thirds of the stalks from a given plant, then wait 5 weeks before next harvest (you can also selectively harvest individual stalks as needed). In the northern parts of North America, expect 2 to 3 harvests per year (2 in the spring, possibly 1 in the fall). Regrowth slows in summer as temperature increases. Don't harvest rhubarb the year of planting; during the second season, harvest lightly; full harvest begins the third season.

PERENNIAL GARDEN FRUITS

Blackberries

Pluck berries when fully ripe. Harvest regularly for best quality (2 or 3 times per week).

Blueberries

Pluck berries when fully ripe (entire berry is dark blue). Harvest 1 or 2 times per week.

Raspberries

Pluck berries when fully ripe. Harvest regularly for best quality (2 or 3 times per week).

Strawberries

Pluck berries when fully ripe (entire berry is red with no white on the tip). Harvest twice a week for best quality.

PERENNIAL HERBS

Anise Hyssop

Pick flowers and leaves as needed, or cut entire plant 6 inches above soil level for bunching or drying. Avoid consuming in large quantities or when pregnant.

Bay

Pick leaves as desired.

Chervil

Break off individual branches, or harvest like lettuce mix for cut and come again culture.

Chives

Cut chives 1 inch above soil level when leaves are 9–18 inches tall, but before flower stalks appear. If you miss the window, the leaves get tough but the flowers are tasty for salads or light cooking. You can cut chives repeatedly throughout the season.

Chives, Garlic

See Chives.

Fennel

Cut foliage with scissors or a knife as desired.

Horseradish

Dig roots in early spring, late fall, or winter at least one year after planting. Gently loosen soil with a spade or garden fork around the plant, and locate the main taproot (likely running horizontally). Additional harvestable roots will be growing downward from this main root. Replant root pieces as desired, or leave some portion of the root structure in the ground for regrowth the following season.

Lavender

Cut flower stalks a few inches above the woody growth of the plant when they appear. To maintain shape of the plant, cleanly cut all flower stalks at the same level at one time.

Lemon Balm

For highest oil content and manageable regrowth, cut entire plant a few inches above soil level in late spring-early summer, just before blossoms appear. Otherwise, harvest leaves as needed.

Lemongrass

Pull off or cut largest stalks from the outside of the plant (usually ¼–½ inch thick). The edible portion of the plant is the center of the bulbous area at the base of the stalk. Remove foliage and peel back outer layers of the bulb to reach the white and green inner section.

Lemon Verbena

For highest oil content, harvest stems and leaves as first blossoms are opening. Don't cut more than one-quarter of the length of a stem at a given harvest. Cut individual stems as necessary, or shear the entire plant at one time to maintain its shape. Plant flowers throughout the season, so multiple harvests are possible.

Marjoram

For best management of regrowth, cleanly cut all stems when about 8–10 inches long. New stems will regrow from base of plant for repeated harvests.

Mint

For best management of regrowth, cleanly cut all stems when about 8–10 inches long. New stems will regrow from base of plant for repeated harvests.

Oregano

Harvest as you would marjoram.

Purple Coneflower

For foliage, cut entire plant just below lowest leaf set during the second year of growth. For flowers, cut buds just as they're beginning to open.

Rosemary

For best regrowth and plant shape, cut young stems (whitish color) back to the older woody growth (brownish color) when they reach 6–8 inches long. Harvest just before flowering for best flavor.

Sage

Harvest by cutting back the outer 6–8 inches of the plant's stems and leaves. Do this uniformly at one time to maintain the plant's shape. Pluck leaves from stems for use. First harvest can be made about 2½ months after planting.

Savory, Winter

Harvest as you would marjoram.

Stevia

When plant reaches 8 inches, pinch back growing tips to encourage lateral branching. Cut plant back to 8 inches several times over the course of the season to harvest.

Tarragon

For best regrowth, cut entire plant back to 6 inches above soil level when plant is 12–14 inches tall.

Thyme

Harvest as you would marjoram.

Valerian

To harvest roots, cut back top growth and dig in late summer–early fall of second season of growth. Replant root pieces as desired for new plants. Harvest leaves as desired throughout the season.

Other Plant Parts to Eat

- *Arugula:* flowers, seed pods
- *Basil:* flowers
- *Beans, Fava (Broad):* shoots, young leaves, flowers
- *Beets:* leaves
- *Bok Choy:* flowers, flower stems
- *Broccoli:* secondary florets, flowers, flower stems and leaves
- *Brussels Sprouts:* top leaf cluster, leaves
- *Cabbage:* outer leaves
- *Cabbage, Chinese:* outer leaves
- *Carrots:* Greens (tops)
- *Cauliflower:* leaves
- *Celeriac:* tops
- *Chard, Swiss:* stalks
- *Cilantro:* flowers, seeds
- *Collards:* flowers
- *Cucumbers:* flowers
- *Dill:* fronds, flowers, seeds
- *Fennel, Bulbing:* fronds
- *Garlic:* scapes (flower stalks)
- *Kale:* flowers
- *Kohlrabi:* leaves
- *Leeks:* flowers
- *Mustard Greens:* flowers
- *Okra:* flowers
- *Onions, Bulb:* tops, flowers
- *Parsley:* flowers
- *Peas, Shelling:* growing tips, flowers, tendrils, shoots
- *Peas, Snap:* growing tips, flowers, tendrils, shoots
- *Raab:* flowers
- *Radishes:* flowers, seed pods
- *Rutabagas:* flowers, seed pods
- *Scallions:* flowers
- *Squash, Gourds:* flowers
- *Squash, Pumpkins:* flowers
- *Squash, Summer:* flowers
- *Squash, Winter:* flowers
- *Sweet Potatoes:* leaves
- *Turnips:* flowers
- *Watermelon:* flowers

Edible Weeds

This might already be obvious to you, or it may be a revelation: many weeds in and around your garden are very edible, and are often nutritious and tasty. Chickweed may grow rampant in the garden. Why not harvest it and add it to salads? Many people will pay top dollar for dried nettle leaves, but it can often be harvested all around the neighborhood. Young dandelion leaves are surprisingly tasty when mixed with kale or other cooking greens. If your goal is to maximize the food production potential of your space, identifying and using free-growing weeds is an effortless way to increase your harvest.

You might want to limit harvest of weeds to your own property or those you know to be safe. If you do choose to harvest off-site, be careful to only pick weeds from places you know to be free of chemical usage; weeds along roadsides and even in city parks may be sprayed with herbicides. Also be sure to harvest from sites that aren't used for animal wastes (if your dog uses the lawn for a bathroom, avoid eating edible weeds from this area).

Gleaning outside the Garden

Fruit trees can be common in established neighborhoods, and it is possible that much or all of that fruit goes unharvested each year. Making a map of these opportunities, identifying the owner, getting permission to harvest (if applicable), and keeping tabs on the plant through the season (to make sure you don't miss peak harvest time) can pay off.

You might find, for example, a single apple tree near your house that can provide you with months of fresh apples and a year's supply of applesauce, all for a few hours of harvesting! Pay back these sorts of favors and improve your yield by pruning the trees you visit for harvest and cleaning up any dropped fruit.

HARVEST SAFELY

As a sustainability-minded production gardener, you have the opportunity to enjoy some of the safest food in the nation. You have control over every step of the growing process, from choosing what goes into the soil, what you use to care for the crops, and how to harvest them. Your crops won't ever be transported long distances or moved through multiple warehouses, so chances for outside contamination are slim.

However, just because you are a small producer using environmentally sound techniques doesn't mean you can turn a blind eye to food safety, especially if you're sharing crops with friends, donating them to a food bank, or selling them to a restaurant down the street. You'll need to be sure to keep crops free of pathogens.

As a home gardener who doesn't sell produce, you won't be subject to federal regulations (specifically, the Food Safety Modernization Act of 2011, which dictates food safety practices for growing and handling produce for all commercial farmers). But you owe it to yourself, your family, and other like-minded growers to take some simple steps to keep your food clean. The steps covered here are extremely basic; for those who are interested in learning more, check out Resources, page 307, for more information.

Avoiding Fecal Contamination

The main pathogenic concern as production gardeners is fecal matter (human and animal). Fecal matter is a well-known carrier of many pathogens, so obviously it's best if you can keep it off of your food. Potential sources of contamination could be your hands, pets, wildlife, dirty water, poorly composted manure, or garden footwear. It's worth noting that you should be principally concerned with crops that will be eaten raw (e.g., salad mix; carrots). Cooking or processing foods eliminates the vast majority of common pathogens.

Clean hands, tools, and containers. This is an easy one. Wash your hands before harvesting. Wash them for a full 30 seconds, using soap and warm water. While you're at it, wash your harvest knife and harvesting containers, especially if you're harvesting something that will be eaten raw. Consider rinsing them with a sanitizing agent (a 10 percent bleach solution works well (1 part bleach to 9 parts water), as does an organically approved sanitizer).

Dispose of animal waste appropriately. A big pile of dog poo in the garden does not count as extra fertilizer. If you find feces among your vegetables, remove the waste and the soil that's been in contact with it, and then wash your hands. Don't put any of this in your home compost pile; dispose of it by burying it far from the garden or put it in the trash. If this becomes a recurring problem, consider fencing your garden to keep out pets and wildlife.

Irrigate with clean water. If you're irrigating with municipal water, you don't need to be too concerned about it as a source of pathogens. If you're irrigating from a well, we recommend testing it for coliform about once a year (you'll want to do this anyway if this is your drinking water source). If you're irrigating with surface water (from a pond, stream, collected in a rain barrel from your roof, or so forth), you'll definitely want to test it because it could be contaminated. Consider using drip irrigation to keep pathogens off the leaves of crops that will be eaten raw.

Wash with clean water. You should use only potable water for washing crops. Avoid soaking crops in water: crops can draw pathogens into their tissues along with the water. A better method is to spray the crops clean on a mesh table. If you need to use a soaking tub to cool or clean certain crops, see below for best practices when using this method.

Use only well-composted manure. Manure has the potential to carry pathogenic bacteria, which is why we recommend composting it completely before applying it to the garden. Many home compost piles won't ever reach the desired temperature of 140°F that is required to kill pathogens. If you're concerned that you haven't gotten your pile hot enough, it's still safe to apply to your garden as long as you wait four months before planting crops in that space (this is a good reason to apply your compost in the fall and let it age before spring planting).

Consider separate footwear. If you're worried about tracking pathogens into the garden, you might consider keeping a dedicated pair of shoes just for the garden.

You owe it to yourself, your family, and other like-minded growers to take some simple steps to keep your food clean.

HARVESTING FOR MAXIMUM FRESHNESS AND QUALITY

Your produce is undergoing cellular respiration while it is growing in the garden and it continues to do so after you pick it. To put that another way, your food is still alive after you harvest it. This is a great concept, to be sure, but while you're still thinking about it, your produce is already breaking down and losing quality.

Cool Them Down

Some vegetable crops have much higher cellular respiration rates than others; and the higher this rate, the faster the deterioration after harvest. Crops with high cellular respiration should be cooled quickly to an appropriate temperature to preserve their quality. These are also the crops that are best eaten as soon as possible after harvest.

You may have already learned this fact with sweet corn: fresh-picked ears that are purchased from a farmers' market or a roadside stand are always tastier than corn that's been sitting in a grocery store for a few days. Sweet corn is a very high respiration crop, which is why it tastes best if eaten the day that it is harvested (unless it is very quickly cooled to 33°F and held there). High respiration crops can be very satisfying to grow at home because you get to eat them at their peak.

For some crops (winter squash, onions, garlic), you'll need to cure them at a higher temperature for a short period to reduce moisture levels, and then move them into colder storage for long-term keeping (see page 287 for more on this).

Daily Harvest Timing

One of the easiest ways to ensure post-harvest quality is to pick your crops at an appropriate time of day. If a crop needs to be cooled to preserve its post-harvest quality, it makes sense to harvest it when the air temperature is cooler. You may have already learned this by trial and error. If you cut a head of lettuce or pick a bunch of kale at noon when it's 80°F outside, and leave it in the sun for even a few minutes, the leaves will quickly wilt. However, if you pick it at 7:00 in the morning when the temperature is 60°F, it will hold its quality much longer.

This happens because plant metabolic activity is higher when air temperatures are higher. When you pick lettuce at midday, its cells are cranking away to help the plant grow, and they're still cranking away after you remove the plant's water supply by cutting it from its roots. Conversely, if you pick lettuce early in the morning, the cells are relatively inactive, so the leaves don't break down as quickly after cutting.

Additionally, many crops store best at high humidity levels because this allows them to stay hydrated and crisp. If you pick these crops when there's still dew on them, it's easier to maintain an appropriate humidity level after harvesting. Some large commercial lettuce operations actually do their harvesting at night because it saves them a lot of time and energy that would otherwise need to be spent on cooling and hydrating the lettuce.

In contrast to lettuce, some crops keep best when harvested after the dew has burned off, like tomatoes and cucumbers. These crops can be more prone to rot after harvest if their outer surface is wet. A good strategy is to pick crops that like to be cool and wet early in the morning, and pick crops that like to be dry in the midday or evening when dew has burned off.

Remember, these are suggestions, not rules. You'll most likely harvest whenever you have time, but not to worry: crops can easily be cooled, hydrated, or dried off after harvest.

Harvesting Crops That Like It Cool and Wet

For small quantities, all you need to do is harvest your crops when it's cool outside and there's still dew on the leaves. From there, you can place the harvest in a plastic bag and set it in the fridge. The bag keeps the humidity high, and the fridge quickly cools things down. Be careful not to jam too much produce into a small drawer or compartment; air circulation around the bags is important to cool the crops. If you need to keep the produce outside for a while, bag it to maintain humidity, and be sure to keep it in the shade. You might give each bag a

A mesh laundry bag can be used to remove excess water from salad greens after washing them.

spritz of water if the crop is completely dry at harvest time.

If the crops are dirty and/or were harvested during the heat of the day, place them in a colander or on a drain table (see page 283) and give them a good rinsing. This will clean them up and cool them down. For mixed lettuces and salad greens like arugula, mizuna, or baby spinach, a salad spinner works well for drying before packing. For larger quantities, fill a mesh laundry bag and spin it around by hand (be sure to wash and dry the mesh bag between uses).

Crops that are best harvested cool and wet include salad greens, cooking greens, leeks, scallions, sweet corn, all brassicas (broccoli, cabbage, cauliflower, kale, bok choy, mustard greens), and all root crops with tops (beets, carrots, radishes, rutabagas, turnips).

Harvesting Crops That Like It Dry

These crops — including all solanums, cucurbits, beans, berries, storage onions and garlic — are pretty easy. All you need to do is wait until the dew has dried, then harvest away. If the crops need to be cleaned or are still a little damp with dew, most of them can be wiped off with a dry rag. Alternatively, you can wear soft cotton gloves while you're harvesting and wipe them off as you pick.

Most crops that like to be dry also don't mind being a little warmer at harvest time. If you'll be eating them soon, don't worry about cooling solanums and cucurbits at all (just pick them and store them at room temperature until they're ready to use). Beans do appreciate a cooling rinse if it's above 70°F.

Onions and garlic (and sometimes potatoes) need to be cured before storage (see page 287); most growers will wait to clean them until after curing.

Washing and Cooling

The primary cleaning equipment of the home garden is the garden hose. Water from a hose also serves as a great cooling agent (using cold water to cool produce is called hydrocooling by professional growers). Make sure you use a drinking water–approved hose; most common garden hoses contain bactericides and unacceptable levels of lead.

For most home production growers, the primary cooling and storage equipment is the refrigerator. If you are growing large amounts of produce or will be sharing or distributing your harvest, you might consider buying an auxiliary fridge, or even setting up a small walk-in cooler to hold your harvests.

If you need to wash and/or cool large quantities of produce, consider building a drain table. Vinyl-coated welded wire fencing lets dirty water drain through and is easy to clean. If you want to get fancy, consider purchasing a manufactured plastic or stainless steel drain table. Spreading a few inches of gravel underneath the table will help keep the area from getting muddy. When you're finished cleaning, shake off the crops or let them air-dry a bit (they shouldn't be completely dry), pack them into plastic bags, and move them into the refrigerator.

Tub Washing

We generally don't recommend soaking produce in a tub to clean it. This is because immersing produce into water can cause the crops to absorb pathogens. It also allows pathogens to spread from one piece of produce to many.

That said, tub washing is a useful technique that is often used on professional organic farms. This method is especially efficient for washing baby lettuce and salad greens, and it can be safely done using two or three wash tubs. Professional growers often add an organically approved sanitizer to keep pathogens from multiplying and spreading in the water.

To prepare for tab washing, select two or three plastic or stainless steel tubs that are appropriately sized for your harvest (#2 plastic is inert and won't leach or react with the sanitizer). Using three separate tubs is the gold standard (triple washed), but using two tubs is also acceptable. Make sure they're clean before use. Along with the

A drain table is a great way to cool and clean large amounts of produce.

tubs, you'll need an organically approved sanitizer such as SaniDate or Tsunami, if desired, and a colander.

Wash your hands before getting started, and then fill all tubs with potable water. If desired, add sanitizer as directed on the package. Some growers use sanitizer in all three tubs, some use it in the third and final rinse, some use it in the second, some use it in the first, and some don't use it at all. We use a triple rinse system and use sanitizer in the first two tubs. (We feel the risk of pathogen transfer is greatest in these tubs, and we like to completely rinse off our produce in the final tub.)

Place greens into the first tub. Stir gently, and then use the colander to move them into the second tub. Stir again and move to the third tub. Stir gently, and then place them in the colander to drain and next into a salad spinner or mesh bag to dry.

Harvesting Tools

In addition to the tools you use during your growing season, consider keeping a few specialized tools and pieces of equipment on hand for harvesting. Here's what we recommend:

Scissors, Knives, Pruning Shears

Scissors are a great harvest tool for harvesting salad greens, soft herbs, and any other thin plant matter. Knives are great for harvesting salad greens and head lettuce, and for cutting through thicker plant stems (broccoli, cabbage, cauliflower). Pruning shears are excellent for cutting through tough stems on summer and winter squash, cucumbers, tomatoes, and peppers. We recommend keeping a dedicated pair of each of these tools for harvesting to avoid

contamination of produce, especially for crops that will be eaten raw.

Harvesting Containers

You'll need something to pack your produce into so that you can carry it back to the house. We love using traditional baskets for harvesting a wide variety of produce. A metal colander is great for washing and cooling crops, and a large plastic tub is useful for crops that need to be soaked.

Scale

This isn't essential but is useful if you like to keep accurate harvest records or if you're selling any of your crops. A simple kitchen scale works well, or you can actually purchase a digital produce scale if you want to get fancy.

Hose for Washing Produce

Most garden hoses contain surprisingly high levels of lead, so we recommend finding a lead-free hose to use for produce washing. Lead-free hoses are relatively easy to come by, but it's important to check, rather than assume. Manufacturers are eager for you to know about their new lead-free hoses, so look around and find one that you feel good about.

Soap/Hand Sanitizer

You should always wash your hands before handling produce. Keep a small bottle of biodegradable soap or hand sanitizer with your harvest tools. These soaps and sanitizers can also be used to clean your cutting implements, containers, and the top of your scale.

STORING THE HARVEST

With appropriate storage techniques, you can keep your produce fresh for weeks, or even months, after you harvest it. Storage crops usually need some type of temperature-controlled space such as a refrigerator, walk-in cooler, or root cellar. A few crops can even be successfully stored in the garden, buried under the soil during the winter months.

When large-scale growers are storing crops for extended periods, they might have three or four walk-in coolers that are set to precise temperature and humidity levels. This allows them to store and sell crops over the longest period possible. Most gardeners don't have the space or equipment to make this happen, but you can actually do a pretty good job using what you probably already have at home.

Production-Scale Tools

If you're scaling up your operation, then you should know about some of the specialty tools that small farmers use to make their harvesting and produce-washing systems more efficient. These tools include commercial-size salad spinners, handheld mechanical greens harvesters, barrel washers to quickly clean large quantities of root crops, and large harvesting tubs for picking bulk amounts of produce. Many of these ingenious tools are available for retail purchase, though many farmers choose to design and build their own tools to meet their specific needs. These tools may be helpful if you find that the harvesting and processing of a particular crop is taking a lot of your time. See Resources, page 307, for more information.

Large-scale greens harvesting can be made easier with a greens cutter powered by a cordless drill. See Resources, page 307, for suppliers.

A commercial salad spinner is useful for drying large amounts of salad greens after they've been washed.

Storage Locations

The specific crops you are storing, the types of space you have available, and your end use will dictate which storage option is most appropriate for a particular harvest.

In the refrigerator. The home refrigerator is the best place to store crops that like it cold (32 to 39°F) and humid (90 to 100 percent relative humidity). Placing crops in plastic bags or in a box or bin with a plastic liner helps maintain high levels of humidity. If crops are very dry when bagging, you can spray a quick spritz of water in the bag (you don't want standing water in the bag, just enough to moisten the crop itself).

As you scale up your garden, consider a second refrigerator for long-term produce storage. We encourage you *not* to buy the oldest, cheapest fridge you can find; most old refrigerators are very inefficient and operate at high monetary and environmental costs.

On the counter. For short-term storage of crops that like warmer temperatures and low humidity, simply place them in a bowl at room temperature. Try this with tomatoes, cured onions and garlic, cucumbers, and summer and winter squash.

In the garden. Some root vegetables — such as carrots, parsnips, and potatoes — can be overwintered in the garden. The key here is to keep the ground and the roots from freezing. The best way to do this is to cover the planting with a thick layer of mulch (8 inches or more) before air temperatures drop below freezing.

Even with the mulch, this technique may not work in areas with extremely cold winter temperatures. In warmer climates, where the soil doesn't freeze during the winter, this technique works but crops may be more susceptible to pest problems as they sit in garden storage. For example, in the Pacific Northwest, potatoes stored in the ground for too long become a tasty treat for marauding wireworms.

In a root cellar. Many people consider the root cellar to be an antiquated piece of farm history. But in truth, it is an ingenious, time-saving, low-energy storage system. Traditionally, a root cellar was simply a framed-in hole dug into the ground or side of a hill. Geothermal energy and insulation from the earth moderated the temperature in the cellar (cooler in summer, ideally above freezing in winter). These are still an effective storage method. If you have the space, time, and skills to construct one, you can give it a try. Be sure to install vents to maintain air circulation and allow cooler outdoor air to enter.

Make Your Own Cooler

Many small farmers have begun using a new piece of technology called the CoolBot (see Resources, page 307). This device allows you to convert a normal air conditioner into a refrigeration unit. To use a CoolBot, you'll need a working air conditioner and a space that can be insulated and converted into a walk-in style cooler. Possible opportunities are basement rooms, sheds, portions of a garage, or used steel shipping containers.

In your house, the simplest "root cellar" might be a corner of a basement or a spot in a garage or shed that stays cooler than the rest of your house (but doesn't get below freezing). A heated garage works well for crops that like relatively warmer temperatures and low humidity (cured potatoes, sweet potatoes onions, garlic, and winter squash). These low-humidity crops keep best in well-ventilated containers like wooden crates or cardboard boxes with vent holes in the sides.

Keeping the space dark is important to discourage crops from sprouting. This is especially true for potatoes, which can develop a toxic green coloration if exposed to light. (If this occurs, peel them before use to remove any trace of the green coloration.) If it's cold(er) in your garage or shed, you can use that location to store root crops that like lower temperatures and higher humidity (such as carrots, beets, radishes, and turnips). These crops store best in the 30s, but will keep for a while in the 40s or 50s. Store them in plastic bags for best results.

Buried containers. Another take on a root cellar is simply to bury a container underground. Try burying a food grade plastic bucket or large drum with a lid, so that the rim protrudes a few inches above ground. Fill it with produce, packed between layers of sawdust, clean straw, or peat moss (root crops such as beets, carrots, or turnips are probably best for this type of storage), secure the lid, and cover it with 8 or more inches of soil or straw mulch. This method is definitely not perfect, because you have no control over air circulation or temperature, but it does work.

Curing for Longevity

Certain crops can be cured before eating and storing so as to improve flavor and increase storage life. Curing is the process of holding a crop at a relatively high temperature for a short period after harvest. Because the curing process varies by the crop, we'll discuss a few specific crops here.

Onions. If you harvest onions while the tops are still green, you can use both bulbs and tubular leaves for raw eating or cooking. However, to store onions for more than a few weeks it's necessary to cure them. To do so, stop irrigating when bulbs are mature and tops are starting to die back. Wait until the onion tops begin to brown and fall over, then pull them from the ground. If the weather is forecasted to be warm and sunny, you can

A Note about Ethylene

Ethylene is a gas that serves as a plant growth regulator. It's naturally produced by plants, and helps certain crops continue to ripen after harvest. However, ethylene causes problems with vegetables in storage because it causes many crops to rot prematurely. Notorious ethylene producers such as apples, bananas, cantaloupe, pears, and tomatoes should be stored separately from other vegetable crops. Conversely, you can use ethylene producers to your advantage — if you want to hasten the ripening process for greenish tomatoes harvested at the end of the growing season, try storing them with a few apples.

leave the onions out in the field in the sun for several days to begin the curing process. If it's extremely hot or rain is in the forecast, skip this step.

Store the onions (with tops and roots still attached) in a dry, well-ventilated location until the tops are fully brown and dried (about two to three weeks). At this point, you can trim the roots and tops to within 1 inch of the bulb, and move the bulbs into long-term storage. A greenhouse with the doors open is a great place for curing. Ideal curing temperature is 75 to 80°F. For maximum airflow, spread the onions on racks or a mesh-top table in a single layer or bundle the onions by their tops and hang them under cover.

Garlic. As with onions, garlic must be cured for long-term storage. Withhold water when bulbs are approaching maturity. Harvest garlic when about half the leaves are brown and half are still green. Don't wait until all the leaves are dead or storage life and flavor will be compromised. At that point, follow the steps for curing onions (however, omit the few days of curing in the field as direct sun exposure after harvest can break down flavor compounds). Softneck garlic can be braided together and hung when the tops are fully dry, which makes for an attractive storage option.

Winter squash and storage pumpkins. Winter squash does not need to be cured before eating, but it will keep best after curing for 7 to 10 days at 70 to 80°F. For best flavor, wait to harvest winter squash and pumpkins until their stems are dry and they have a yellowish/brownish mark where they've been in contact with the ground. If you need to harvest your squash early to protect it from rain or adverse weather in the fall, curing it can greatly improve flavor. Wipe down squash fruits with a very mild bleach solution (1 tablespoon bleach to 1 gallon of water) to eliminate fungal spores and extend storage life.

Potatoes. "New potatoes" are harvested before the top growth has started to brown. These early potatoes are eaten uncured and have amazing flavor and texture. However, for long-term storage, potatoes should be cured to slightly toughen the skin and heal any wounds from harvesting. Dig potatoes when the tops have died back. Hold them in a dark, well-ventilated space at 55 to 60°F for one to two weeks. For longest storage life, don't wash until immediately before use. For moderate-term storage, you can wash after curing and then air-dry.

Sweet potatoes. For long-term storage, dig sweet potatoes after the foliage has started to yellow and die back. You can leave them in the field exposed to the sun for a few hours to begin the curing process (optional). Before washing, cure at 70 to 90°F in a well-ventilated space for about two weeks.

Crop Storage

ANNUAL VEGETABLES AND HERBS	IDEAL STORAGE TEMPERATURE (°F)	SUGGESTED STORAGE % RELATIVE HUMIDITY	PREFERRED STORAGE CONTAINER	BEST HOME STORAGE PRACTICE
ARUGULA	33	95	plastic bag/liner	bagged in refrigerator
BASIL	50	90	paper bag/plastic bag with vents	paper bag at room temperature
BEANS, EDIBLE SOY (EDAMAME)	33	95	plastic bag/liner	bagged in refrigerator
BEANS, FAVA (BROAD)	41–45	95	plastic bag/liner	bagged in refrigerator
BEANS, LIMA	41–45	95	plastic bag/liner	bagged in refrigerator
BEANS, SHELL	41–5	95	plastic bag/liner	bagged in refrigerator
BEANS, SNAP	41–45	95	plastic bag/liner	bagged in refrigerator
BEETS	33	95	plastic bag/liner	bagged in refrigerator
BOK CHOY	33	95	plastic bag/liner	bagged in refrigerator
BROCCOLI	33	95	plastic bag/liner	bagged in refrigerator
BRUSSELS SPROUTS	33	95	plastic bag/liner	bagged in refrigerator
CABBAGE	33	95	plastic bag/liner	bagged in refrigerator
CABBAGE, CHINESE	33	95	plastic bag/liner	bagged in refrigerator
CARROTS	33	95	plastic bag/liner	bagged in refrigerator
CAULIFLOWER	33	95	plastic bag/liner	bagged in refrigerator
CELERIAC	33	95	plastic bag/liner	bagged in refrigerator
CELERY	33	95	plastic bag/liner	bagged in refrigerator
CHARD, SWISS	33	95	plastic bag/liner	bagged in refrigerator
CILANTRO	33	95	plastic bag/liner	bagged in refrigerator
COLLARDS	33	95	plastic bag/liner	bagged in refrigerator
CORN, SWEET	33	95	plastic bag/liner	bagged in refrigerator
CUCUMBERS	50–55	95	paper bag/plastic bag with vents/wrap in paper towel/on the counter	at room temperature, with or without paper bag
DILL	33	95	plastic bag/liner	bagged in refrigerator

ANNUAL VEGETABLES AND HERBS	IDEAL STORAGE TEMPERATURE (°F)	SUGGESTED STORAGE % RELATIVE HUMIDITY	PREFERRED STORAGE CONTAINER	BEST HOME STORAGE PRACTICE
EGGPLANT	50–55	90	paper bag/plastic bag with vents/wrap in paper towel/on the counter	at room temperature, with or without paper bag
ENDIVE	33	95	plastic bag/liner	bagged in refrigerator
FENNEL, BULBING	33	95	plastic bag/liner	bagged in refrigerator
GARLIC	33	60–70	mesh bag/well-ventilated box/on the counter	at room temperature in well-ventilated mesh bag
KALE	33	95	plastic bag/liner	bagged in refrigerator
KOHLRABI	33	95	plastic bag/liner	bagged in refrigerator
LEEKS	33	95	plastic bag/liner	bagged in refrigerator
LETTUCE, BABY MIX	33	95	plastic bag/liner	bagged in refrigerator
LETTUCE, HEADS	33	95	plastic bag/liner	bagged in refrigerator
MÂCHE	33	95	plastic bag/liner	bagged in refrigerator
MELON, CANTALOUPE, HONEYDEW	36–41	95	well-ventilated cardboard box/on the counter	unbagged in refrigerator
MUSTARD GREENS	33	95	plastic bag/liner	bagged in refrigerator
OKRA	45–50	95	paper bag/plastic bag with vents/wrap in paper towel/on the counter	at room temperature
ONIONS, BULB	33	60–70	mesh bag/well-ventilated cardboard box/on the counter	at room temperature in well-ventilated location
PARSLEY	33	95	plastic bag/liner	bagged in refrigerator
PARSNIPS	33	95	plastic bag/liner	bagged in refrigerator
PEANUT	34–41	55–70	paper bag	room temperature for a few months, refrigerated for up to a year
PEAS, SHELLING	33	95	plastic bag/liner	bagged in refrigerator
PEAS, SNAP	33	95	plastic bag/liner	bagged in refrigerator
PEPPERS, HOT	41–50	85–95	paper bag/well-ventilated cardboard box/on the counter	at room temperature

ANNUAL VEGETABLES AND HERBS	IDEAL STORAGE TEMPERATURE (°F)	SUGGESTED STORAGE % RELATIVE HUMIDITY	PREFERRED STORAGE CONTAINER	BEST HOME STORAGE PRACTICE
PEPPERS, SWEET	45–50	90–95	paper bag or well-ventilated cardboard box	at room temperature
POTATOES	40–50	90–95	paper bag or well-ventilated cardboard box	at room temperature in the dark
RAAB	33	95	plastic bag/liner	bagged in refrigerator
RADICCHIO	33	95	plastic bag/liner	bagged in refrigerator
RADISHES	33	95	plastic bag/liner	bagged in refrigerator
RUTABAGAS	33	95	plastic bag/liner	bagged in refrigerator
SCALLIONS	33	95	plastic bag/liner	bagged in refrigerator
SPINACH	33	95	plastic bag/liner	bagged in refrigerator
SQUASH, GOURDS	50–55	50–75	paper bag/well-ventilated cardboard box/on the counter	at room temperature
SQUASH, PUMPKINS	54–59	50–75	paper bag/well-ventilated cardboard box/on the counter	at room temperature
SQUASH, SUMMER	41–50	95	paper bag/well-ventilated cardboard box/on the counter	at room temperature
SQUASH, WINTER	50–55	50–75	paper bag/well-ventilated cardboard box/on the counter	at room temperature
SWEET POTATOES	55–59	85–95	paper bag/well-ventilated cardboard box/on the counter	at room temperature
TOMATILLOS	45–55	85–95	paper bag/well-ventilated cardboard box/on the counter	at room temperature
TOMATOES	45–55	85–95	paper bag/well-ventilated cardboard box/on the counter	at room temperature
TURNIPS	33	95	plastic bag/liner	bagged in refrigerator
WATERMELON	50–59	90	well-ventilated cardboard box	at room temperature

PERENNIAL VEGETABLES	IDEAL STORAGE TEMPERATURE (°F)	SUGGESTED STORAGE % RELATIVE HUMIDITY	PREFERRED STORAGE CONTAINER	BEST HOME STORAGE PRACTICE
ARTICHOKE	32	95	plastic bag/liner	bagged in refrigerator
ASPARAGUS	35	95	plastic bag/liner	bagged in refrigerator
CARDOON			plastic bag/liner	bagged in refrigerator
JERUSALEM ARTICHOKE, SUNCHOKE	33	95	plastic bag/liner	bagged in refrigerator
RHUBARB	33	95	plastic bag/liner	bagged in refrigerator

PERENNIAL GARDEN FRUITS	IDEAL STORAGE TEMPERATURE (°F)	SUGGESTED STORAGE % RELATIVE HUMIDITY	PREFERRED STORAGE CONTAINER	BEST HOME STORAGE PRACTICE
BLACKBERRIES	33	90–95	in cardboard berry boxes (tills) or well-ventilated plastic clamshell containers	in boxes in refrigerator
BLUEBERRIES	33	90–95	in cardboard berry boxes (tills) or well-ventilated plastic clamshell containers	in boxes in refrigerator
RASPBERRIES	33	90–95	in cardboard berry boxes (tills) or well-ventilated plastic clamshell containers	in boxes in refrigerator
STRAWBERRIES	33	90–95	in cardboard berry boxes (tills) or well-ventilated plastic clamshell containers	in boxes in refrigerator

PERENNIAL HERBS	IDEAL STORAGE TEMPERATURE (°F)	SUGGESTED STORAGE % RELATIVE HUMIDITY	PREFERRED STORAGE CONTAINER	BEST HOME STORAGE PRACTICE
BAY	33	95	plastic bag/liner	bagged in refrigerator
CHERVIL	33	95	plastic bag/liner	bagged in refrigerator
CHIVES	33	95	plastic bag/liner	bagged in refrigerator
CHIVES, GARLIC	33	95	plastic bag/liner	bagged in refrigerator
FENNEL	33	95	plastic bag/liner	bagged in refrigerator
HORSERADISH	33	95	plastic bag/liner	bagged in refrigerator
LAVENDER	33	95	plastic bag/liner	bagged in refrigerator
LEMON BALM	33	95	plastic bag/liner	bagged in refrigerator
LEMONGRASS	33	95	plastic bag/liner	bagged in refrigerator
LEMON VERBENA	33	95	plastic bag/liner	bagged in refrigerator
MARJORAM	33	95	plastic bag/liner	bagged in refrigerator
MINT	33	95	plastic bag/liner	bagged in refrigerator
OREGANO	33	95	plastic bag/liner	bagged in refrigerator
ROSEMARY	33	95	plastic bag/liner	bagged in refrigerator
SAGE	33	95	plastic bag/liner	bagged in refrigerator
TARRAGON	33	95	plastic bag/liner	bagged in refrigerator
THYME	33	95	plastic bag/liner	bagged in refrigerator

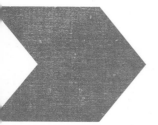

Appendix

Distributing the Harvest

Not every production grower has the goal of distributing their produce beyond their personal use. But for those who do, this section provides an overview of several different marketing options.

We assume that your distribution goals are dependent on the size of land you are working with, your climate, your local culture, and your own personal food needs. If you are living in an urban or suburban area (typically working with half an acre of land or less), we caution that it's probably an unrealistic goal to make your entire income from home food production sales. However, growing a significant portion of your own food and having some extra to distribute are realistic goals.

PRODUCE SALES AND DISTRIBUTION

Let's take a look at some of the most common systems for small-scale food distribution. If you have a distribution idea that is not covered in this section, try it out; you never know what new ideas will catch on.

Friends and Family

For many home food gardeners, the most logical outlet for distributing excess vegetables is to the people who are already part of your community. Bringing homegrown food to any occasion is usually appreciated and can enhance the experience of any dinner party or barbeque. Distributing produce to friends and family can remain an informal affair, or it can be highly organized.

The benefit of creating an organized distribution program is that it allows for better garden planning before the season starts, ensures a happy home for your produce, and may encourage your participants to assist with the garden labor and/or costs. The timing and quantity of distribution will obviously be very specific to your personal situation. Here are a couple of general tips, though:

Schedule ahead. Set a predetermined day and time for friends to pick up vegetables. This allows you to plan the week's schedule to make sure you are available when they come by to pick up. You might even be able to convince them to help harvest and weed while they are there.

Try a U-pick operation. If your friends know the garden well and you are confident that they know which crops to harvest and how to pick them, you can let them have free rein at harvest time. This means less work for you, of course. But this strategy also helps ensure that people are only harvesting the crops they'll be able to use, thus leaving the remainder to be picked by somebody else.

Donations to Food Banks

Donating produce to food banks is a great way for growers to help provide fresh, local produce to those in need. If you'd like to pursue this option, check in with food banks located near you to see if they can accept homegrown produce (some are not able to), and what crops are most useful to them.

If you'd like to make regular deliveries to a food bank, add appropriate crops and quantities to your planting schedule to help meet their needs. For more information and ways to get other growers in your community involved, check out the Plant a Row for the Hungry program, managed by the Garden Writers Association (see Resources, page 307).

Roadside Stands

Probably the easiest system for selling excess produce is to set up a produce stand. Produce stands are often created at the edge of a property, near the end of a driveway or another right of way. You can open a produce stand during certain days and hours of the week, when you expect the most opportunity for sales. For example, you can open on Saturday and Sunday mornings when people are out socializing, exercising, and shopping; or you can open at the end of the workday to catch customers and neighbors on their way home.

Produce stands can be staffed or unstaffed. Many produce stands are unstaffed and operate on the honor system. Growers like this system because it frees up their time for essential garden management tasks; customers like it because it feels good to harken back to the olden days when people felt more confident in the honesty of

Legal Considerations for Produce Sales

If you are growing your own food and sharing it with friends and family, you are generally not subject to legislation that affects commercial growers. However, if you are selling produce for money, many legal issues begin to come into play. These issues vary by state, county, and municipality, and may cover where your produce is grown, how you sell it, how you report your income, what your food safety practices are, and what kind of insurance you carry.

This is especially important if you are selling at a farmers' market or an off-site produce stand. It's your responsibility to know which laws affect you if you're selling produce, and it's important for you to understand what your personal liabilities are in today's highly litigious society. A good place to start this process is by checking to see if your region has an organization that represents local farmers or produce growers. They may have good advice on where to read up on local laws governing your area. Barring that, check in with your local health department or county or municipal government offices.

Elements of a Roadside Stand

1. **SHELTER.** The stand should have a solid roof to protect vegetables from sun, rain, and wind.

2. ***STORAGE CONTAINERS.*** Depending on the crop and the length of time you plan to leave vegetables at the site, you might want to invest in produce coolers. Coolers are essential for certain temperature-sensitive crops such as salad mix.

3. ***CASH BOX.*** You want it to be easy for people to pay for their produce. Plan to buy or build an easy to see and easy to use system for payment. Very small honor system stands might rely on a jar for customers to deposit cash. For a bit more security, you can use a locking box that you bring to and from the stand during operating hours.

4. ***SIGNAGE.*** It should be easy for people to recognize the various crops at your display. It's easy to forget that not everybody knows what kohlrabi is or what Brussels sprouts look like on the stalk. Create attractive, clear signs for each crop, and indicate the price per unit. Include signs that enable customers to interact with you beyond the farm stand: leave out a newsletter signup sheet with your phone number, website, or other contact information for your farm. You can use this information to build a customer base and let them know of upcoming crops, price changes, or any other relevant news.

5. ***CROPS.*** Make sure to refresh the crops under the stand. Clean, good-looking, fresh crops sell best, so ensure that you are providing a quality product.

FOOD SAFETY. Make sure your produce is protected from contamination by animals or other sources. This is especially critical if your stand is unstaffed. Use appropriate food handling skills when stocking and managing the stand. Consider taking a food safety course or do research on your own to expand your knowledge on this subject.

their community. Honor system stands can be a unique way to build community.

The advantage of staffing the stand is that you can meet your customers, answer questions, learn what vegetables are most requested, make sure people pay the correct amount for their goods (and make change as necessary), and not worry that the produce or cash box might walk away. If you want to locate the farm stand somewhere other then your own property, or if you have a large amount of produce to sell, it pays to staff the stand during business hours. The only drawback is the relatively large amount of time you will have to spend hanging out at the stand.

Your presence at the stand, however, allows you to connect directly with your customers. You might become someone's "farmer" who not only produces food but who also answers questions about certain crops and even provides advice for cooking a particular vegetable. As a small-scale grower you have the opportunity to cultivate personal relationships with your client base. Your customers will better appreciate the vegetables and be more likely to return to the stand if they like you. Also it gives your clients a story to tell, which leads to referrals for more customers.

Before setting up a roadside stand, be sure to check your zoning restrictions to make sure it's legal to do so.

Farmers' Markets

An extension of the produce stand, a farmers' market is essentially a group of local purveyors who all set up temporary produce stands in a single location to attract more customers. Collective selling markets will attract many more customers than a single farm stand. Most farmers' markets are managed by an organization and run by a market manager. Check with this organization in your area for information on how to apply for a stand and what regulations you must follow to sell at the market.

Considerations for Farmers' Market Selling

Price your produce appropriately. It is important to respect the culture of the market and keep prices competitive with other producers. Keep in mind that even if your income is not dependent upon your sales (i.e., you can lower prices without worrying about it), other growers at the market may depend exclusively on these sales for their income. Lowering your prices below fair market value can threaten the livelihood of the other growers in your community.

Time commitment. Selling at a farmers' market requires a lot of time. In addition to the duration of the market (often between two and five hours), you will need time to load up your harvested crops, set up the stand, break down the stand at the end of the market, and unload when you get home. Most markets require that you arrive on site at least 30 minutes prior to market opening and that your stand remain up for the duration of the market (taking down a stand can cause a disturbance of the market, detract from the experience of customers, and lead to lower sales for everyone).

Market fees. Many markets (although not all) require that you pay a market fee for participating in the event. These fees cover expenses that the market incurs for marketing, permits, and staffing. Fees may be flat rate (a fixed amount for each booth), they may relate to the size of your stand, or they may increase incrementally with sales. Some markets require that you report your sales at the end of the market day and pay a certain percentage of sales as your market fee.

Respect other producers. Before signing up for a stand, go to the market and see what other people are selling. Learn which crops are in short supply from growers and which crops are overstocked. Consider matching your offerings with what is needed in the market; avoid oversaturating it with produce that's already in good supply.

Materials. A stand at a farmers' market uses materials that are similar to a produce stand. A farmers' market stand is not a permanent structure, however, so create a stand that can be quickly set up and broken down. Many growers use a 10 × 10-foot pop-up tent to cover their market stand. These tents require weights for each corner. You can buy tent weights or make your own using sandbags, PVC tubes filled with concrete, 5-gallon buckets filled with sand, or any other heavy object that is easy to tie up to the tent canopy structure. Also you will need tables, produce displays, signage, chairs, cash box, receipts, and a calculator to run an effective market stand.

Restaurant Supply

Restaurants that are keen on local produce and like unique varieties are one of the best markets for many small-scale farmers. Smaller, high-end restaurants can often utilize small quantities of produce and are often willing to work with less-regular delivery schedules.

Effective Restaurant Sales

Assess the market before planning your crops. Go to restaurants. Meet the folks who work there and find out what they would consider buying. You may discover that your ability to supply a unique crop or variety will open up doors for restaurant sales.

Make sure the proprietor understands the value of your product. Your produce may be more expensive than from other sources, but the quality and freshness of your produce should be higher. The restaurant can also use the story of your relationship and how you grow your crops to engage their clientele.

Be professional. To keep an ongoing relationship with another small business, it is important to communicate regularly and honestly, be on time with your deliveries, and bring them only the highest-quality goods.

CSA: Community Supported Agriculture

Community Supported Agriculture (CSA) is a marketing model where a group of consumers pay a farmer in advance for regular deliveries of produce (it's like signing up for a magazine subscription). The CSA model provides customers with a steady supply of fresh, seasonal produce throughout the season, and helps the grower cover costs at the start of the season (traditionally a time when growers have very limited cash flow). It also helps a grower share the inherent risks of agriculture with his or her customers. If the weather during a season is poor, customers might receive less produce in their share; if the season is good, customers benefit from extra food.

The CSA model is alluring for small producers, but can be very management intensive. Your planning needs to be top-notch to be able to supply a variety of produce in appropriate quantities on a regular basis (usually weekly) for your customers. If you're interested in running a CSA, we strongly encourage you to do some extensive research to make sure it's the right model for you. In addition, we strongly recommend that you have a few years of production experience under your belt.

There are many ways to manage a CSA program. Some farms take full payment up front, others take a deposit and several other payments, and others set up a monthly payment for customers. Some growers have their customers come to the garden to pick up their share of produce, and some deliver shares to a distribution point. Some CSAs set up to be work-share programs where a customer can receive a discounted or free share in exchange for working in the garden. Whatever the scheme, taking the time to plan the logistics of your CSA in advance is vital.

Tips for Running a Successful CSA

Start small. Working with a very small membership to start will allow you to establish a workable scheme, correct mistakes, and get your systems in place without harming your reputation or business. A small group of well-informed members (maybe your friends and family) will be much more accepting of stumbles, and can provide you with important feedback before you expand the program.

Set reasonable expectations. Let your members know how many deliveries they'll receive over the course of the season, how much and what types of produce they'll receive, and how the crop selection might vary with the season.

Offer supplemental benefits. Recipes, newsletters, and farm open houses help to keep members happy and engaged.

Set a schedule for yourself. It is essential that you are able to harvest and deliver produce shares at regular intervals for your customers. This means developing a strict planting and harvesting schedule for all of your crops. Good recordkeeping is vital so you can improve your systems from year to year.

Educational Programming

If you're interested in inspiring others to grow their own food, consider turning your garden into an outdoor classroom. Engaging new and beginning growers, students, and at-risk youth can be a great way to give back.

Workshops and regular classes. These are a fun way to teach gardening skills, and you can even make a little money. To pull off a high-quality workshop, you need lots of preparation time. Develop a coherent and linear curriculum, and prepare enough (but not too much) information to pass along. Make sure you have adequate materials and supplies for hands-on activities.

Large events. A big event can be a way for you to connect to the community and make it easy for interested folks to drop in and learn about what you're doing. Spring strawberry festivals or fall harvest festivals are classic examples.

After-school programs. This is probably the most serious type of educational endeavor, and requires lots of time, patience, a regular schedule, and maybe even some insurance to set up. Get in touch with your local school district if you're interested in pursuing this idea.

Planning for Perennials

PERENNIAL VEGETABLES

Artichoke
Genus and species: Cynara scolymus
Mature height*: 5–6'
Spacing†: 3–4'
Life span‡: 1–3 years
Fertility needs: medium
Spreading: yes
Yield§: expect 20–30 buds from an established plant; an average bud weighs about 12 ounces
USDA Hardiness Zones: 7 and above

Asparagus
Genus and species: Asparagus officinalis
Mature height*: 12"
Spacing†: 12"
Life span‡: 15 years
Fertility needs: medium
Spreading: yes
Yield§: total harvest from 1 year; expect to pick about 1 ounce/1 spear per week per row foot over 8 weeks from an established plant
USDA Hardiness Zones: 2–7

Cardoon
Genus and species: Cynara cardunculus
Mature height*: 6–10'
Spacing†: 3–4'
Life span‡: indeterminate
Fertility needs: low
Spreading: yes
Yield§: several bushels of basal leaves
USDA Hardiness Zones: 7–8

Jerusalem Artichoke, Sunchoke
Genus and species: Helianthus tuberosus
Mature height*: 6–10'
Spacing†: 12"
Life span‡: indeterminate
Fertility needs: low
Spreading: yes
Yield§: 0.1–1 pound per row foot, generally from two diggings per year
USDA Hardiness Zones: 2–8

Rhubarb
Genus and species: Rheum rhabarbarum
Mature height*: 24–36"
Spacing†: 3–4'
Life span‡: indeterminate
Fertility needs: low
Spreading: yes
Yield§: expect to harvest 1–3 pounds per picking (2–3 pickings/year) from an established plant
USDA Hardiness Zones: 3–8

PERENNIAL FRUITS

Blackberry
Genus and species: Rubus fruticosus
Mature height*: 5–15'
Spacing†: 2–5'
Life span‡: 5–10 years
Fertility needs: low
Spreading: yes
Yield§: expect to harvest 3–10 pounds per plant over the course of a season
USDA Hardiness Zones: dependant on variety

Blueberry
Genus and species: Vaccinium spp.
Mature height*: 3–6'
Spacing†: 5–6'
Life span‡: 30 years
Fertility needs: medium
Spreading: no
Yield§: expect 1–2 pints per plant total during the 2nd–3rd year, and up to 4 gallons per plant at 5–7+ years; 1 pint of blueberries is about 12 ounces
USDA Hardiness Zones: dependant on variety

Currant

Genus and species: Ribes spp.
Mature height*: 3–5'
Spacing†: 3–5'
Life span‡: 15–30 years
Fertility needs: medium
Spreading: no
Yield§: 4–8 quarts (5–8 pounds) per plant once mature
USDA Hardiness Zones: 3–8

Elderberry

Genus and species: Sambucus nigra
Mature height*: 8–25'
Spacing†: 5–20'
Life span‡: indeterminate
Fertility needs: low
Spreading: no
Yield§: 10–15 pounds per plant
USDA Hardiness Zones: variable; generally 3–9

Goji Berry

Genus and species: Lycium barbarum
Mature height*: 6–10'
Spacing†: 3–8'
Life span‡: indeterminate
Fertility needs: low
Spreading: no
Yield§: 2–4 pounds per plant
USDA Hardiness Zones: 5–9

Gooseberry

Genus and species: Ribes uva-crispa
Mature height*: 3–5'
Spacing†: 3–5'
Life span‡: 15–30 years
Fertility needs: medium
Spreading: no
Yield§: 4–8 quarts (5–8 pounds) per plant once mature
USDA Hardiness Zones: variable; generally 3–8

Huckleberry

Genus and species: Vaccinium and *Gaylussacia* spp.
Mature height*: 2–8'
Spacing†: 3–8'
Life span‡: 50+ years
Fertility needs: low
Spreading: no
Yield§: 5–10 pounds per plant
USDA Hardiness Zones: 5–8

Jostaberry

Genus and species: Ribes × nidigrolaria
Mature height*: 3–5'
Spacing†: 3–5'
Life span‡: 15–30 years
Fertility needs: medium
Spreading: no
Yield§: 4–8 quarts (5–8 pounds) per plant once mature
USDA Hardiness Zones: 3–8

---

*Height of perennial crops can vary based on variety, light levels, soil conditions, climate, pruning, and grafting. In particular, the size of fruit trees can be incredibly wide ranging; nearly all fruit trees are grafted onto a rootstock that determines their mature size. With nearly all perennials, pruning and management play a very significant role in plant size.

† Spacing of perennial edibles can vary dramatically based on variety. Ranges given in the chart indicate average spacing for popular types; refer to variety-specific information before planting any perennial edible.

‡ Life span of perennial edibles can vary considerably based on variety, soil conditions, climate conditions, and pest or disease presence. When used in the chart, the term indeterminate means that life span can vary so greatly that it is hard to predict or that the crop spreads or self-propagates vigorously, generally eliminating the need for future plantings.

§ Yield from perennials can vary widely depending on variety, climate, if it is grafted and what type of rootstock was used, how it is pruned, and how old it is.

Planning for Perennials CONTINUED

Lingonberry
Genus and species: *Vaccinium vitis-idaea*
Mature height*: 12–24"
Spacing[†]: 2–3'
Life span[‡]: indeterminate
Fertility needs: low
Spreading: yes
Yield[§]: 1–2 pounds per plant
USDA Hardiness Zones: 3–8

Raspberry
Genus and species: *Rubus idaeus*
Mature height*: 4–10'
Spacing[†]: 1–3'
Life span[‡]: 10–20 years
Fertility needs: low
Spreading: yes
Yield[§]: expect about 0.6–0.8 pound per row foot over the course of an entire season; 1 pint = approx. 0.75 pound
USDA Hardiness Zones: variable; generally 3–9

Strawberry
Genus and species: *Fragaria × ananassa*
Mature height*: 6"
Spacing[†]: 8–12"
Life span[‡]: 2–12 years
Fertility needs: medium
Spreading: yes
Yield[§]: day-neutral types: expect 0.5–1 pound per row foot for the whole season during the 2nd and 3rd years; harvest period varies, but is generally about 3–4 months
USDA Hardiness Zones: variable; generally 3–8

Wintergreen
Genus and species: *Gaultheria procumbens*
Mature height*: 6–12"
Spacing[†]: 2–3'
Life span[‡]: indeterminate
Fertility needs: low
Spreading: yes
Yield[§]: 1 pound per plant
USDA Hardiness Zones: variable; generally 3–8

PERENNIAL HERBS

Anise Hyssop
Genus and species: *Agastache foeniculum*
Mature height*: 24"
Spacing[†]: 12–24"
Life span[‡]: indeterminate
Fertility needs: low
Spreading: yes
Yield[§]: variable
USDA Hardiness Zones: 4–9

Bay
Genus and species: *Laurus nobilis*
Mature height*: 3–30' (pruned to shape)
Spacing[†]: 3–15'
Life span[‡]: 50+ years
Fertility needs: low
Spreading: no
Yield[§]: variable
USDA Hardiness Zones: 8–11

Chives
Genus and species: *Allium schoenoprasum*
Mature height*: 12–18"
Spacing[†]: 12–18"
Life span[‡]: indeterminate
Fertility needs: low
Spreading: yes
Yield[§]: variable
USDA Hardiness Zones: 3–10

Chives, Garlic
Genus and species: *Allium tuberosum*
Mature height*: 12–18"
Spacing[†]: 12–18"
Life span[‡]: indeterminate
Fertility needs: low
Spreading: yes
Yield[§]: variable
USDA Hardiness Zones: 3–9

Fennel

Genus and species: Foeniculum vulgare
Mature height*: 6–8'
Spacing†: 2–3'
Life span‡: indeterminate
Fertility needs: low
Spreading: yes
Yield§: variable
USDA Hardiness Zones: 5–9

Horseradish

Genus and species: Armorica rusticana
Mature height*: 24"
Spacing†: 2–3'
Life span‡: indeterminate
Fertility needs: low
Spreading: yes
Yield§: variable
USDA Hardiness Zones: 2–9

Lavender

Genus and species: Lavandula spp.
Mature height*: 24–36"
Spacing†: 3–5'
Life span‡: 3–5 years
Fertility needs: low
Spreading: no
Yield§: variable
USDA Hardiness Zones: 5 and above

Lemon Balm

Genus and species: Melissa officinalis
Mature height*: 24–36"
Spacing†: 12–24"
Life span‡: indeterminate
Fertility needs: low
Spreading: yes
Yield§: variable
USDA Hardiness Zones: 3–10

Lemongrass

Genus and species: Cymbopogon citratus
Mature height*: 24–36"
Spacing†: 2–3'
Life span‡: indeterminate
Fertility needs: low
Spreading: yes
Yield§: variable
USDA Hardiness Zones: 9 and above

Lemon Verbena

Genus and species: Aloysia triphylla
Mature height*: 12"–6'
Spacing†: 12–24"
Life span‡: indeterminate
Fertility needs: low
Spreading: no
Yield§: variable
USDA Hardiness Zones: 8–10

Marjoram

Genus and species: Origanum majorana
Mature height*: 12"
Spacing†: 12–24"
Life span‡: 3–5 years
Fertility needs: low
Spreading: yes
Yield§: variable
USDA Hardiness Zones: 7–9

Mint

Genus and species: Mentha spp.
Mature height*: 24–36"
Spacing†: 12–24"
Life span‡: indeterminate
Fertility needs: low
Spreading: yes
Yield§: variable
USDA Hardiness Zones: 3–11

Oregano

Genus and species: Origanum vulgare
Mature height*: 12"
Spacing†: 12–24"
Life span‡: 3–5 years
Fertility needs: low
Spreading: yes
Yield§: variable
USDA Hardiness Zones: 4–10

Purple Coneflower

Genus and species: Echinacea purpurea
Mature height*: 24"
Spacing†: 2–3'
Life span‡: indeterminate
Fertility needs: low
Spreading: yes
Yield§: variable
USDA Hardiness Zones: 3–9

Rosemary
Genus and species: Rosmarinus officinalis
Mature height*: 3–5'
Spacing†: 2–5'
Life span‡: 5–10 years
Fertility needs: low
Spreading: no
Yield§: variable
USDA Hardiness Zones: 8 and above

Saffron
Genus and species: Crocus sativus
Mature height*: 6–12"
Spacing†: 6–12"
Life span‡: 7–10 years
Fertility needs: low
Spreading: yes
Yield§: variable
USDA Hardiness Zones: variable; generally 6–8

Sage
Genus and species: Salvia officinalis
Mature height*: 24–36"
Spacing†: 3–5'
Life span‡: 3–5 years
Fertility needs: low
Spreading: no
Yield§: variable
USDA Hardiness Zones: 5–9

Savory, Winter
Genus and species: Satureja spp.
Mature height*: 12–24"
Spacing†: 12–24"
Life span‡: 3–5 years
Fertility needs: low
Spreading: yes
Yield§: variable
USDA Hardiness Zones: 6–10

Sorrel
Genus and species: Rumex acetosa
Mature height*: 12"
Spacing†: 12"
Life span‡: 5+ years
Fertility needs: low
Spreading: no
Yield§: variable
USDA Hardiness Zones: 4–9

Stevia
Genus and species: Stevia rebaudiana
Mature height*: 24–36"
Spacing†: 2–3'
Life span‡: 3–5 years
Fertility needs: low
Spreading: no
Yield§: variable
USDA Hardiness Zones: 9–10

Tarragon
Genus and species: Artemisia dracunculus
Mature height*: 24–36"
Spacing†: 2–3'
Life span‡: 3–5 years
Fertility needs: low
Spreading: yes
Yield§: variable
USDA Hardiness Zones: 5–9

Tea Camellia
Genus and species: Camellia sinensis
Mature height*: 6–10'
Spacing†: 4–6'
Life span‡: 50+ years
Fertility needs: low
Spreading: no
Yield§: variable
USDA Hardiness Zones: 7–10

Thyme
Genus and species: Thymus vulgaris
Mature height*: 12"
Spacing†: 12–24"
Life span‡: 3–5 years
Fertility needs: low
Spreading: yes
Yield§: variable
USDA Hardiness Zones: 5–9

Valerian
Genus and species: *Valeriana officinalis*
Mature height*: 2–6'
Spacing†: 2–3'
Life span‡: indeterminate
Fertility needs: low
Spreading: yes
Yield§: variable
USDA Hardiness Zones: 5–9

FRUIT AND NUT TREES

Almond
Genus and species: *Prunus dulcis*
Mature height*: 10–30'
Spacing†: 5–20'
Life span‡: 20–30 years
Fertility needs: low
Spreading: no
Yield§: 10–20 pounds per tree
USDA Hardiness Zones: 7–9

Apple
Genus and species: *Malus domestica*
Mature height*: 5–50'
Spacing†: 5–20'
Life span‡: 25–50+ years
Fertility needs: low
Spreading: no
Yield§: 50–300 pounds per tree
USDA Hardiness Zones: variable; generally 3–8

Asian Pear
Genus and species: *Pyrus pyrifolia*
Mature height*: 5–50'
Spacing†: 5–20'
Life span‡: 20–30 years
Fertility needs: low
Spreading: no
Yield§: 50–300 pounds per tree
USDA Hardiness Zones: variable; generally 5–9

Cherry
Genus and species: *Prunus* spp.
Mature height*: 5–50'
Spacing†: 5–20'
Life span‡: 10–30 years
Fertility needs: low
Spreading: no
Yield§: 50–150 pounds per tree
USDA Hardiness Zones: variable; generally 5–9

Citrus
Genus and species: *Citrus* spp
Mature height*: 3–30'
Spacing†: 3–15'
Life span‡: 50+ years
Fertility needs: low
Spreading: no
Yield§: 50–150 pounds per tree
USDA Hardiness Zones: variable; generally 7 and above

European Pear
Genus and species: *Pyrus* spp.
Mature height*: 5–50'
Spacing†: 5–20'
Life span‡: 20–30 years
Fertility needs: low
Spreading: no
Yield§: 50–300 pounds per tree
USDA Hardiness Zones: dependent on variety

Fig
Genus and species: *Ficus* spp.
Mature height*: 5–30'
Spacing†: 5–20'
Life span‡: 10–30 years
Fertility needs: low
Spreading: no
Yield§: 10–30 pounds per plant
USDA Hardiness Zones: variable; generally 8–10

Planning for Perennials <small>CONTINUED</small>

Hazelnut
Genus and species: Corylus spp.
Mature height*: 10–40'
Spacing†: 5–20'
Life span‡: 20–30 years
Fertility needs: low
Spreading: no
Yield§: 1–10 pounds per plant
USDA Hardiness Zones: 4–8

Mulberry
Genus and species: Morus spp.
Mature height*: 10–70'
Spacing†: 5–20'
Life span‡: 50+ years
Fertility needs: low
Spreading: no
Yield§: 5–25 pounds per tree
USDA Hardiness Zones: 4–8

Peach
Genus and species: Prunus persica
Mature height*: 5–15'
Spacing†: 5–20'
Life span‡: 10–15 years
Fertility needs: low
Spreading: no
Yield§: 50–200 pounds per tree
USDA Hardiness Zones: 5–8

Plum
Genus and species: Prunus spp.
Mature height*: 5–40'
Spacing†: 5–20'
Life span‡: 10–20 years
Fertility needs: low
Spreading: no
Yield§: 10–100 pounds per tree
USDA Hardiness Zones: dependent on variety

Walnut
Genus and species: Juglans spp.
Mature height*: 15–50'
Spacing†: 5–20'
Life span‡: 50+ years
Fertility needs: low
Spreading: no

Yield§: 30–60 pounds per tree
USDA Hardiness Zones: 4–9

VINES

Akebia
Genus and species: Akebia spp.
Mature height*: indeterminate
Spacing†: 8–10'
Life span‡: 10–20 years
Fertility needs: low
Spreading: yes
Yield§: 5–25 pounds per vine
USDA Hardiness Zones: 4–9

Grape
Genus and species: Vitis spp.
Mature height*: indeterminate
Spacing†: 8–10'
Life span⁴: 50+ years
Fertility needs: low
Spreading: no
Yield§: 5–15 pounds per vine
USDA Hardiness Zones: dependent on variety

Hop
Genus and species: Humulus lupulus
Mature height*: 10–30'
Spacing†: 3–10'
Life span‡: 20–30 years
Fertility needs: low
Spreading: yes
Yield§: .5–2 pounds per vine
USDA Hardiness Zones: variable; generally 4–8

Kiwi
Genus and species: Actinidia spp.
Mature height*: indeterminate
Spacing†: 8–15'
Life span‡: 50+ years
Fertility needs: low
Spreading: no
Yield§: 25–100 pounds per vine
USDA Hardiness Zones: dependent on variety

Resources

Books

Appelhof, Mary. *Worms Eat My Garbage: How to Set Up and Maintain a Worm Composting System,* 2nd ed. Flower Press, 1997.

Ashworth, Suzanne. *Seed to Seed: Seed Saving and Growing Techniques for Vegetable Gardeners,* 2nd ed. Seed Saver's Exchange, 2002.

Ball Brothers Company. *Ball Blue Book Guide to Preserving,* rev. ed. Hearthmark, 2013.

Ball, Jeff. *The Self-Sufficient Suburban Gardener.* Rodale, 1983.

Barbarow, Peter. *Give Peas a Chance! Organic Gardening Cartoon-Science.* Naturegraph Publishers, 1990.

Coleman, Eliot. *Four-Season Harvest: Organic Vegetables from Your Home Garden All Year Long,* rev ed. Chelsea Green, 1999.

——. *The New Organic Grower: A Master's Manual of Tools and Techniques for the Home and Market Gardener,* 2nd ed. Chelsea Green Publishing, 1995.

——. *The Winter Harvest Handbook: Year Round Vegetable Production Using Deep-Organic Techniques and Unheated Greenhouses.* Chelsea Green Publishing, 2009.

Damerow, Gail. *Storey's Guide to Raising Chickens,* 3rd ed. Storey Publishing, 2010.

Elias, Thomas S., and Peter A. Dykeman. *Edible Wild Plants: A North American Field Guide to Over 200 Natural Foods.* Sterling, 2009.

Engeland, Ron L. *Growing Great Garlic: The Definitive Guide for Organic Gardeners and Small Farmers,* 9th ed. Filaree Productions, 1998.

Fortier, Jean-Martin. *The Market Gardener.* New Society Publishers, 2014.

Greene, Janet, Ruth Hertzberg, and Beatrice Vaughan. *Putting Food By,* 5th ed. Plume, 2010.

Greenwood, Pippa, and Andrew Halstead. *Pests & Diseases: The Definitive Guide to Prevention and Treatment,* rev. ed. Dorling Kindersley, 2009.

Hart, Rhonda Massingham. *Bugs, Slugs & Other Thugs: Controlling Garden Pests Organically.* Storey Publishing, 1991.

Henderson, Elizabeth, and Robyn Van En. *Sharing the Harvest: A Citizen's Guide to Community Supported Agriculture,* rev. ed. Chelsea Green Publishing, 2007.

Hoffmann, Michael P., and Anne C. Frodsham. *Natural Enemies of Vegetable Insect Pests.* Cornell University Press, 1993.

Katz, Sandor Ellix. *Wild Fermentation: The Flavor, Nutrition, and Craft of Live-Culture Foods.* Chelsea Green Publishing, 2003.

Kourik, Robert. *Designing and Maintaining Your Edible Landscape Naturally.* Chelsea Green Publishing, 2005.

——. *Drip Irrigation for Every Landscape and All Climates,* 2nd ed. Metamorphic Press, 2009.

Lanza, Patricia. *Lasagna Gardening: A New Layering System for Bountiful Gardens: No Digging, No Tilling, No Weeding, No Kidding!* Rodale, 1998.

Logsdon, Gene. *Small-Scale Grain Raising: An Organic Guide to Growing, Processing, and Using Nutritious Whole Grains for Home Gardeners and Local Farmers,* 2nd ed. Chelsea Green, 2009.

McCrate, Colin and Brad Halm. *Food Grown Right, In Your Backyard: A Beginner's Guide to Growing Crops at Home.* Skipstone, 2012.

Minnich, Jerry, Marjorie Hunt, and the editors of *Organic Gardening* magazine. *The Rodale Book of Composting: Easy Methods for Every Gardener,* rev ed. Rodale, 1992.

Nau, Jim. *Ball Perennial Manual: Propagation and Production*. Ball Publishing, 1996.

Noyes, Nick. *Easy Composters You Can Build*. A Storey Country Wisdom Bulletin, A-139. Storey Publishing, 1995.

O'Brien, Julie, and Richard J. Climenhage. *Fresh & Fermented: 85 Delicious Ways to Make Fermented Carrots, Kraut, and Kimchi Part of Every Meal*. Sasquatch, 2014.

Riotte, Louise. *Carrots Love Tomatoes: Secrets of Companion Planting for Successful Gardening*, rev ed. Storey Publishing, 1998.

Rynk, Robert, ed. *On-Farm Composting Handbook*. Natural Resource, Agriculture, and Engineering Service, 1992.

Slama, Jim, and Atina Diffley, eds. *Wholesale Success: A Farmer's Guide to Food Safety, Selling, Postharvest Handling, and Packing Produce*, 3rd ed. FamilyFarmed.org, 2013.

Smillie, Joe, and Grace Gershuny. *The Soul of Soil: A Soil-Building Guide for Master Gardeners and Farmers*, 4th ed. Chelsea Green Publishing, 1999.

Smith, Miranda. *Your Backyard Herb Garden: A Gardener's Guide to Growing Over 50 Herbs Plus How to Use Them in Cooking, Crafts, Companion Planting and More*. Rodale, 1997.

Storey Publishing. *Cover Crop Gardening: Soil Enrichment with Green Manures*. A Storey Country Wisdom Bulletin, A-5. Storey Publishing, 1977.

Sustainable Agriculture Network. *Managing Cover Crops Profitably*, 3rd ed. SARE, 2007.

Tozer, Frank. *The New Vegetable Grower's Handbook: A User's Manual for the Organic Vegetable Garden*. Green Man Publishing, 2013.

Wigmore, Ann. *The Sprouting Book: How to Grow and Use Sprouts to Maximize Your Health and Vitality*. Avery Publishing, 1986.

Wiswall, Richard. *The Organic Farmer's Business Handbook: A Complete Guide to Managing Finances, Crops, and Staff — and Making a Profit*. Chelsea Green Publishing, 2009.

Publications

Farm Hack
http://farmhack.net
Online resource for DIY farm tool builders

Growing for Market
Fairplain Publications
800-307-8949
www.growingformarket.com

Mother Earth News
Ogden Publications
www.motherearthnews.com

Authors' Recommended Suppliers

ARBICO Organics
800-827-2847
www.arbico-organics.com

Baker Creek Heirloom Seed
417-924-8917
www.rareseeds.com

FarmTek
800-327-6835
www.farmtek.com

Fedco Seeds
207-426-9900
www.fedcoseeds.com

High Mowing Organic Seeds
866-735-4454
www.highmowingseeds.com

J.W. Jung Seed Company
800-297-3123
www.jungseed.com

Johnny's Selected Seeds
877-564-6697
www.johnnyseeds.com

Planet Natural
800-289-6656
www.planetnatural.com

Seed Savers Exchange
563-382-5990
www.seedsavers.org

Store It Cold (CoolBot)
888-871-5723
http://storeitcold.com
For a DIY walk-in cooler

Territorial Seed Company
800-626-0866
www.territorialseed.com

Flame Weeding Supplies

Flame Engineering
888-388-6724
www.flameengineering.com

Flame Weeders
304-462-7606
www.rtol.net/jonathanmeyer/flameweeder

Irrigation Supplies

The Drip Store
877-597-1669
www.dripirrigation.com

DripWorks
800-522-3747
www.dripworks.com

Non-Toxic Wood Preservatives for Raised Beds

Timber Pro Coatings
888-888-6095
www.timberprocoatings.com
Internal wood stabilizer

Valhalla Wood Preservatives
250-358-2661
www.valhalco.com
LifeTime Wood Treatment

Produce Donation

Plant a Row for the Hungry
Garden Writers Association
877-492-2727
www.gardenwriters.org

Soil and Plant Tissue Testing

A&L Eastern Laboratories
804-743-9401 (Richmond, Virginia)
252-206-1721 (Wilson, North Carolina)
www.al-labs-eastern.com

Industrial Test Systems
800-861-9712
www.sensafe.com
Home test kit for arsenic

UMass Soil and Plant Tissue Testing Lab
University of Massachusetts
413-545-2311
http://soiltest.umass.edu

Useful Apps

Sun Seeker
Ozpda
www.ozpda.com
Useful for figuring out sun exposure/shading on a potential garden space at any time of year

Wild Edibles
www.wildmanstevebrill.com

Online Farm Recordkeeping

AgSquared
www.agsquared.com

COG Pro
https://cog-pro.com

Seattle Urban Farm Company
www.seattleurbanfarmco.com

Last Frost Date Calculator

Garden Wizards
The Gastronomic Gardener
www.gastronomicgardener.com/garden-wizard/

USDA Hardiness Zone Map

Agricultural Research Service
planthardiness.ars.usda.gov

Converting Measurements to Metric

Use the following formulas for converting US measurements to metric.

WHEN THE MEASUREMENT GIVEN IS	MULTIPLY IT BY	TO CONVERT TO
WEIGHTS/MEASURES		
tablespoons	14.79	milliliters
fluid ounces	29.57	milliliters
cups	236.59	milliliters
cups	0.236	liters
pints	473.18	milliliters
pints	0.473	liters
quarts	946.36	milliliters
quarts	0.946	liters
gallons	3.785	liters
ounces	28.35	grams
pounds	0.454	kilograms
LENGTHS		
inches	2.54	centimeters (cm)
inches	25.4	millimeters (mm)
inches	0.0254	meters (m)
feet	0.305	meters (m)
yards	0.9144	meters (m)
yards	91.44	centimeters (cm)

Index

Page numbers in *italic* indicate illustrations; numbers in **bold** indicate charts or worksheets.

R

radishes
    companion planting, 42
    crop rotation, 81
    fall/winter crops, 255
    short-season crops, 29
    sprouting, 178
Recipes for Preventive Sprays, 230
recordkeeping, 309
    additional things to include, 93–95
    cloud-based, 70
    creating a planting plan, 6, 26, 43
    logs to keep, 94
    mapping your crops, 78, *78*
relay planting, 40–42
restaurant supply, 298
rhizobium, 109
roadside stands, 281, 295–97, *296*
root maggots, 229, *231*
roots
    root cutting, 212
    root pruning, *210*, 210–11
    Tolerance of Root Disturbance (transplants),
        184
row covers. *See* low tunnels
Ryan and Kiwi, 8
    Connecting a Single Timer Hose Bib Line to
        Garden Beds, 140, *141*
    Nonstop Arugula, 74
    Rotation and Microclimate, 86, *87*
    Seed for Ryan's Arugula, 106
    Typical City Lot, 9, *9*

S

salad greens
    Cold-Hardy Salad Crops, **256**
    cool-weather crops, 253, 255–57, 267, *267*
    harvesting tips, 282–85
    relay planting, 42
    shading, 269
    succession planting, 34
    year-round nursery production, 176, 178
salad spinner, 284–85, *285*
season extension, 252–69. *See also* high tunnels and
  greenhouses
    choosing a structure, 255, 257–60
    choosing cold-weather crops, 254–56

cooling in summer, 268–69
    extending harvest in fall and winter, 254
    strategies for heat-loving crops, 253–54
    warming up and cooling down, 253
seed selection, 96–110
    climate factors, 103
    disease resistance, 103–4
    how much to order, 104, 106
    hybrid vs. open-pollinated, 102
    organic seed stock, 97
    seasonality, 102–3
    seed definitions, 101
    Seed Life Span, **108**
    Seed Order Worksheet, **98–99**
    selecting varieties, 100
    sources and suppliers, 97
    storing seeds, 107
    treatments that improve yield, 109–10
seed starting. *See also* direct seeding
    refresher, 166, *166*
    scheduling, 165, 167
seed treatments
    scarification, 110
    seed soaking, 110
shade map, *20*
site considerations, 17–24
    annual beds, 19, 21–23
    size, 18–19
site maps
    Dave and Erin garden, *11*
    elements of a high-yield landscape, *25*
    Jason's garden, *10*
    Ryan and Kiwi's garden, *9*
    shade map, *20*
size of garden
    site considerations, 8
    by square feet, 16–17
snap peas
    relay planting, 41
    succession planting, 40
soil prep and care. *See also* amendments to soil, *and*
  composting
    adjusting nutrient levels, 123–25
    adjusting pH, 122
    conversions for amendent application rates, 126
    cover crops, 245–48, **248–50**
    humus and organic matter, 238–39
    incorporating new materials, 114–15

Other Storey Books You Will Enjoy

EPIC TOMATOES
by Craig LeHoullier
Grow your best tomatoes with this fascinating and artful guide by expert grower Craig LeHoullier. Packed with insights and enthralling photography, Epic Tomatoes explains everything a tomato enthusiast needs to know about growing more than 200 varieties of hybrid and heirloom tomatoes. 256 pages. Paper. ISBN 978-1-61212-208-3. Hardcover. ISBN 978-1-61212-464-3.

THE FRUIT GARDENER'S BIBLE
by Lewis Hill and Leonard Perry
This complete guide to growing fruits and nuts in the home garden covers everything from choosing the best varieties to planting, pruning, protecting from wildlife, and harvesting. 320 pages. Paper. ISBN 978-1-60342-567-4. Hardcover. ISBN 978-1-60342-984-9.

THE VEGETABLE GARDENER'S BIBLE, 2ND EDITION
by Edward C. Smith
The 10th anniversary edition of the best-selling vegetable gardening classic features Ed Smith's time-tested W-O-R-D system for growing an abundance of vegetables, fruits, and herbs in your own back-yard using completely organic methods! 352 pages. Paper. ISBN 978-1-60342-475-2. Hardcover. ISBN 978-1-60342-476-9.

WEEK-BY-WEEK VEGETABLE GARDENER'S HANDBOOK
by Ron Kujawski and Jennifer Kujawski
Use these detailed, customizable to-do lists to break down gardening into manageable tasks. Whether it's planting strawberries, pinching off pumpkin blossoms, or checking for tomato hornworm, the Kujawskis show exactly what to do — and exactly when and how to do it. 200 pages. Paper with partially concealed wire-o. ISBN 978-1-60342-694-7.

THE YEAR-ROUND VEGETABLE GARDENER
by Niki Jabbour
Learn how to grow your own food 365 days a year, no matter where you live! Select the best varieties for each season, master the art of succession planting, and make inexpensive protective structures that keep vegetables viable and delicious through the colder months. 256 pages. Paper. ISBN 978-1-60342-568-1. Hardcover. ISBN 978-1-60342-992-4.

These and other books from Storey Publishing are available wherever quality books are sold or by calling 1-800-441-5700. Visit us at *www.storey.com* or sign up for our newsletter at *www.storey.com/signup*.